IMAGES
of America

Green Cove Springs

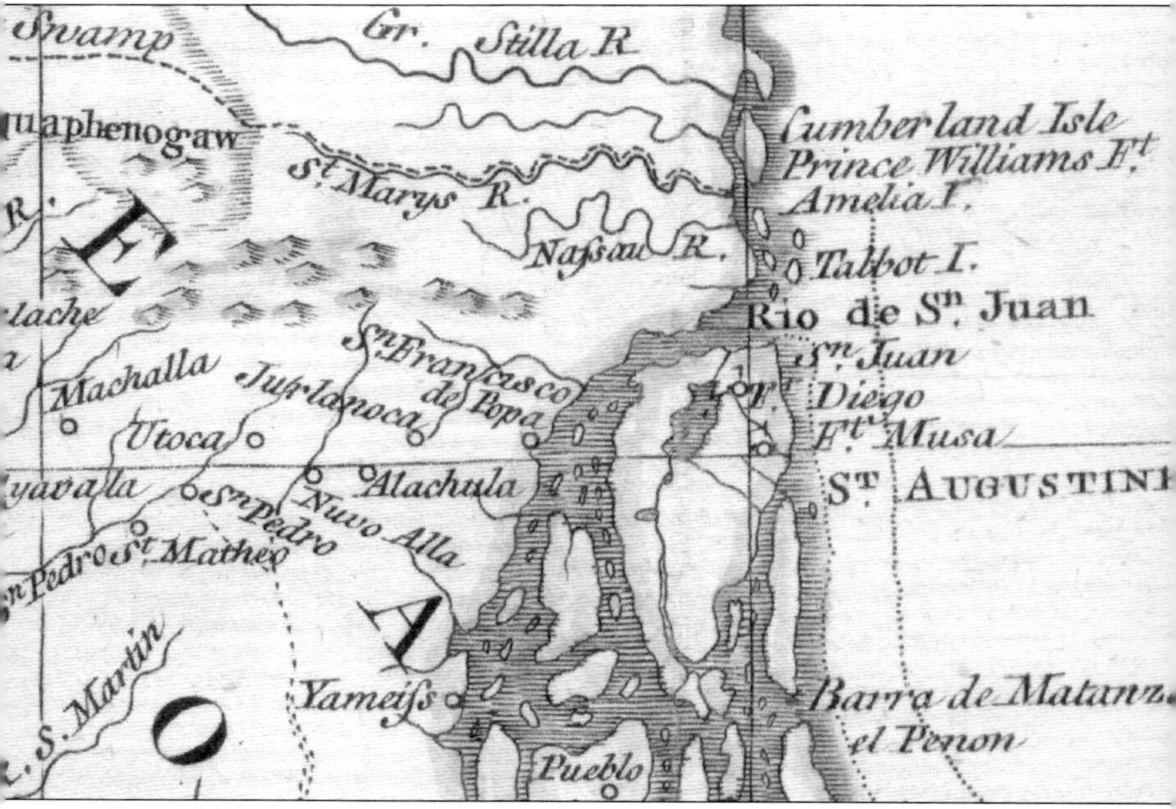

BRITISH MAP, 1765. Green Cove Springs has long been settled since the arrival of the Europeans. To the south of town was an important Spanish river crossing at Fort San Francisco de Pupo, which was established in the early 1700s. This *c.* 1765 map shows Fort Pupo along the St. Johns River. (Author's collection.)

ON THE COVER: A grandfather and his granddaughter sit relaxing on a bench at the spring and casino at Green Cove Springs, around 1920. The family pictured here was from Maine and routinely traveled to Florida for a vacation. (Author's collection.)

IMAGES
of America

GREEN COVE SPRINGS

Kevin S. Hooper

ARCADIA
PUBLISHING

ISBN 978-0-7385-8642-7

Published by Arcadia Publishing
Charleston, South Carolina

Printed in the United States of America

Library of Congress Control Number: 2010924656

For all general information, please contact Arcadia Publishing:
Telephone 843-853-2070
Fax 843-853-0044
E-mail sales@arcadiapublishing.com
For customer service and orders:
Toll-Free 1-888-313-2665

Visit us on the Internet at www.arcadiapublishing.com

This is dedicated to Kammy, Luke, Emmalee, and Levi. Thank you for enduring yet another adventure in writing, research, and travel. Hebrews 12:1

Contents

Acknowledgments

This book would not have been possible without the generous help of many individuals. John Nelson was helpful in sharing his wonderful research that he had done on Magnolia Springs and for providing Web sites that had digitized many northern 19th-century newspapers. Dr. Dan Schafer for providing the image of Dr. Seth Rogers; Claude Bass at the Clay County Archives; the staff at Archives II in College Park, Maryland, for helping to find the photograph on Lee Field and NAAS Green Cove Springs; and to Kasey, Andie, Korey, Shayla, Luke, Emmalee, and Levi for helping to select the final few images to use. Also thanks to my co-workers and boss for covering for me when I flew to Washington, D.C., to research and "play" in the snow; and to my friends who read and reread many of the pages, giving me ideas along the way.

Unless otherwise noted, all images appear courtesy of the author.

Introduction

Before Green Cove Springs and Magnolia Springs became a winter playground for the north, the area was inhabited by the Timucua Indians. The Timucua were a group of people who were split into many different tribes that spoke a similar dialect. These native tribes created small villages along the creeks and the St. Johns River before the arrival of Juan Ponce de Leon in 1513, and buried their dead in small sand mounds. Once St. Augustine had been settled, the Spanish created several small missions within their new territory. By 1702, many of these had been destroyed by Indian uprisings and attacks from the north. Sometime after 1702, Fort San Francisco de Pupo was established to help guard the river crossing along the Camino Real, which was the road that ran between St. Augustine and Pensacola. Fort Pupo gained international attention when Gen. James Oglethorpe invaded Spanish Florida in 1739. Oglethorpe, able to defeat the small garrison of men in January 1740, could not overcome the defenses of St. Augustine and was forced to retreat. During the retreat, Fort Pupo was destroyed. The fort sat long forgotten and unused until 1836 when men of the Georgia militia briefly occupied it as Gen. Winfield Scott started his multipronged attack against the Seminole Indians.

After Great Britain acquired east and west Florida in 1763, large tracts of land were given to individuals who would subdivide the land and entice English citizens to settle the land by farming. Gen. Patrick Tonyn acquired 20,000 acres south of Black Creek and created a successful indigo plantation. William Mills acquired 20,000 acres to the south of Green Cove Springs in 1768; however, there is very little evidence that this land was ever cultivated. Tonyn would be forced to destroy his viable plantation during the Revolutionary War, so articles of value could not benefit the rebellious colonies.

The first permanent settlement to the area came in 1790 when Thomas Travers was awarded 1,000 acres near Magnolia Springs. By 1795, Travers had a large supply of goods shipped from Charleston. After his death, his son William continued to live on the land. The Travers plantation was destroyed during the Indian War, in the summer of 1836. The property around Magnolia Springs would not see new inhabitants until the end of the Second Seminole War in 1842. Men such as Joseph Finegan, Thomas J. Hendricks, Joseph Summerlin, and Dr. Nathan D. Benedict would move into the area and help establish a small town. In 1853, Dr. Nathan D. Benedict, who was the superintendent of the New York State Lunatic Asylum, in ill heath decided that the climate of Florida would be beneficial to him. In 1855, he opened a hotel at Magnolia Springs for the invalid and advertised that it was located in one of the healthiest places in Florida.

During the Civil War, Magnolia and Green Cove Springs were almost entirely deserted. Although the Confederate government had authorized a mail route for Green Cove Spring after closing the one at Magnolia, there is no proof that this route was ever created. Once the Union gunboats had clear supremacy upon the St. Johns River, many residents of the area simply migrated toward the interior of the state. Black Creek was even blocked by fallen trees.

The area saw very little military action during the war, and when it arrived, it remained for only a few months. Once the Union command felt the river was free of Confederate torpedoes, their army spread south and west to the interior. Meeting a strong Confederate force at Gainesville, the Union forces met a devastating defeat and retreated to Magnolia, where they created an earthen work defense on Thomas J. Hendricks plantation. Men from the 4th Massachusetts Cavalry, 17th Connecticut Infantry, 75th Ohio Volunteers, 34th and 102nd U.S. Colored Infantry created a large fort that Gen. John G. Foster would later describe as "very faulty." A few pro-Union citizens of Clay County ventured into the Union defenses to take the oath of allegiance where they found food and jobs. The 4th Massachusetts Cavalry met defeat as they were driving cattle toward Magnolia from Middleburg in late October 1864. Capt. J. J. Dickinson of the 2nd Florida Cavalry fought a 40-minute skirmish against the Yankee cavalry, which resulted in a "complete route" of the 4th Massachusetts Cavalry. On November 4, 1864, Magnolia was abandoned, and by the end of the decade, the tourist industry was gaining momentum at Magnolia Springs while just beginning at Green Cove Springs.

After the war, Dr. Benedict sold his hotel at Magnolia to Seth Rogers, who, with Oliver Harris, in 1872 expanded the hotel. Together they built several cottages along the river. At the same time, the Union and Clarendon Hotels had been constructed and the sulphur spring cleaned and made into a bathing area started to draw visitors. The citizens of the county had voted to make Green Cove Springs the county seat, and the town was incorporated on November 2, 1874. The winter tourist industry soon created a town that catered to the affluent northern visitor and many built fine large winter homes in town. The hotels in town were open only from November through May and closed during the summer months. In 1881, Isaac Cruft rebuilt the Magnolia Springs Hotel after a fire destroyed much of it, and he created the large and magnificent Magnolia Hotel and hired O. D. Seavey, an experienced hotel manger, to manage it. By the turn of the 20th century, Magnolia Springs and Green Cove Springs had a total of nine winter hotels and Isaac Haas, who was born in Middleburg and lived in Green Cove Springs, earned a living providing photographs for the visiting tourists. Green Cove Springs flourished until the 1920s, and the Qui-Si-Sana quietly became the last hotel in business.

World War II brought new challenges and people to the city. Magnolia Springs was no longer. Even the once-grand hotel that stood there was no more, having burned to the ground in 1923. In 1941, the U.S. Navy created Lee Field, which was initially used as an airfield to house aircraft that could not be stored at NAS Jacksonville. Because of the navy's needs, the airfield was expanded. At the end of the war, the bases' roles changed, and Green Cove Springs became the site of the Florida Group, Atlantic Reserve Fleet–NAAS Green Cove Springs. The navy base housed almost 800 naval vessels along 13 piers, while several groups of larger ships were moored together and anchored in the river. The navy base continued until 1963 when the mothballed ships were sent to Orange, Texas, and Norfolk, Virginia. Before the base was closed, NASA even looked at the site for an operations base for the space race.

Even amongst its long-term residents, few are fully aware of the rich and storied history of Green Cove Springs as it remains the county seat of Clay County. This book takes the reader on a journey through those early days of the Spanish colonization to its time as a home of vast plantations and beautiful winter resorts that drew travelers from all over the United States, and it explores the important role the city played after World War II for the U.S. Navy.

One

Spanish, British, and the Civil War

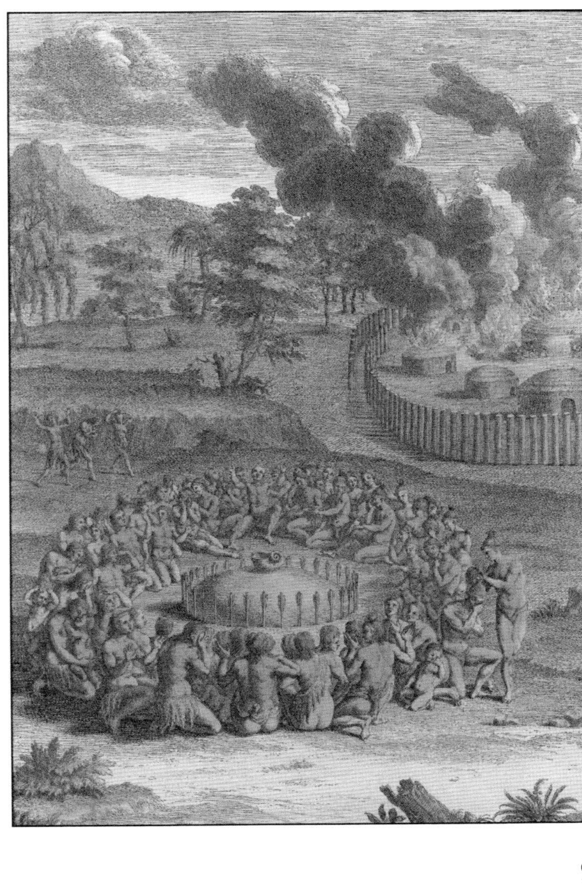

The Manner of Burying Kings and Priests in Florida, around 1722. Although there were no Timucuan villages located near Green Cove Springs, several sand mounds such as the one shown in the middle were constructed by the Indians. Mounds at Peter's Creek, Clark's Creek, Bayard Point, and Magnolia were explored by Clarence Moore in the late 19th century. Moore found that several mounds contained burials. In 1916, Dr. E. J. Thomas and John Kendrick reportedly found three skeletons, six skulls, four arrowheads, and stone axes after two days of digging. The two men said they would "send the skeletons to the museums of natural history in Jacksonville and New York."

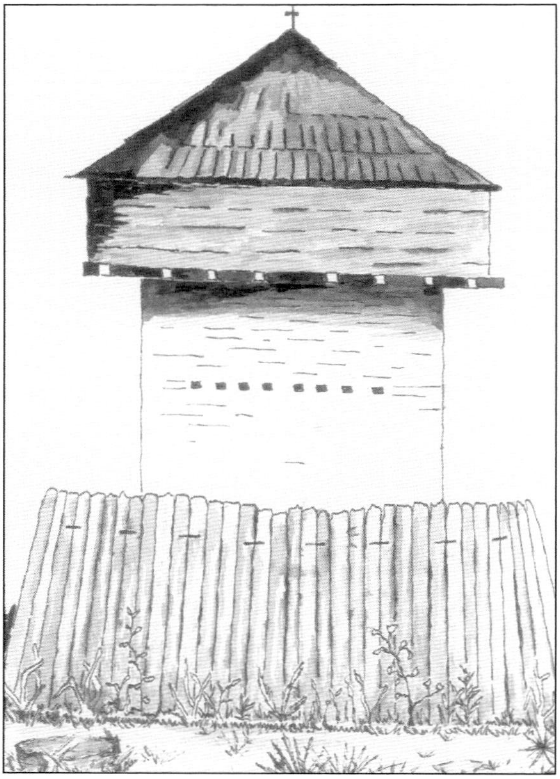

Fort San Francisco de Pupo. The fort was initially built in 1714 south of Green Cove Springs near the present-day Shands Bridge. In 1737, the Spanish military repaired the fort because of the increasing presence of the English in Georgia. The fort along with the one at Picolata on the east bank of the St. Johns provided a defense for the river crossing on the road between St. Augustine and Pensacola. Gen. James Oglethorpe would successfully attack the fort in January 1740. (Courtesy Clay County Archives.)

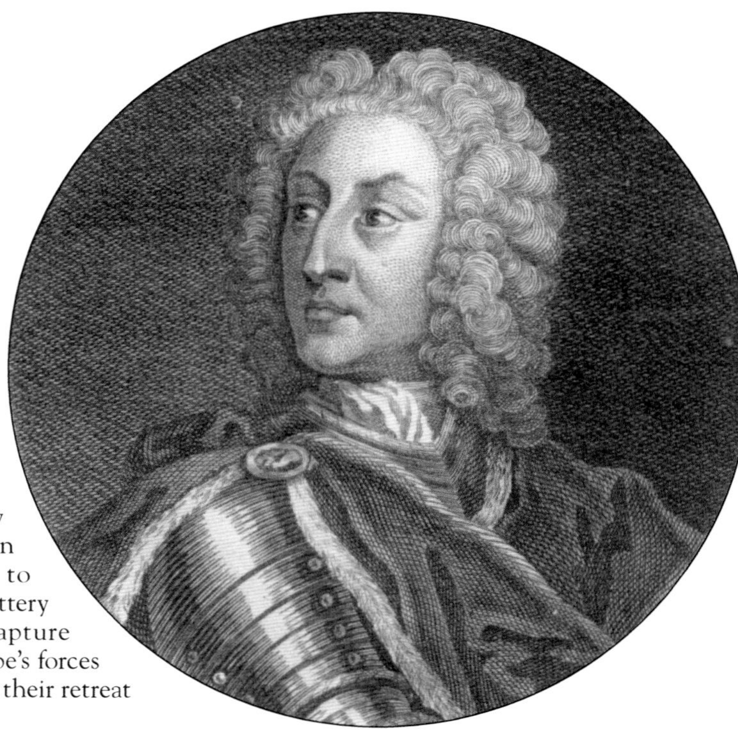

Gen. James Oglethorpe. James Oglethorpe successfully attacked the fortification at Picolata on the east side of the St. Johns first, and then he was able to take Fort Pupo. The small Spanish garrison of approximately 15 men surrendered when Oglethorpe was able to erect a small artillery battery close by. Unable to capture St. Augustine, Oglethorpe's forces burned Fort Pupo during their retreat in July 1740.

INDIGO PROCESSING, AROUND 1759. Patrick Tonyn, who would serve as the second British governor of East Florida, acquired 20,000 acres between Black Creek and Governor's Creek in 1767. Tonyn was initially an absentee plantation owner and had Alexander Gray manage his land until Tonyn's arrival in 1774. Tonyn had cleared and cultivated over 200 acres with the help of two dozen salves. The British military saw the St. Johns River as a natural defense, and thus all the plantations west of the St. Johns were ordered to be destroyed after the colonies started to rebel. Tonyn was forced to destroy his indigo plantation in 1778, which included two dwelling houses, 16 slave houses, and four complete sets of vats for indigo.

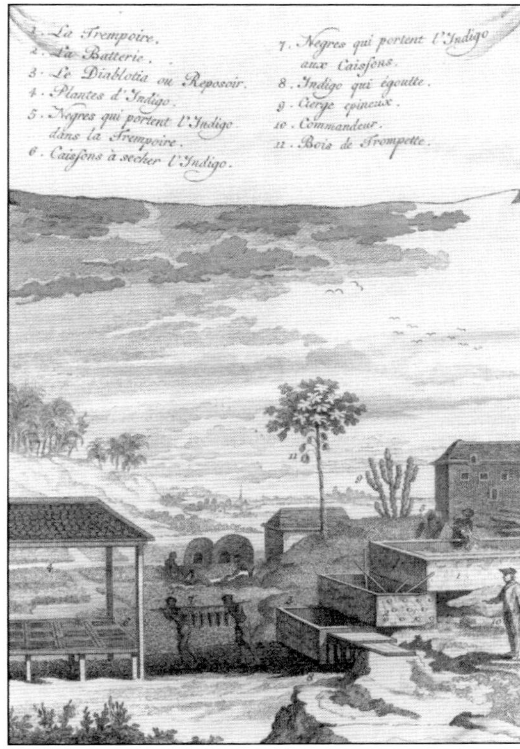

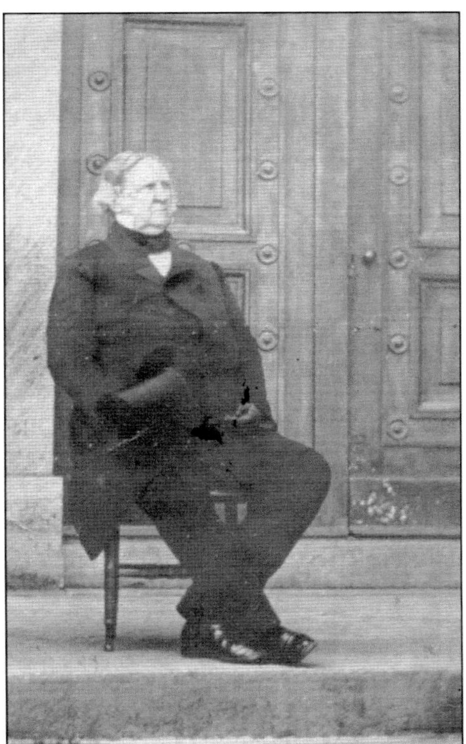

GEN. WINFIELD SCOTT (1786–1866). When Scott launched his unsuccessful attempt at ending the Second Seminole Indian War in spring 1836, he had allowed the Georgia Militia to create a camp at the site of Fort Pupo.

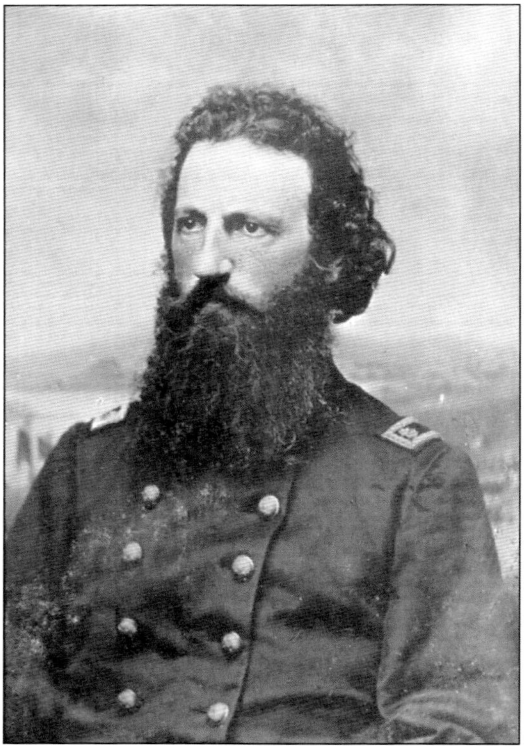

Dr. Seth Rogers (1823–1893). Rogers joined the Massachusetts Medical Society in 1855, and when war broke out in 1862 he became a surgeon in Col. Thomas W. Higginson's black infantry regiment. This regiment would later be designated the 33rd USCT. In 1869, Rogers and his wife purchased the Magnolia Springs Hotel from Dr. Nathan Benedict, who had moved to St. Augustine toward the end of the Civil War. (Courtesy Dr. Daniel L. Schafer and the U.S. Army Military History Institute.)

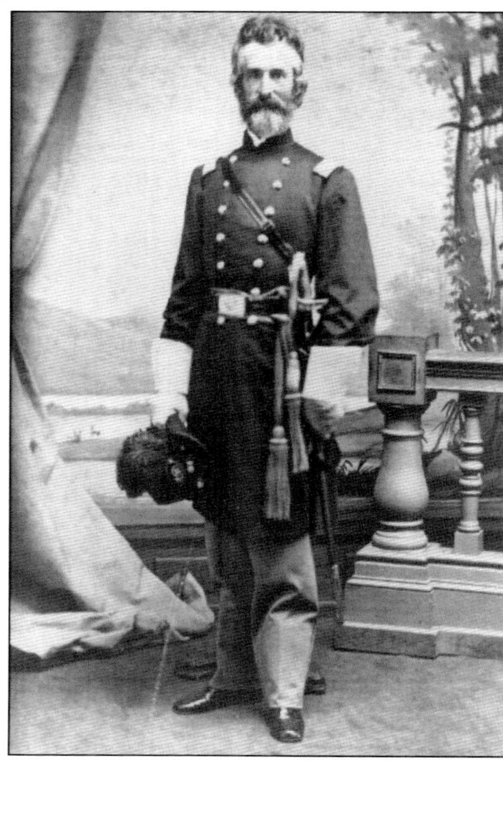

Col. William H. Noble. Colonel Noble commanded the 17th Connecticut and was placed in charge of the Union fort at Magnolia. At the time of the Union occupation, Magnolia contained a "commodious boarding house, a chapel, reading-room, billiard saloon, livery-stable, and out-houses of every description, for the accommodation of such friends and invalids as might seek a Winter home in the soft climate of Florida . . . A public house of far larger proportions—large enough to accommodate three hundred persons—stands nearly completed." (Courtesy the Roger D. Hunt Collection at the U.S. Army Military History Institute.)

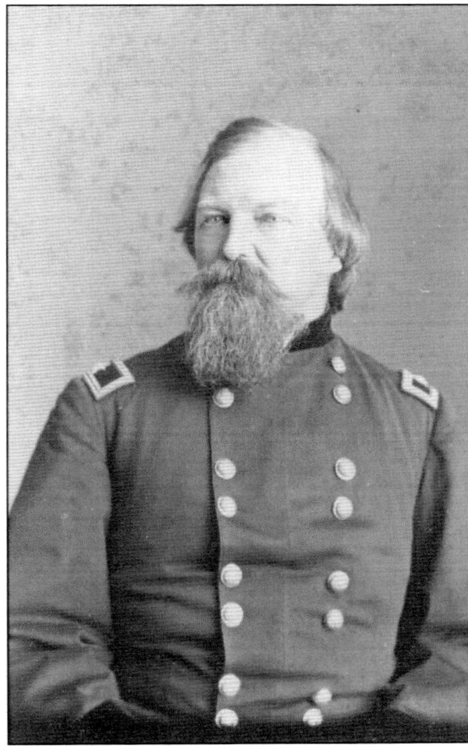

GEN. JOHN P. HATCH (1822–1901). General Hatch designed a multipronged attack into the Confederate defenses in July 1864. After the Union troops were defeated at Gainesville on August 17, 1864, the surviving Union soldiers fled down the Bellamy Road toward Magnolia springs where General Hatch had allowed Col. William Noble of the 17th Connecticut volunteers to set up a strong earthen work fort. Hatch would later be rebuked by Gen. John G. Foster for occupying Magnolia Springs, and the position was abandoned on November 4, 1864.

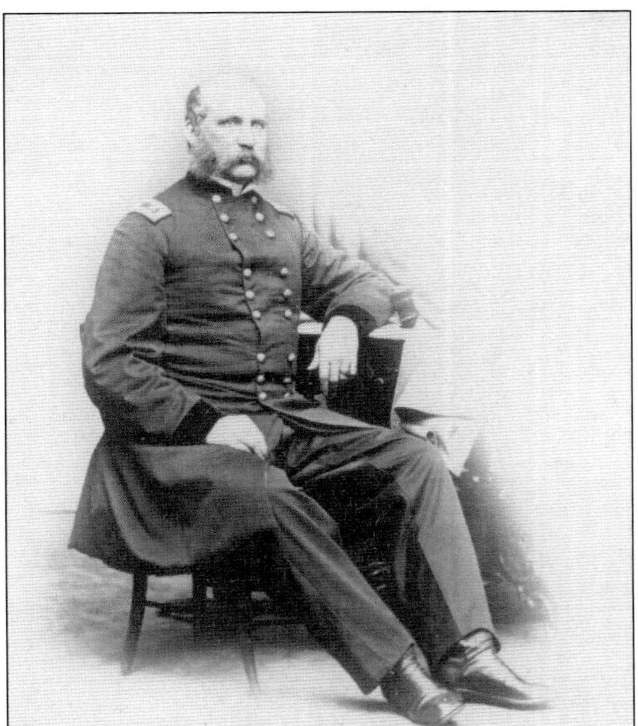

GEN. JOHN G. FOSTER (1823–1874). General Foster issued the order for General Hatch to abandon the Union fortifications at Magnolia. Hatch said that the position only furnished the "rebels with fine arms and horses". After the Civil War, Foster remained in the army.

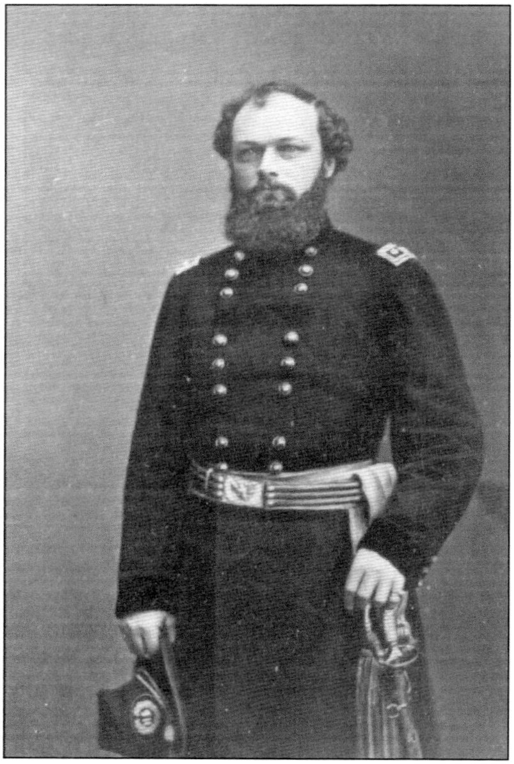

General Quincy A. Gillmore (1825–1888). General Gillmore commanded the Department of the South, and he sent troops to Florida in January 1864, which were defeated at Olustee on February 20, 1864. Gillmore's actions would eventually lead to Union forces establishing a fortified position at Magnolia Springs.

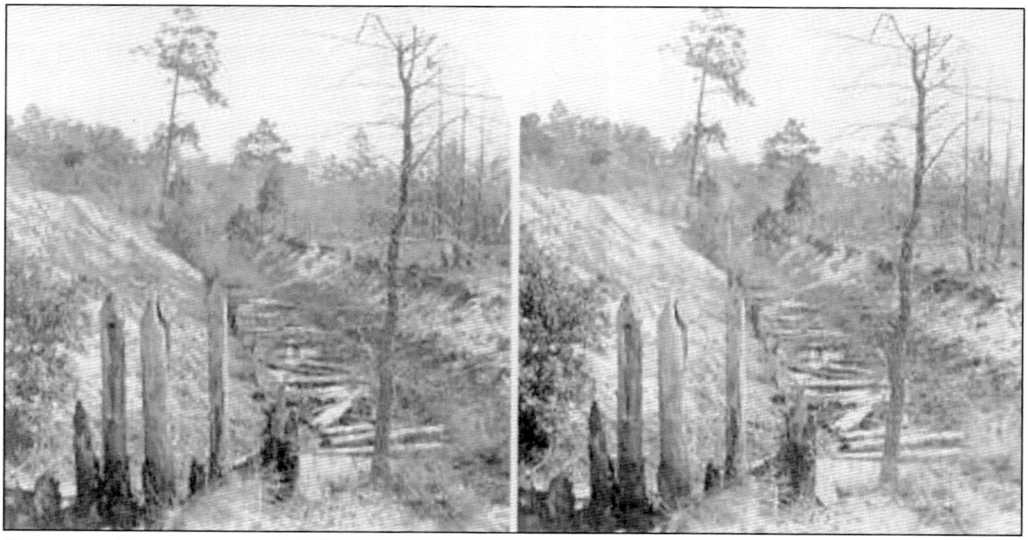

Ruins of Fortifications Near Magnolia. The Union forces, which occupied Magnolia comprised of soldiers from the 17th Connecticut, 4th Massachusetts Cavalry, and the 75th Ohio Volunteers. Men from two black regiments later arrived. While at Magnolia, the Union forces built an earthern work fort, which Gen. John G. Foster would late describe as "very faulty." The Union forces abandoned Magnolia on November 4, 1864. Parts of the fortifications would later be used in the golf course for the Magnolia Hotel. (Photograph by C. Seaver Jr.; courtesy Florida Photographic Archives.)

Two

Magnolia Springs Hotel

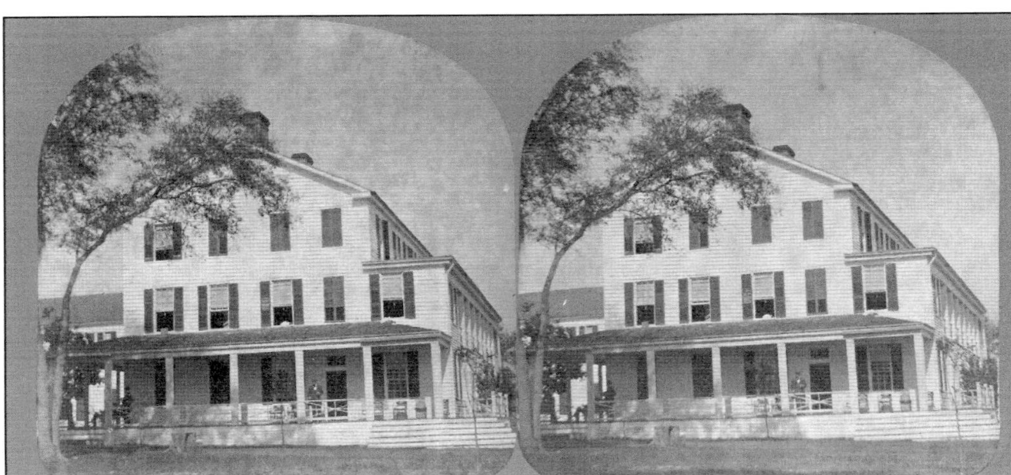

Magnolia Hotel, February 15, 1876. Around 1853, Dr. Nathan D. Benedict decided to move to East Florida on account of poor heath. In 1855, an article from the *St. Louis Medical and Surgical Journal* stated that Dr. Benedict was about to open a hotel in Magnolia for "invalids, where those seeking the benign influence of a southern climate may enjoy the benefits of judicious medication, proper hygienic regulations and comfortable board and lodging."

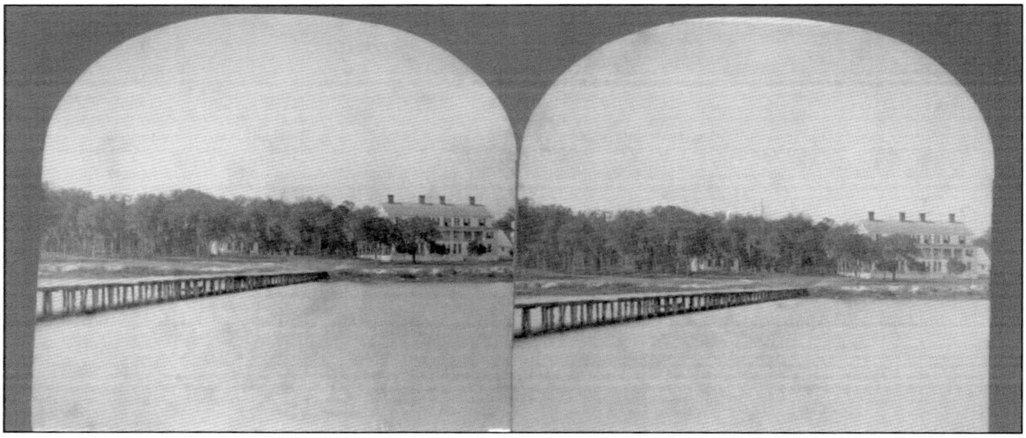

Magnolia Hotel and Cemetery. Because Magnolia was popular with invalids from the north, many who traveled to visit passed away while at the hotel. During the Civil War, a cemetery for Union soldiers was established. This image was taken on February 7, 1876.

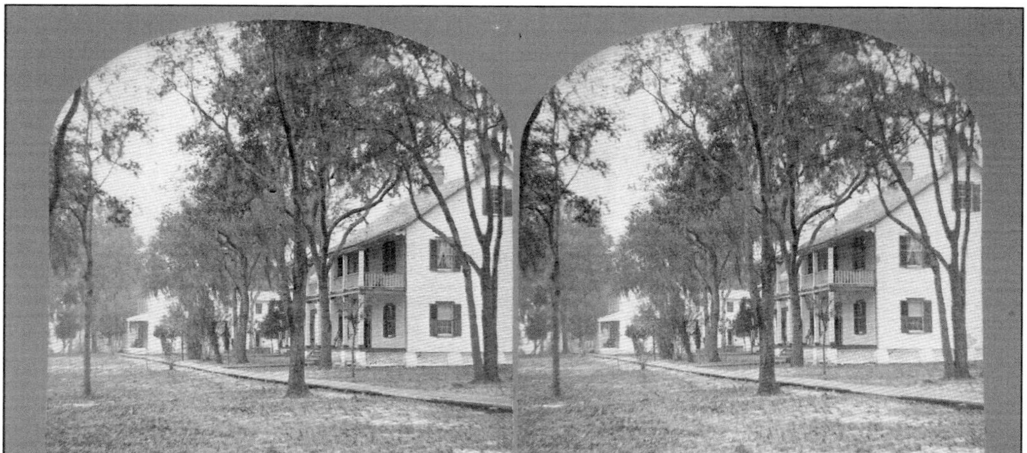

Cottages at Magnolia by Isaac Haas. After the Civil War, Benedict sold his hotel to Dr. Seth Rogers and Oliver Harris. Rogers and Benedict meet during the Civil War—most likely in St. Augustine. Rogers and Harris expanded Benedict's hotel and built five cottages, which catered to larger parties and families.

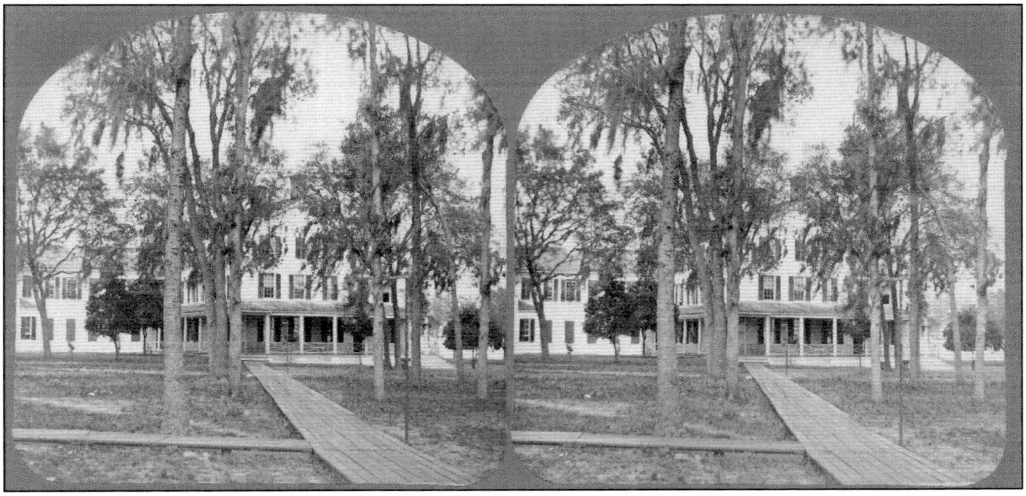

Magnolia by Isaac Haas. When the Union troops abandoned Magnolia in November 1864, Dr. Benedict traveled to Hilton Head, South Carolina, where he met with surgeon Meredith Clymer, who was the medical director in the Department of the South. On November 21, 1864, Benedict agreed to "perform the duties of a Medical Officer, agreeably to Army Regulations, at St. Augustine or elsewhere, and to furnish and keep in good order, and accessible at all times, complete sets of amputating, trephining, and pocket instruments."

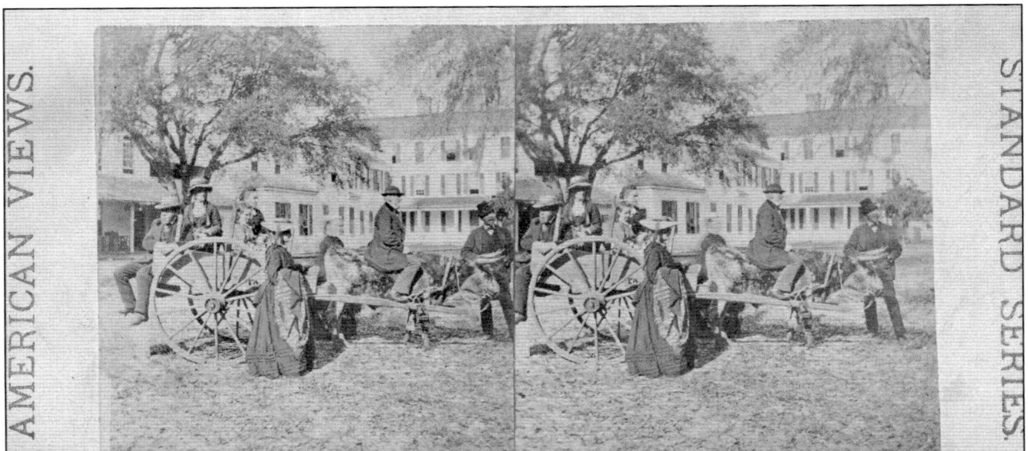

Florida Express at Magnolia Hotel. This image was taken from the back of the old Magnolia Springs Hotel. Guests would often get their picture taken riding an ox-pulled cart that poked fun at native Floridians.

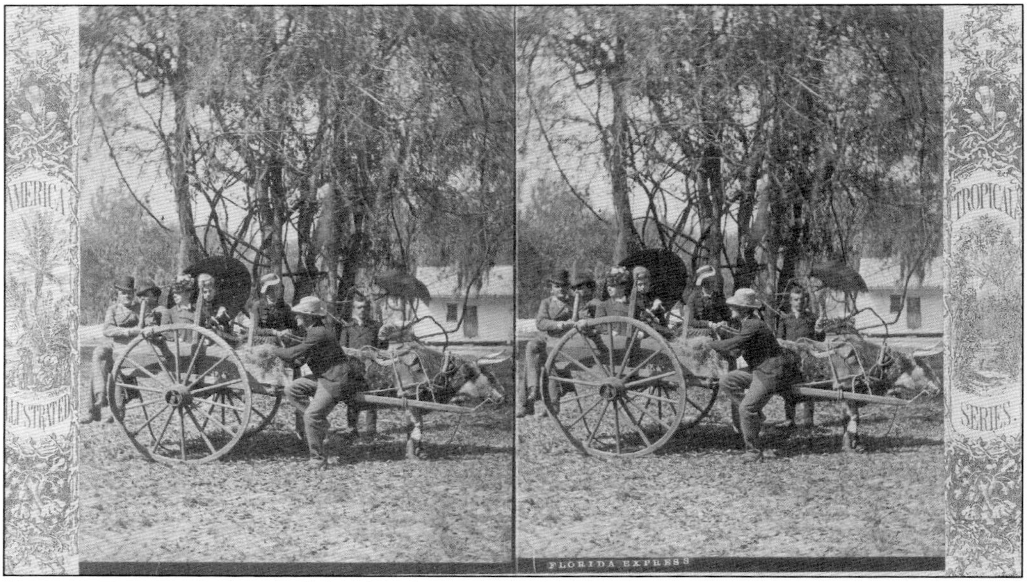

FLORIDA EXPRESS. For a small fee, hotel guest could get their photograph taken. In January 1881, one guest wrote to his cousin that he had some pictures "taken but did not like them," as the photographer could not "take a good photograph."

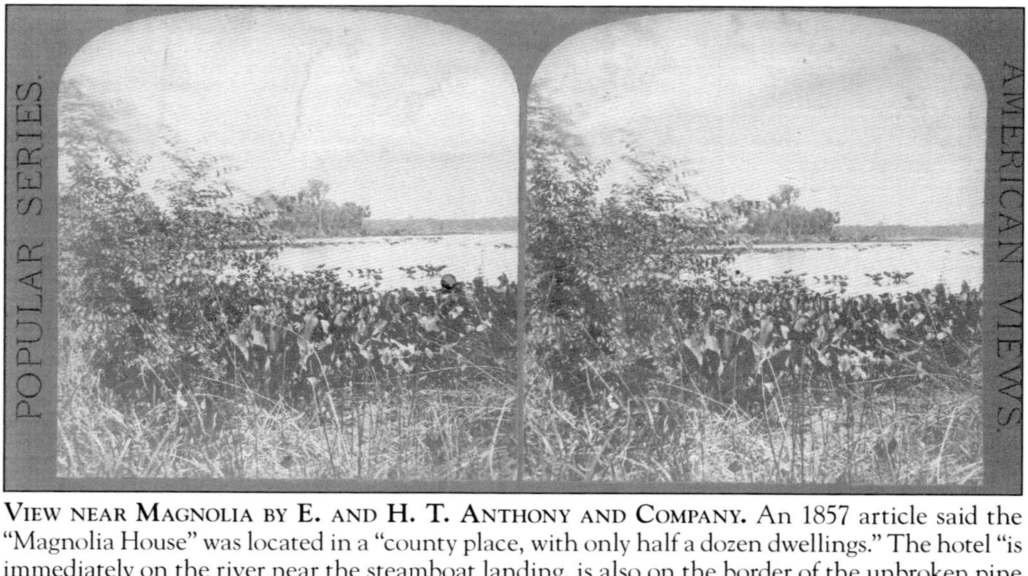

VIEW NEAR MAGNOLIA BY E. AND H. T. ANTHONY AND COMPANY. An 1857 article said the "Magnolia House" was located in a "county place, with only half a dozen dwellings." The hotel "is immediately on the river near the steamboat landing, is also on the border of the unbroken pine forest, where the walks, rides, and hunting grounds, are well sheltered, even in windy weather."

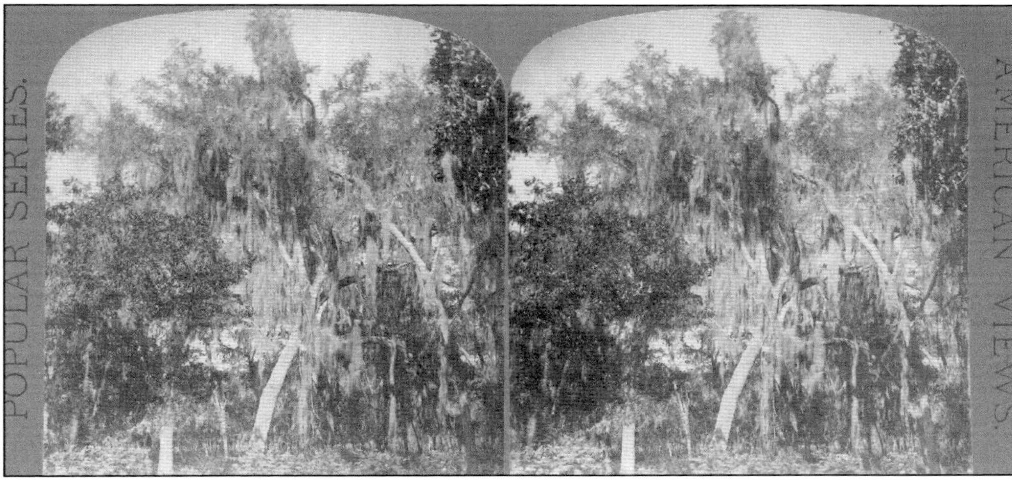

MOSS-COVERED TREE BY E. AND H. T. ANTHONY AND COMPANY. When Dr. Benedict established his hotel for invalids at Magnolia, he chose a site, which would be healthy for its visitor. Benedict would win the praise of the Oneida County Medical Society during his brief tenure as the superintendent of the New York State Lunatic Asylum. A July 10, 1854, resolution in part read "his highest professional qualification, his great moral purity and his gentlemanly deportment . . . entitles him to the highest praise, and lasting gratitude of the people of the State of New York."

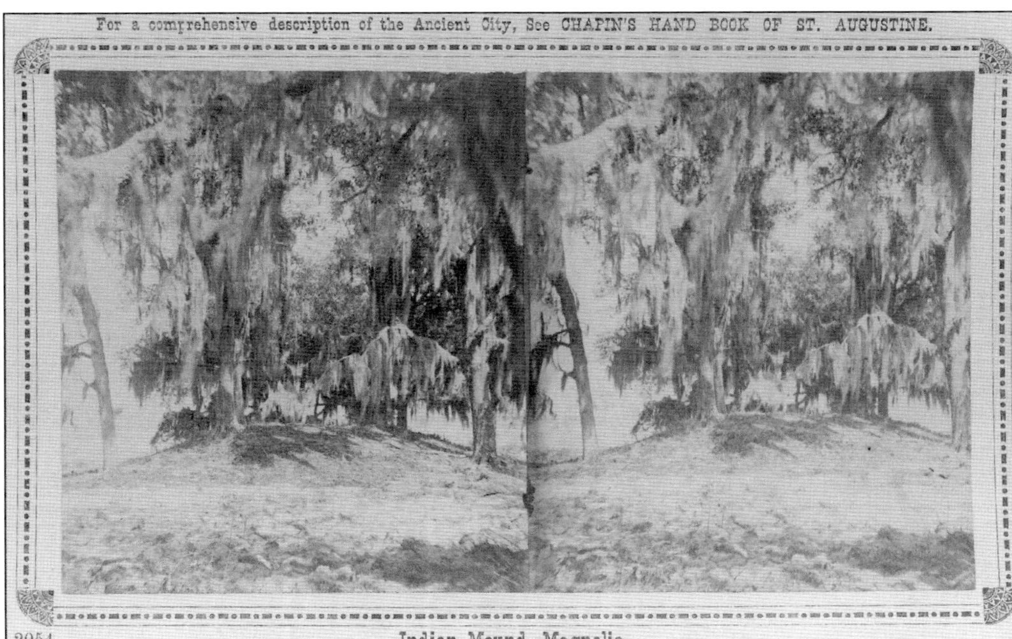

INDIAN MOUND, MAGNOLIA. Clarence B. Moore, a noted archaeologist, explored Florida and recorded hundreds of Indian sand mounds. In 1894, he published a paper noting that the sand mound at Magnolia was within a few yards of the hotel and is "at present a very symmetrical mound, 7 feet high and 60 feet through the base. During the past 30 years, it has been opened a number of times and restored to a more symmetrical shape."

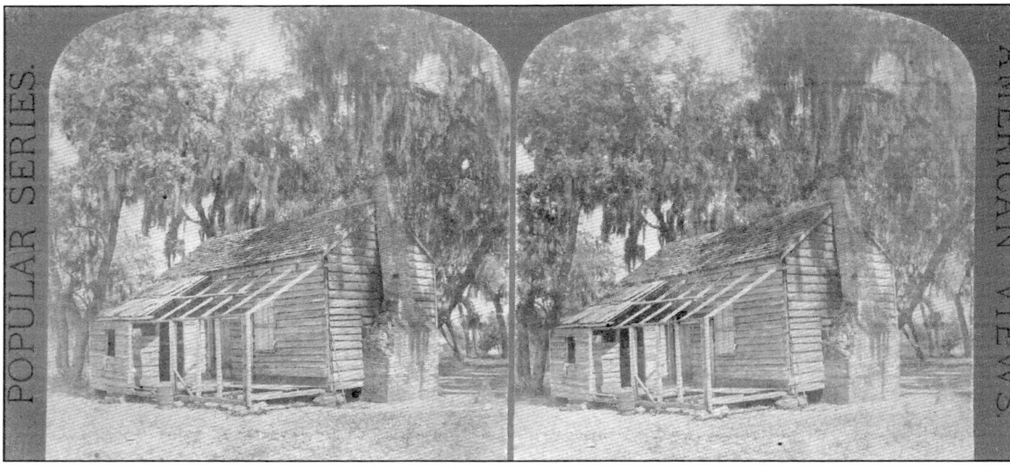

Subject for Reconstruction by E. and H. T. Anthony and Company. During the Civil War, the Union troops occupied the Hendricks plantation. The plantation consisted of a main dwelling house; milk-house; meat house; corn house; hay-house; and three slave quarters, which housed five slaves (three women and two men).

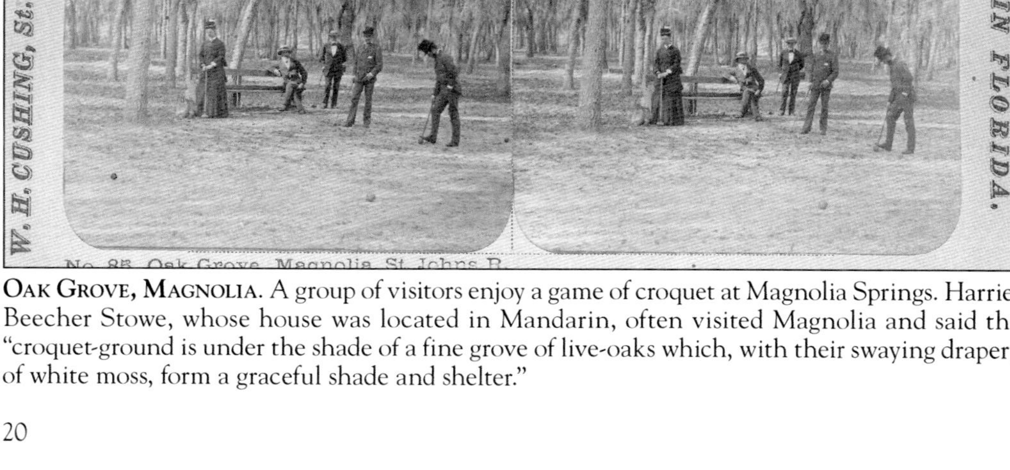

Oak Grove, Magnolia. A group of visitors enjoy a game of croquet at Magnolia Springs. Harriet Beecher Stowe, whose house was located in Mandarin, often visited Magnolia and said the "croquet-ground is under the shade of a fine grove of live-oaks which, with their swaying drapery of white moss, form a graceful shade and shelter."

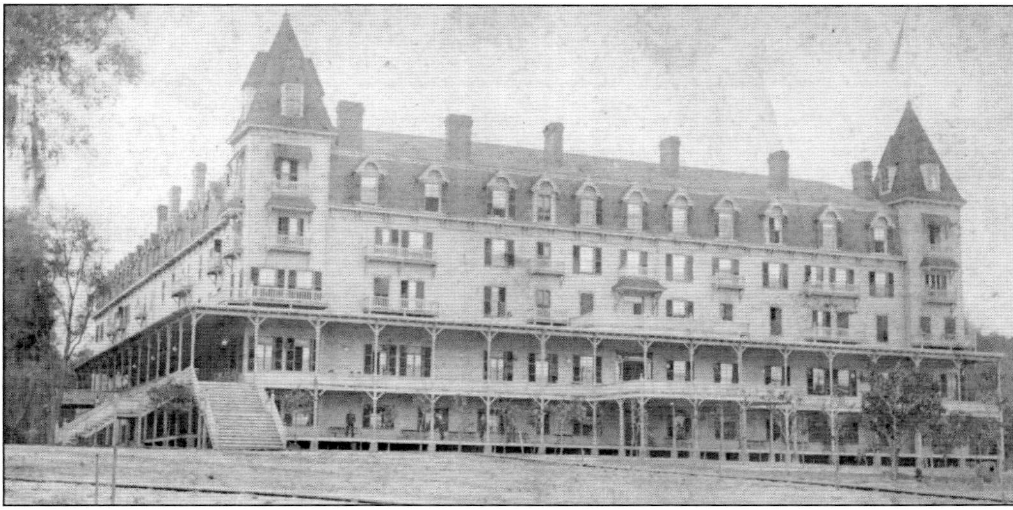

MAGNOLIA HOTEL AROUND 1895. Osborn Dunlap Seavey (1848–1923) was the primary driving force to getting the new Magnolia Springs Hotel built. While managing the Hotel Brunswick in Boston, he met Isaac S. Cruft. When Cruft decided to build hotels in Florida, he chooses Seavey to take charge of the construction and management of the new hotel he built at Magnolia Springs.

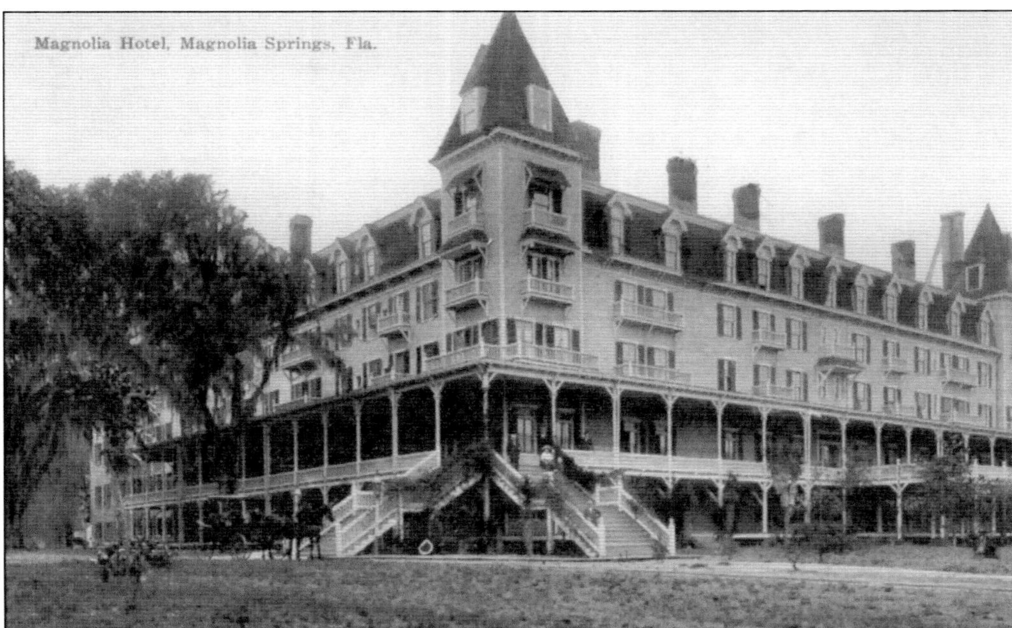

SIDE VIEW OF MAGNOLIA HOTEL. The hotel at Magnolia specifically catered to the northern citizen. One visitor said that the patrons at Magnolia were "the overworked men and women of the north. The people who are not yet invalids, but who are on the verge of a physical bankruptcy in their murderous activity."

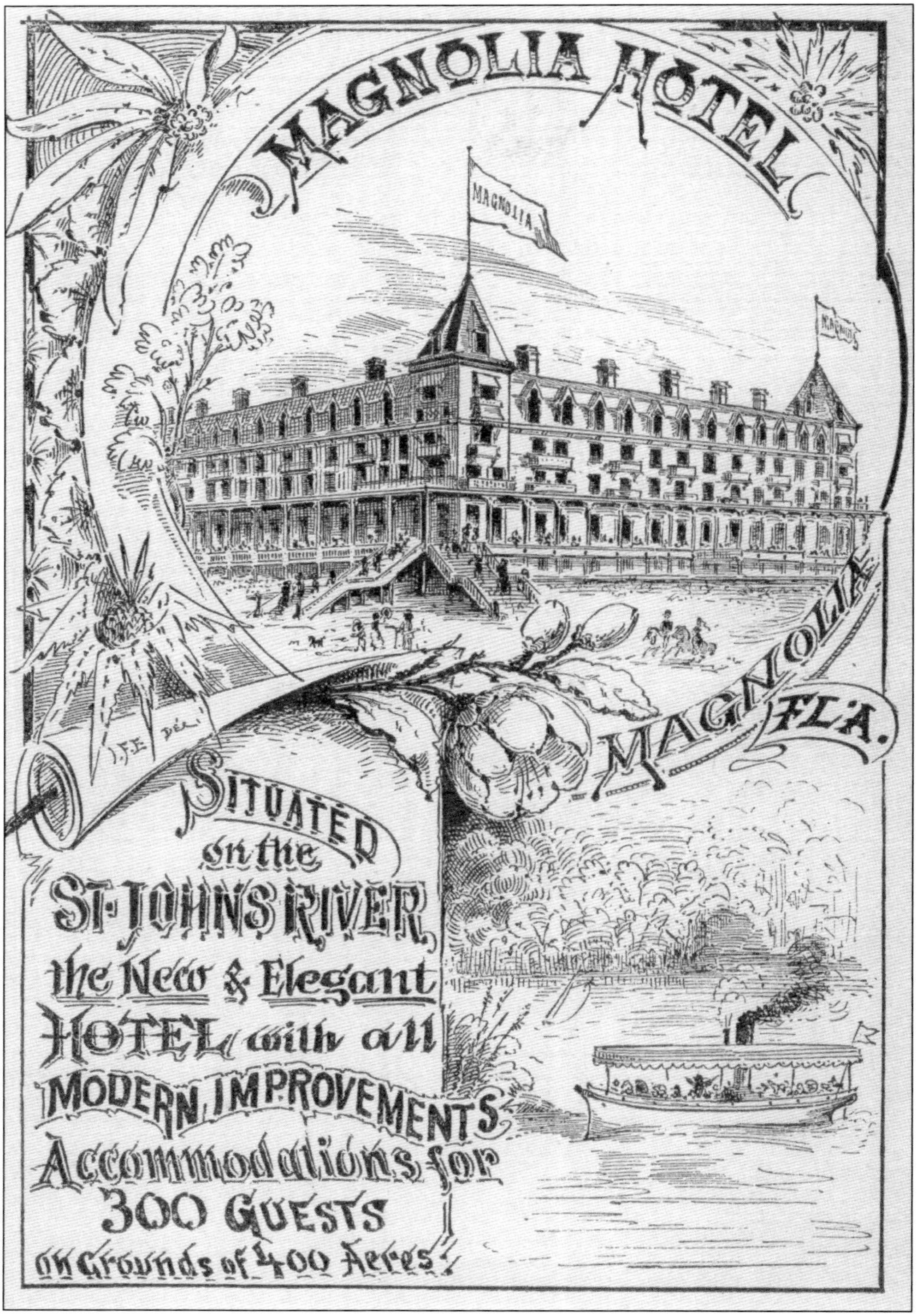

LARGE HOTEL ADVERTISEMENT. The hotel provided modern conveniences such as elevators, steam heating, gas and electric lights, and electric bells. The hotel also provided a music hall with an orchestra, indoor swimming pool, photography darkroom, and fine transportation.

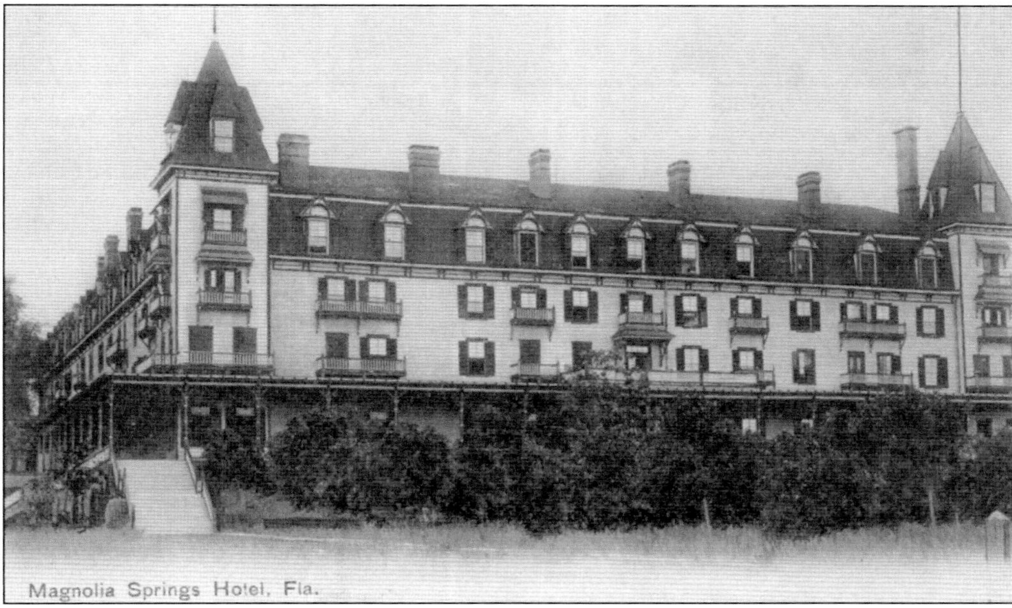

MAGNOLIA SPRINGS HOTEL. When O. D. Seavey decided to retire from the hotel business, he decided to sell the Magnolia Springs Hotel. In 1916, it was listed for sale. Besides a hotel, he said it could have been used for a school or sanitarium. The hotel had 200 rooms and 5 cottages, each with 12 rooms.

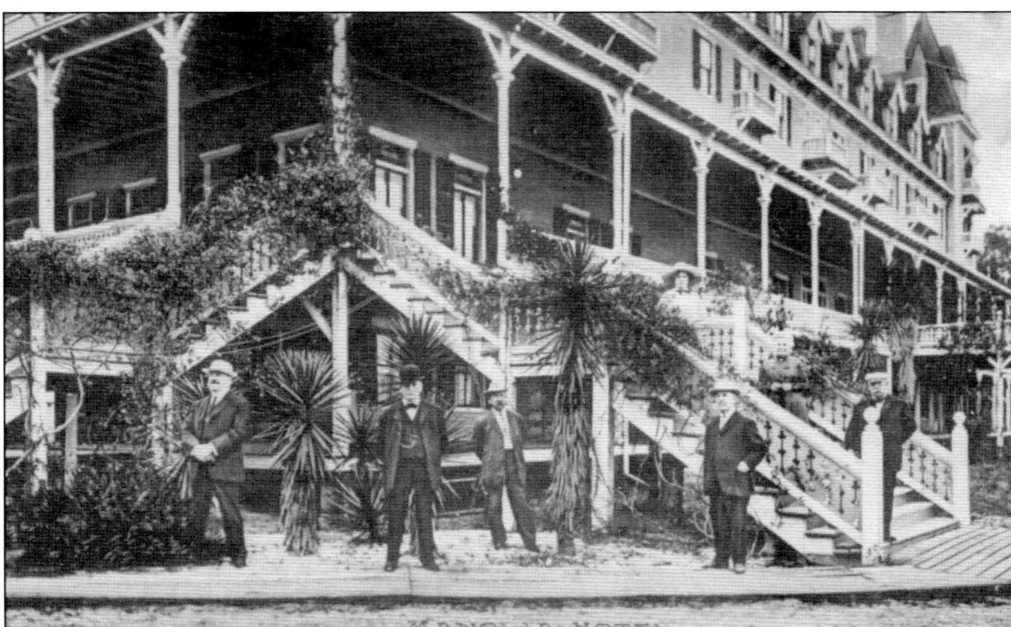

MAGNOLIA HOTEL. O. D. Seavey was around 5 feet, 7 inches in height with blonde hair, blue-gray eyes, a full beard, and was "inclined to be a little stout." His management style was characterized by coolness under fire, and he was always able to act quickly and quietly to solve problems. Seavey moved to St .Augustine when Henry Flagler hired him to manage the Alcazar. This postcard was mailed on March 6, 1914.

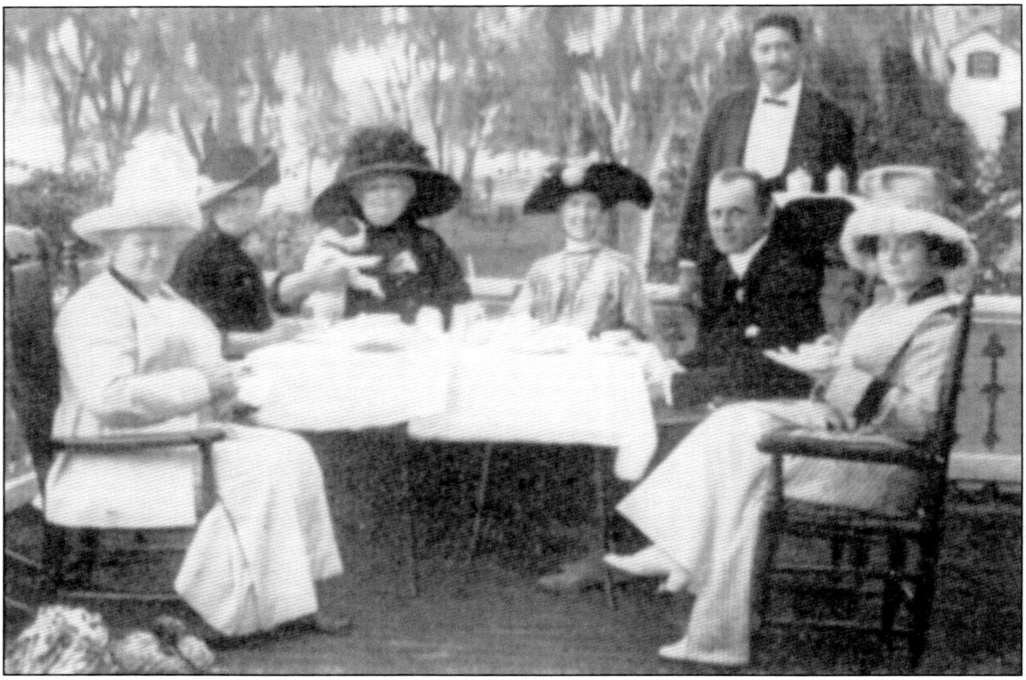

FIVE O'CLOCK TEA ON THE VERANDA. Guest were well taken care of when visiting the Magnolia Hotel. There was an attractive ballroom and theatre, dark room for amateur photography, and the finest fruits and fresh vegetables were available. Also a small herd of cows were kept for "fresh and pure milk."

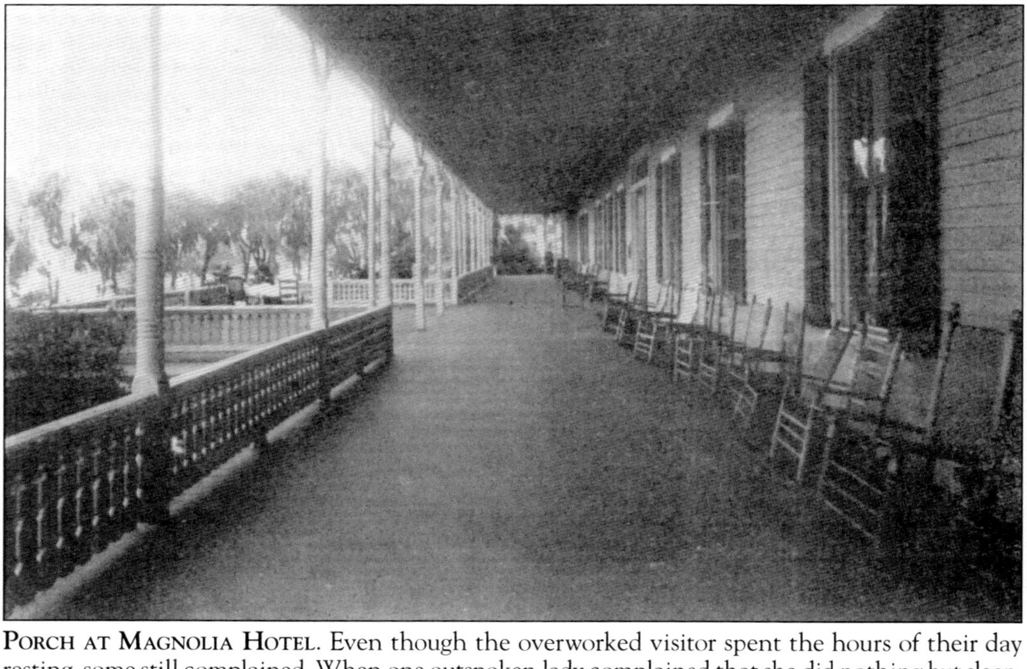

PORCH AT MAGNOLIA HOTEL. Even though the overworked visitor spent the hours of their day resting, some still complained. When one outspoken lady complained that she did nothing but sleep, her friend exclaimed, "well, that is what you came here for, nobody can sleep in New England."

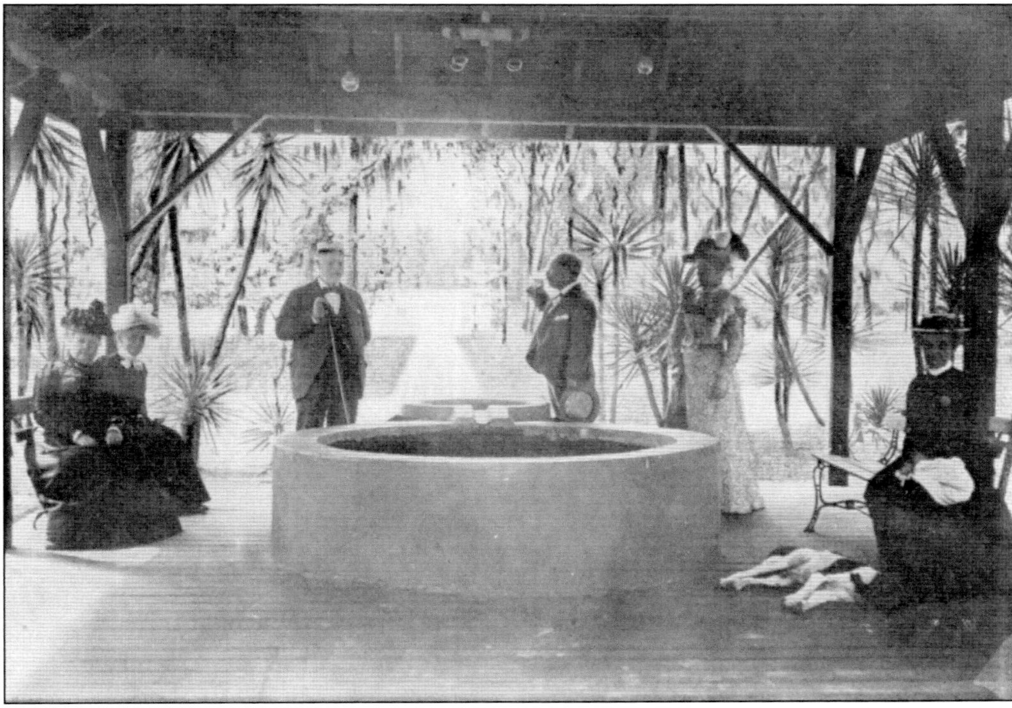

The Spring. A bottling and shipping building were constructed near the Magnolia Spring. The water was bottled in quart and half-gallon bottles, and it could be carbonated or natural. The cost for 50-quart bottles was $6, and 12 half-gallon bottles were $3.

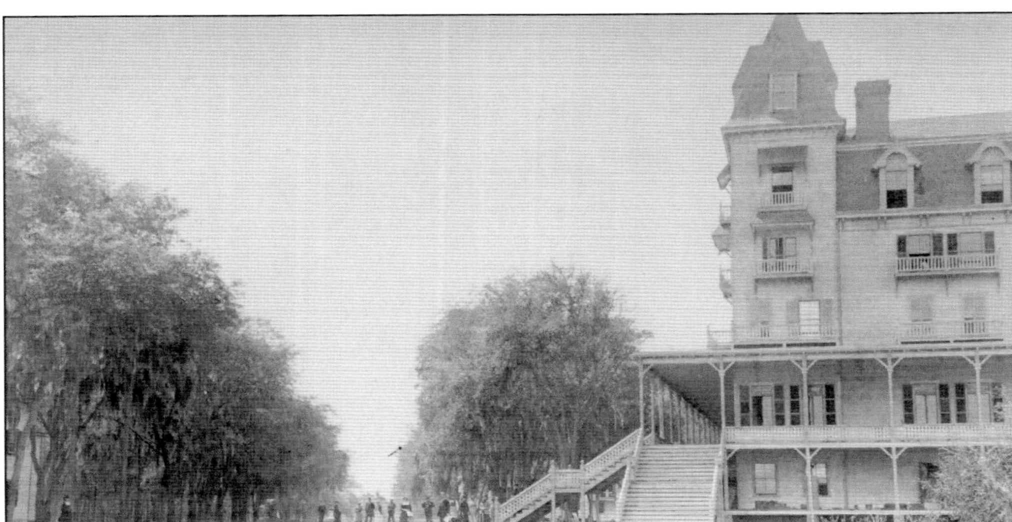

Magnolia Hotel by J. S. Mitchell. On November 11, 1923, the Magnolia Springs Hotel burned. The estimated loss at that time stood at $100,000, and the fire was thought to have originated in the engine room. Assistance from Jacksonville was asked but by the time the Jacksonville firemen arrived, the fire was already under control, and the firemen turned back.

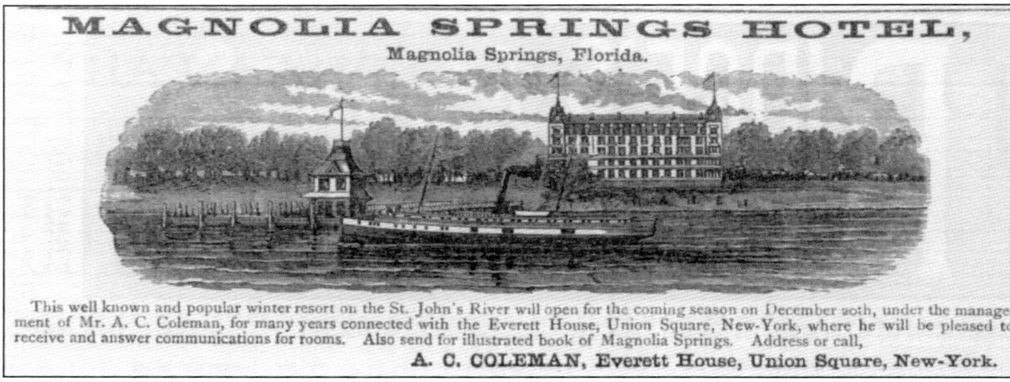

HOTEL ADVERTISEMENT. When President Arthur's steamboat left Jacksonville on an April night in 1883, they noticed a row of electric lights rising and falling and, soon thereafter, rockets bursting into blue lights. The president's steamboat made a quick stop at Magnolia where he was greeted by a cheering crowd. The president stood on the upper deck where he raised his hat to recognize the crowd for their enthusiastic welcome.

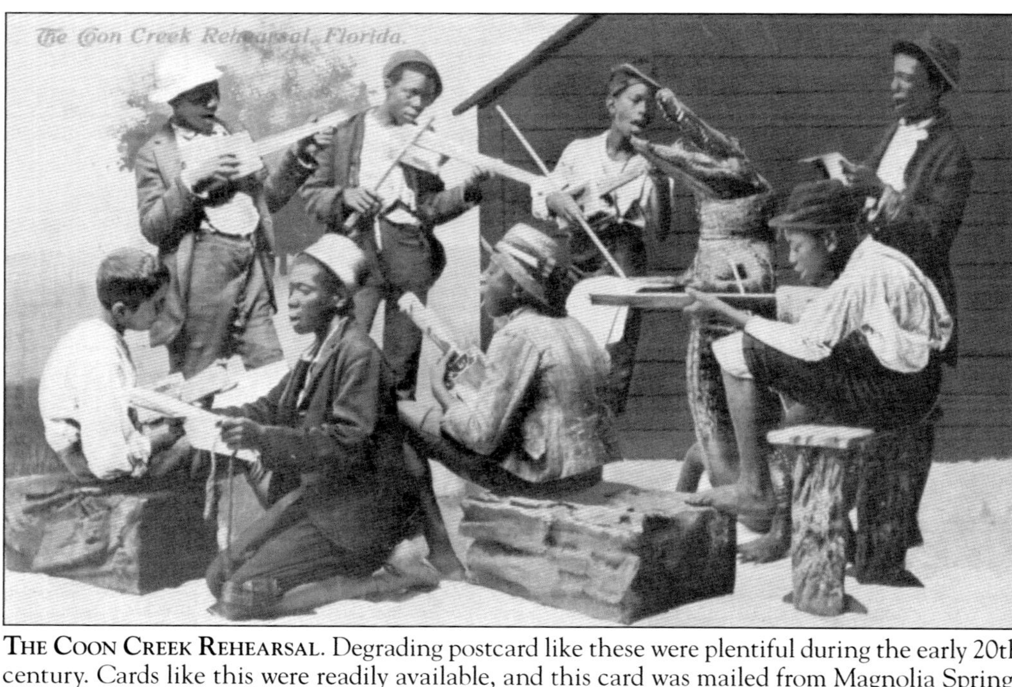

THE COON CREEK REHEARSAL. Degrading postcard like these were plentiful during the early 20th century. Cards like this were readily available, and this card was mailed from Magnolia Springs on February 20, 1913, to New York City.

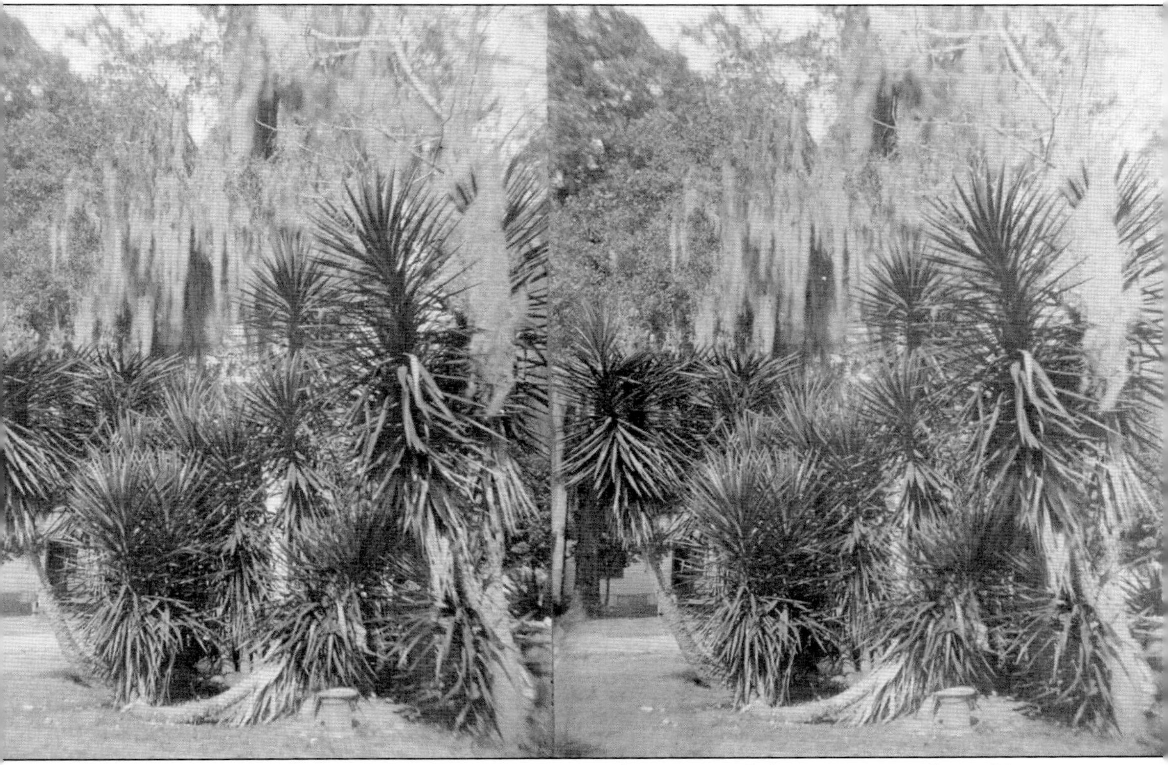

Spanish Bayonet at Magnolia Hotel by Upton. These Spanish bayonet were planted long before the Magnolia Hotel was built. These plants are cold hardy to survive the harshest Florida winter. This grouping was planted near one of the several cottages, so guests could use it as a backdrop in their photographs.

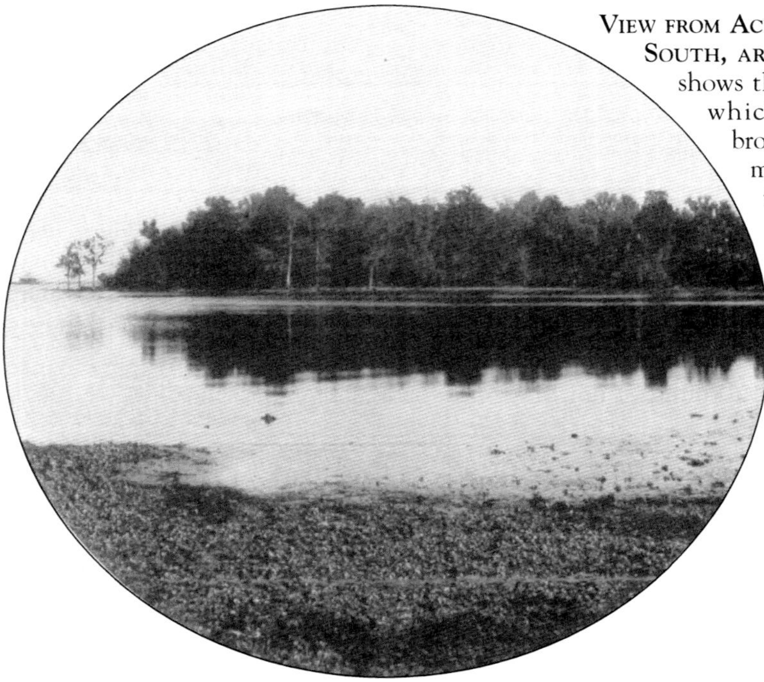

View from Across the Bay Looking South, around 1920. This view shows the excellent riverfront, which an undated hotel brochure described as "five miles wide and the depth for form a half mile to three-quarters of a mile from the shore is not greater than four feet thus affording a safe place for rowing."

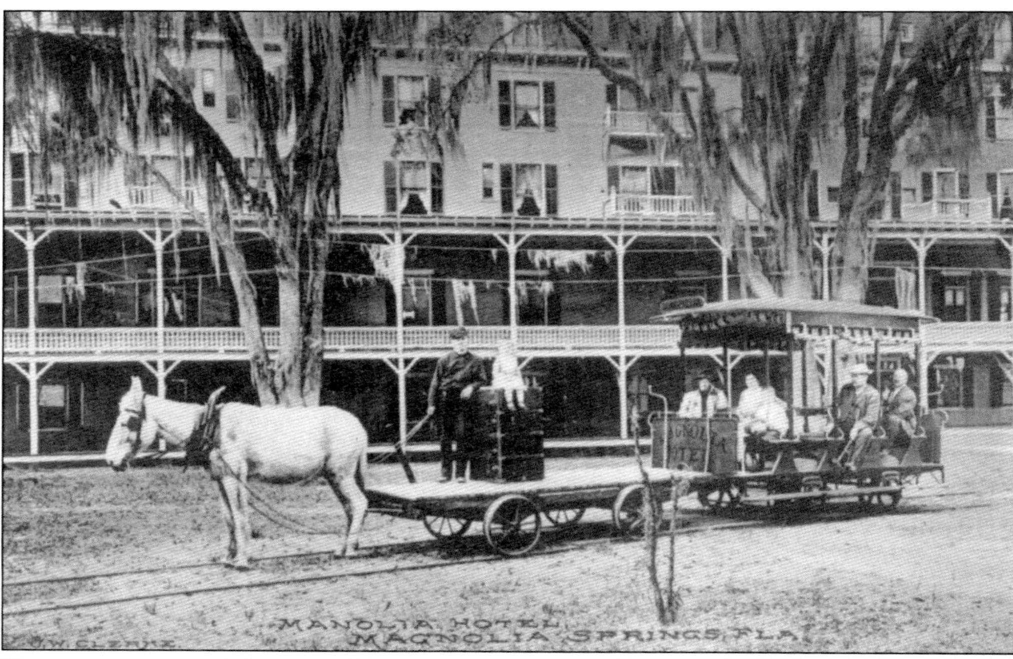

Transportation at Magnolia Hotel. A tramcar met all boats and trains conveying the guests to their splendid hotel. It was said that a "mild day in January from the deck of an approaching steamer, when a band of music occupies the pavilion on the dock, and the hotel piazzas are gay with light colors of fashionably-dressed guests;" it could remind someone of a scene in the Catskills during the height of the summer tourist season. This postcard was mailed on February 25, 1913.

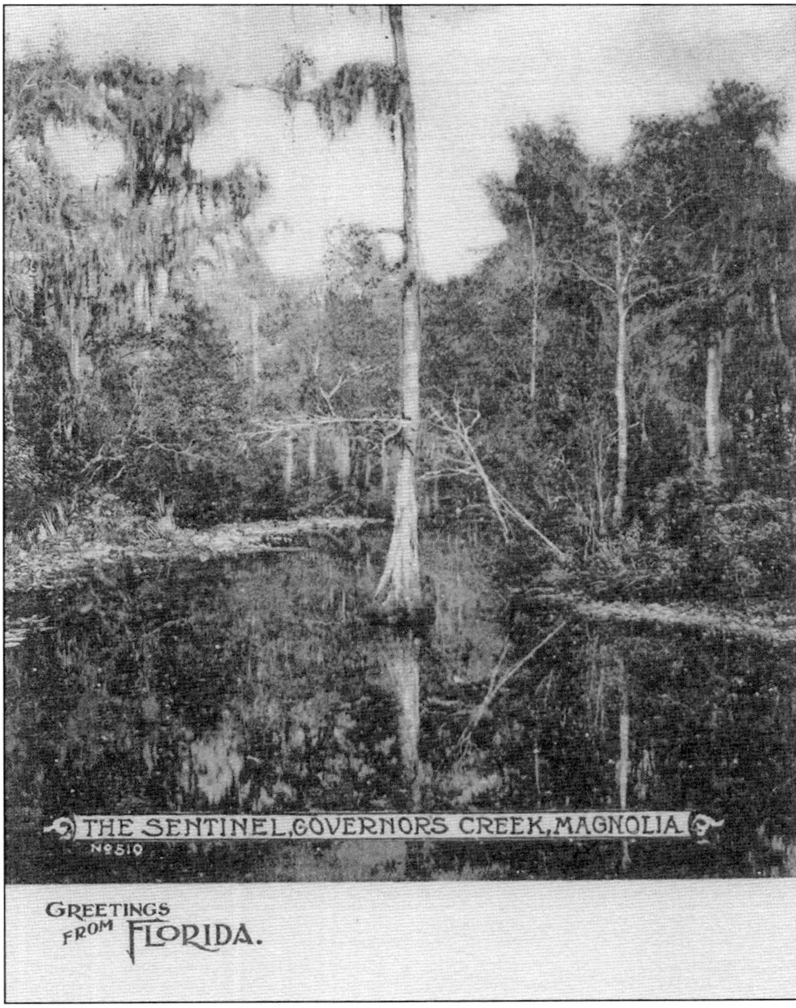

THE SENTINEL. Guests from the north made it a habit of returning year after year to Magnolia. One guest who had been visiting annually for 40 years wrote, "The pleasure of days of bright sunshine during January, February and March, is enhanced by the outdoor life under the shade of the delightful and beautiful grove in which the hotel is situated."

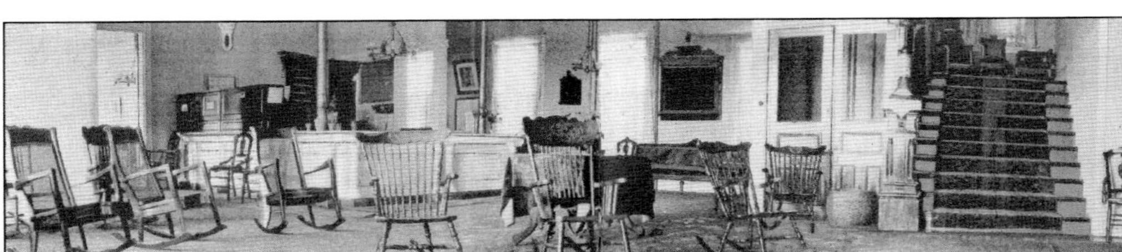

FRONT HOTEL PARLOR. When Seavey was unable to sell the hotel, he rented it to Col. George W. Hulvey of the Florida Military Academy. The military academy had been located at the St. Elmo Hotel, but it was in need of more room. The military academy remained at Magnolia until the hotel and two cottages burned on November 11, 1923.

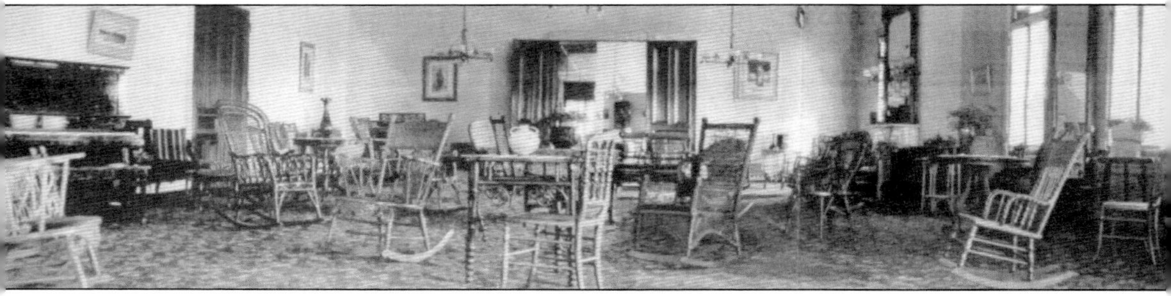

HOTEL PARLOR. "The parlors are large commodious apartments beautifully carpeted and furnished, and when the gas is turned on, illuminating the long room," wrote one newspaper. The hotel staff attended to the wants and needs of the guests in a "skillful manner."

Three

Green Cove Springs Hotels

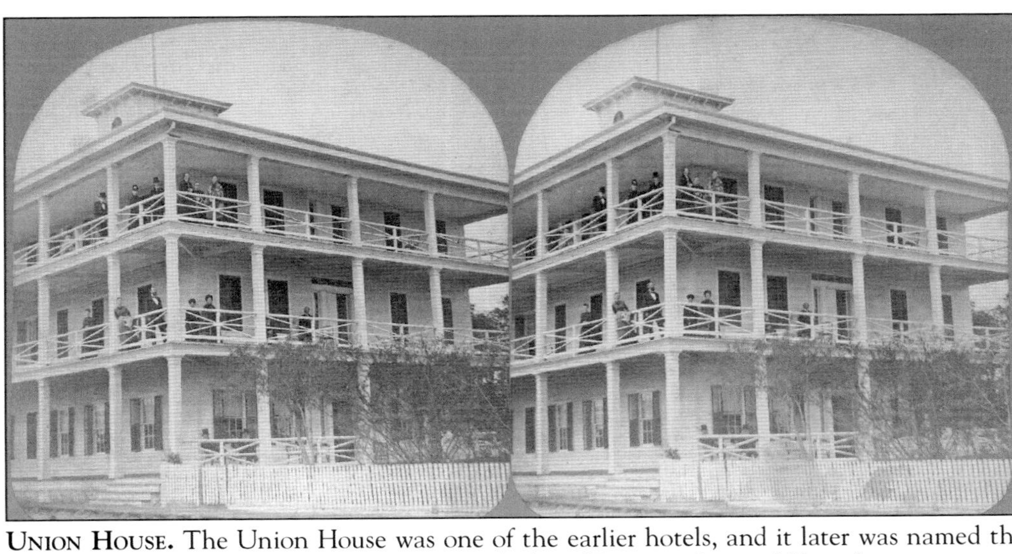

Union House. The Union House was one of the earlier hotels, and it later was named the St. Clair. In 1883, the hotel was managed by Gluck and Rogers, who would later leave to manage a newly built hotel in St. Augustine.

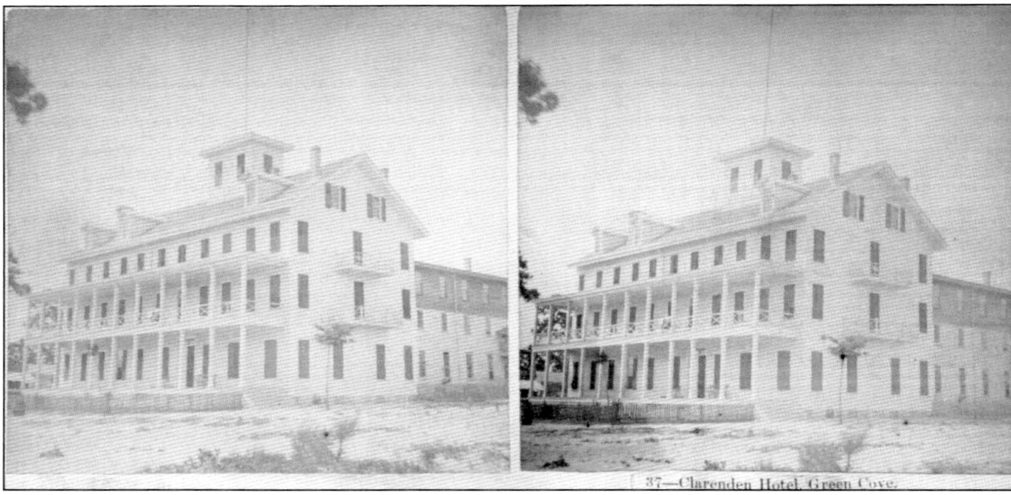

CLARENDON HOTEL BY WOOD AND BICKEL. The Clarendon was one of the first hotels in town, and it helped to promote the town as a "place of health, beauty and happiness."

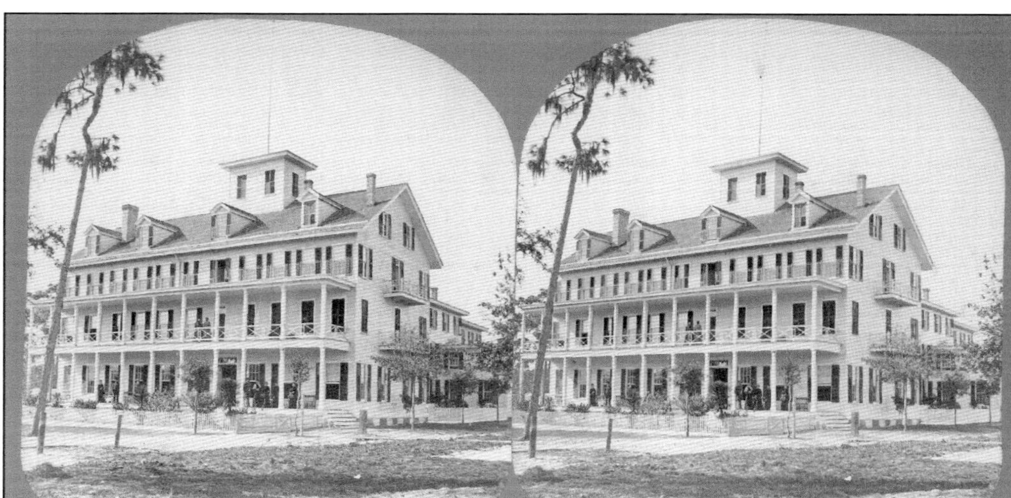

CLARENDON HOTEL. When Arthur T. Aldrich established the Clarendon Hotel around 1871, he said, "I never would have built a hotel, a store, a wharf, in fact, would not be there myself, but for the existence of the spring. The spring adds, to some extent, to the attraction and profit of my house."

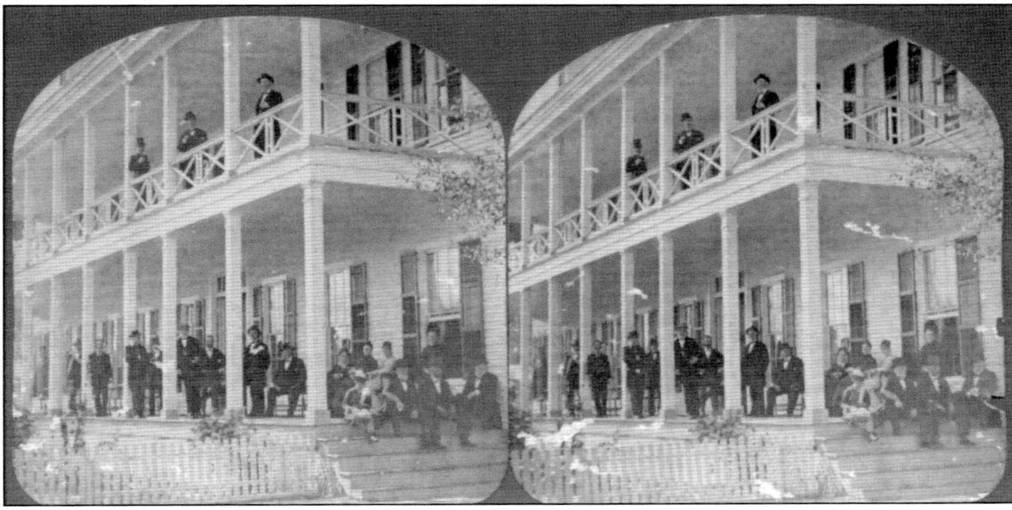

CLARENDON HOTEL BY ISAAC HAAS. After the Clarendon was finished, Arthur Aldrich built a wharf, which induced the steamers to stop at Green Cove Springs. Aldrich said that because of his new hotel, the visiting population had increased and that three-fourths more people pay to patronage the spring.

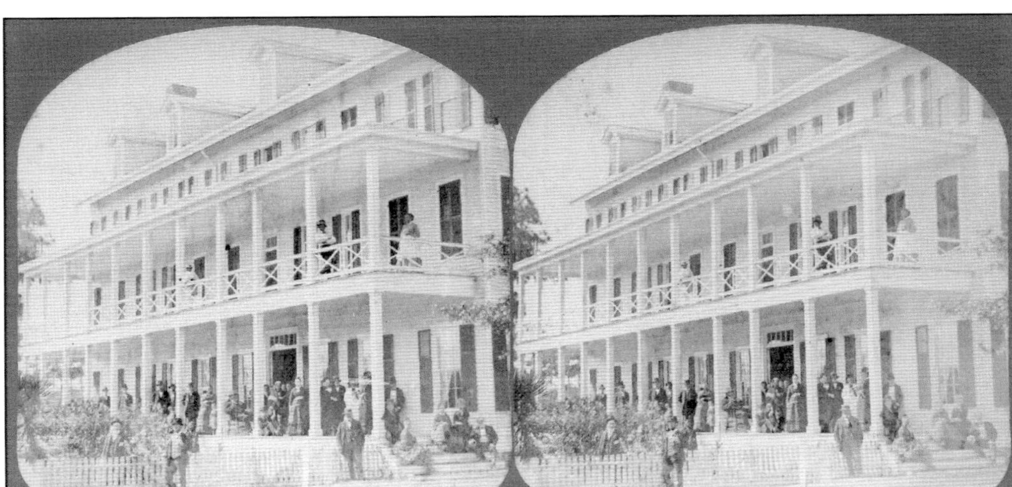

VISITORS AT CLARENDON HOTEL BY ISAAC HAAS. When the tourists would arrive at the train stations or wharfs, one newly transplanted resident wrote, "it is amusing to hear the exclamations of delight and the spontaneous outburst of those who have never been in Florida, and who left home only a few days before . . . in a snow storm."

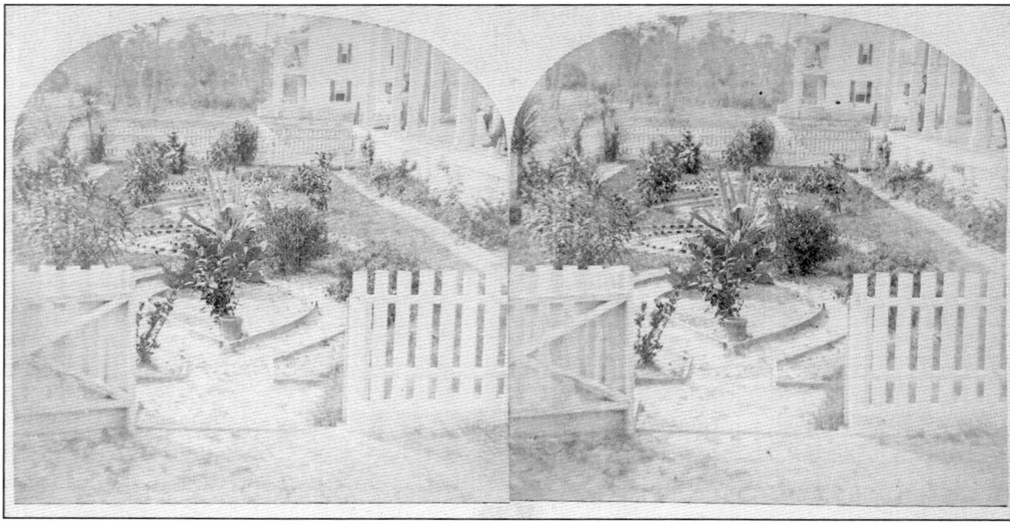

Clarendon Garden by W. H. Cushing. The large hotels maintained small gardens so guests could have fresh fruits and vegetables. This ornamental garden was in front of the Clarendon facing the spring.

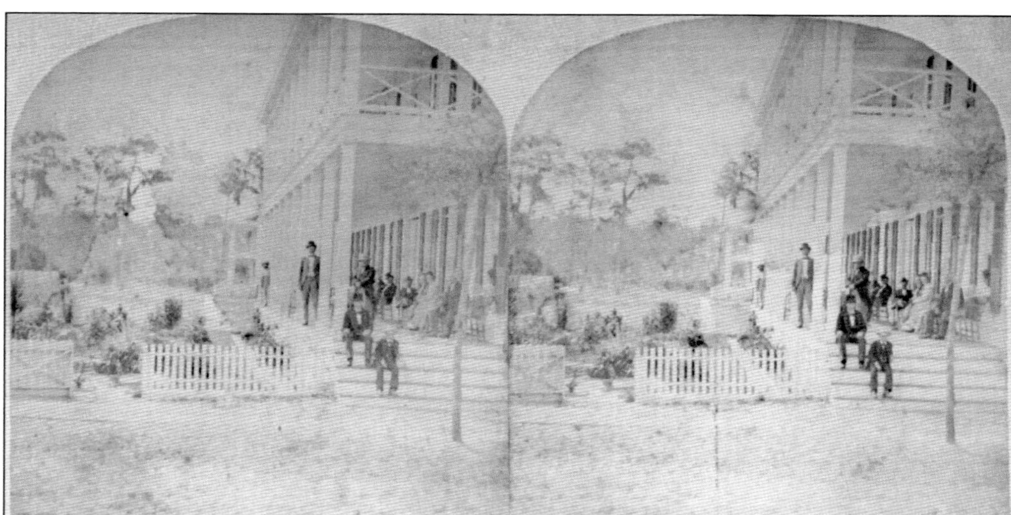

Clarendon Hotel by W. H. Cushing. The hotels made it a point to have lush semitropical gardens looking full for the northern tourist. Many of the visitors would leave the north in snowstorms and within two days, arrive in Florida where they would see "ripe oranges handing on the trees, mocking birds singing in the branches, and all living things seemed basking in the sunlight."

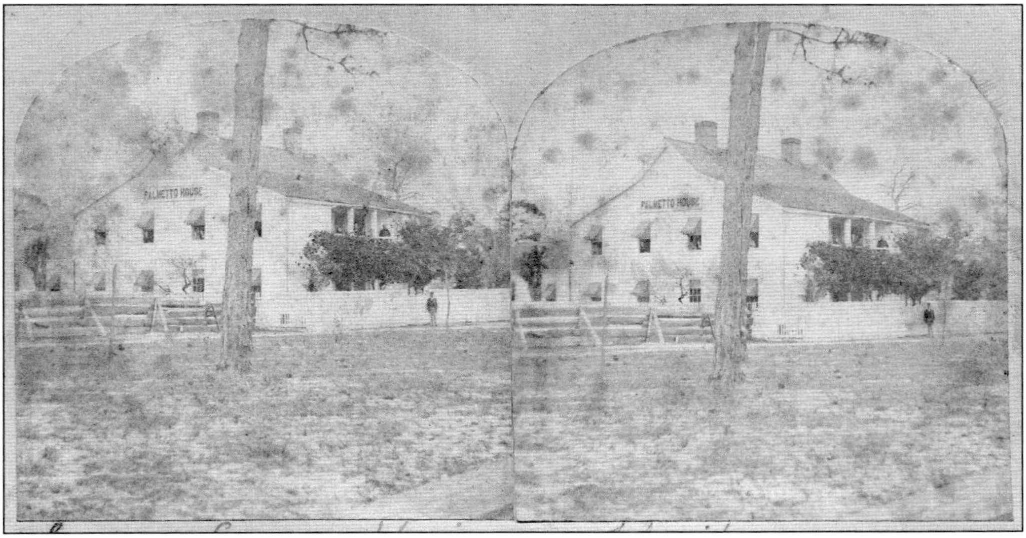

Palmetto House. In 1873, Green Cove "promises to become in time a flourishing and populous village." The Palmetto House was one of the earlier and short-lived hotels. Nothing else is known about this hotel.

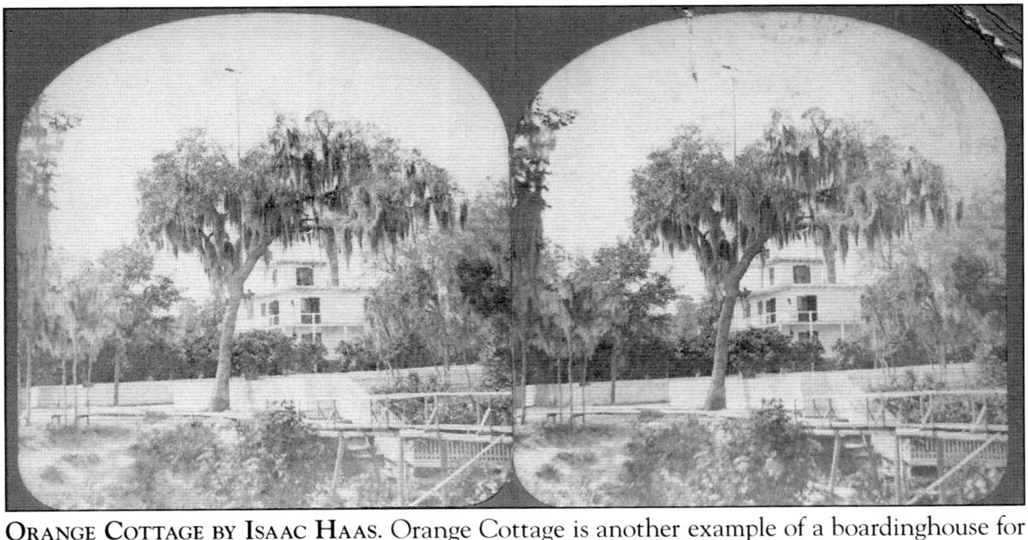

Orange Cottage by Isaac Haas. Orange Cottage is another example of a boardinghouse for visitors. Its location was excellent, since it was very near the springs run. Notice the footbridge across the spring run.

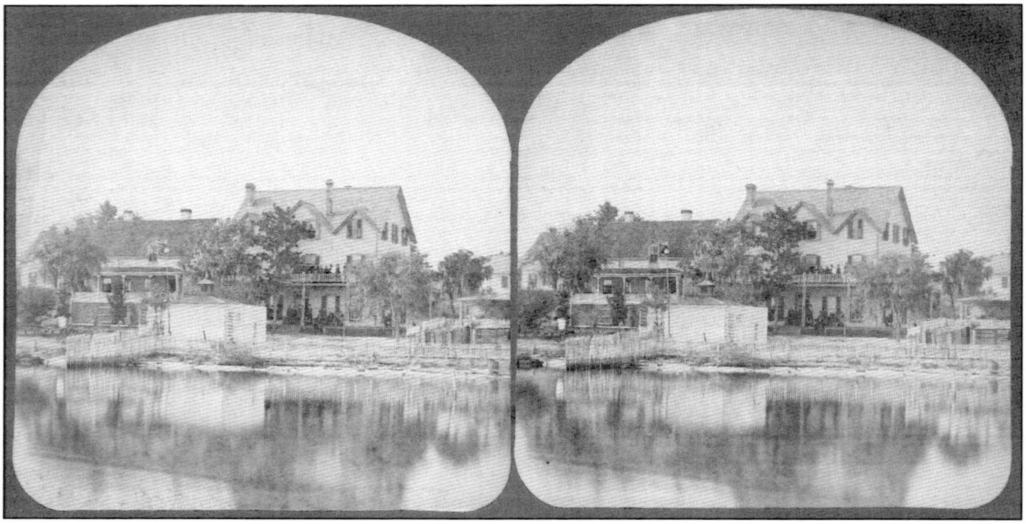

Riverside Cottage by Isaac Haas. This hotel was located on St. Johns Avenue, and its grounds around the house were teaming with "oleanders, fragrant roses, and numerous other fragrant flowers . . . [that] mingles with sub-tropical plants and vines while magnificent shade trees protected them."

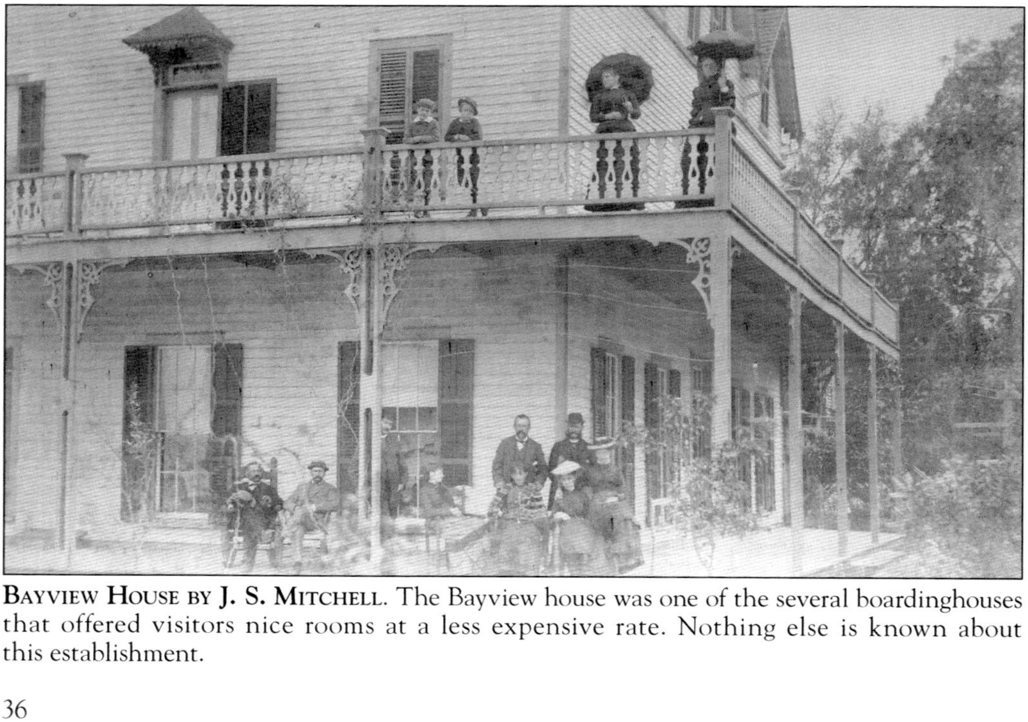

Bayview House by J. S. Mitchell. The Bayview house was one of the several boardinghouses that offered visitors nice rooms at a less expensive rate. Nothing else is known about this establishment.

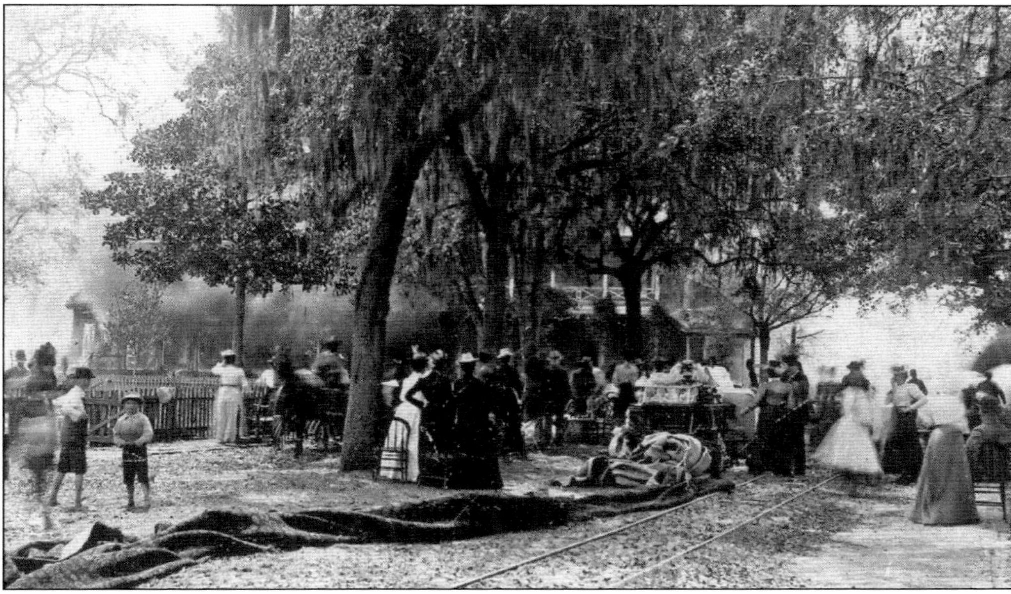

April 3, 1900, Clarendon on Fire. In a letter to the editor of the *New York Times*, a previous visitor recalls the fire that consumed the Clarendon. "The main hotel at Green Cove Springs, Fla was burned down, fortunately at midday, but even at that hour there would probably have been a loss of life to a very estimable aged Philadelphia gentleman had not the porter remembered he was quite deaf. The door was locked and the gentleman was reading and did not hear the knock. The porter kicked the door down and the frightened gentleman had barely time to rush down one flight to the ground and in a few minutes the entire large hotel was a seething mass of flam. But for the thoughtful kicking down of the door, a precious life undoubtedly would have been lost." (Courtesy Clay County Archives.)

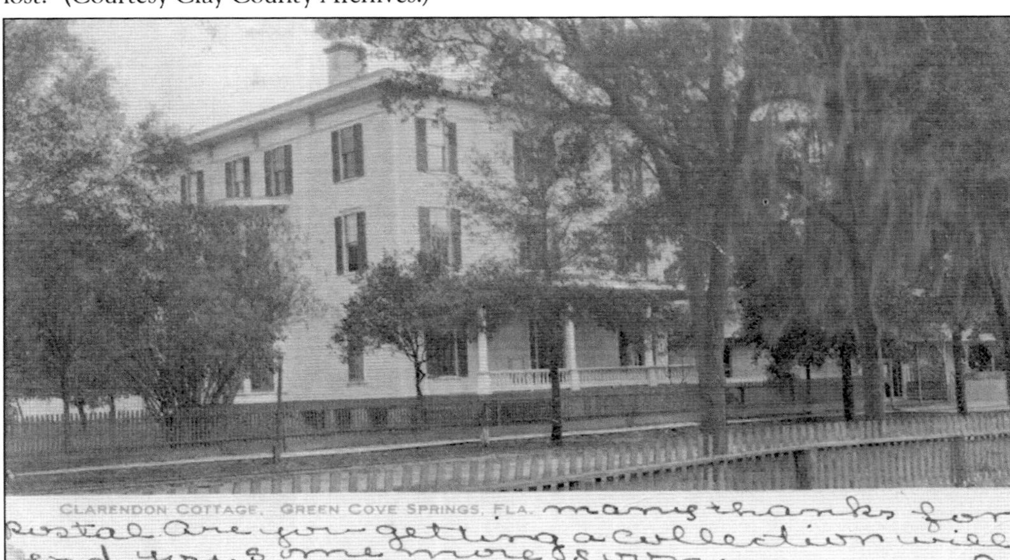

Clarendon Hotel Cottage. When the main building of the Clarendon hotel burned in 1900, only the two cottages survived. Today the remaining cottage is a bed and breakfast. (Courtesy Clay County Archives.)

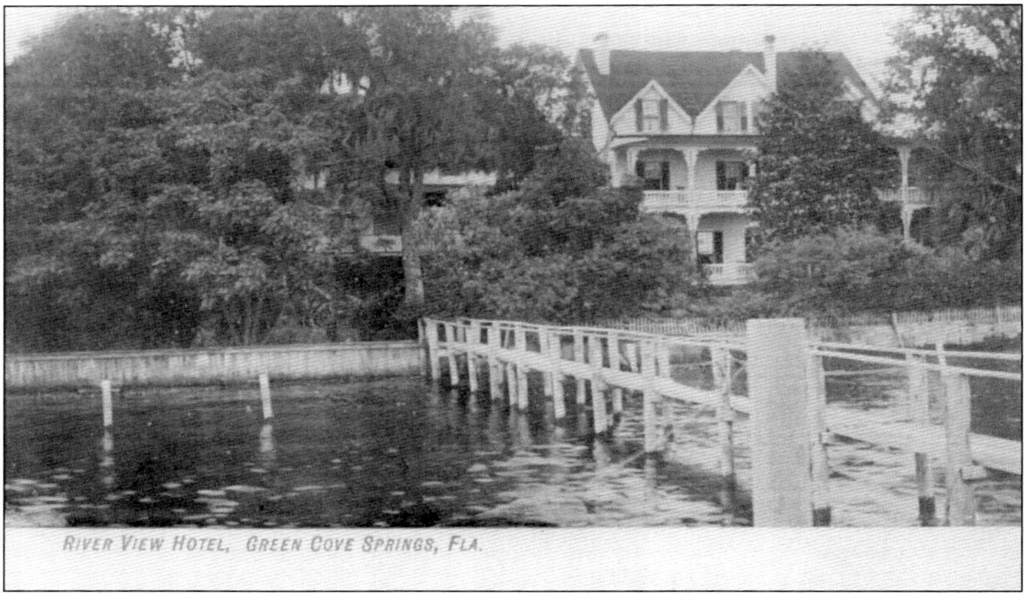

Riverview Hotel. The Riverview hotel was located on St. Johns Avenue. It was a small, private boardinghouse. In an undated letter from March one visitor wrote that there were "some 25 boarders . . . is very pleasant, a large yard, croquet grounds, etc. The boarding is good and the house well kept—such nice attentive servants."

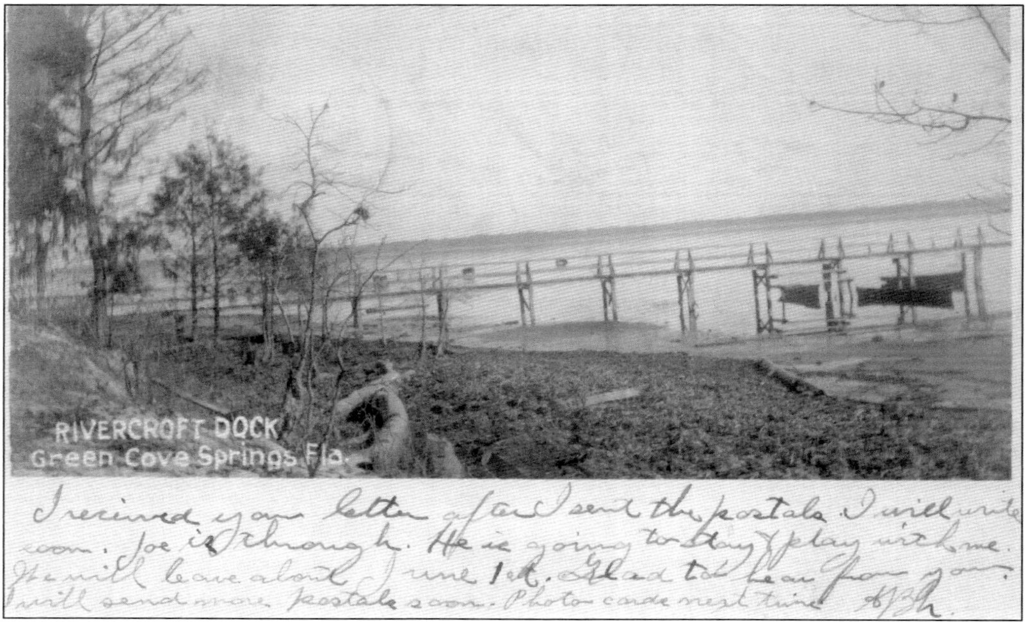

Rivercroft Dock. The docks on the river were used to dispose of table scraps. When Senator James Beck visited, he watched as a servant dumped a tin pan of refuse into the water. Almost immediately, there was a terrible struggle in the water. As Senator Beck watched the fish, he leaned over the railing and out tumbled his spectacles and case. "In a moment a catfish certainly two feet long, took in the case, and made a bee-line for the middle of the river. The Senator yelled, 'Stop him! Stop him! He's got my glasses!' "

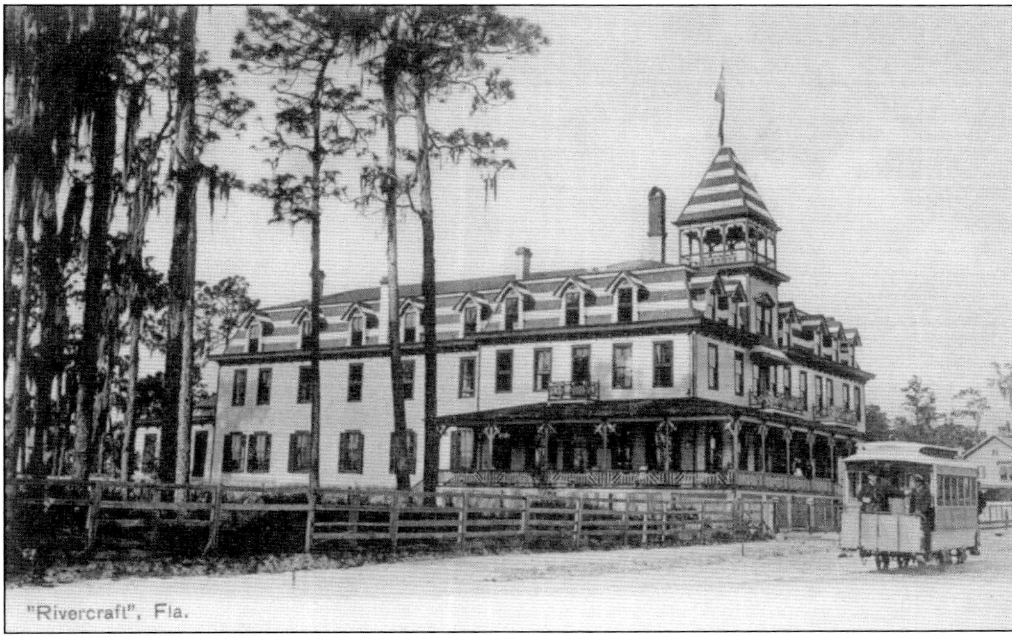

The Rivercraft. Also known as the St. Elmo Hotel (and Hotel St. Elmo) in 1893, a number of improvements were made to the hotel during the summer. Many of the rooms had been repapered, and new carpets were put down and "the whole house thoroughly renovated," said one newspaper story.

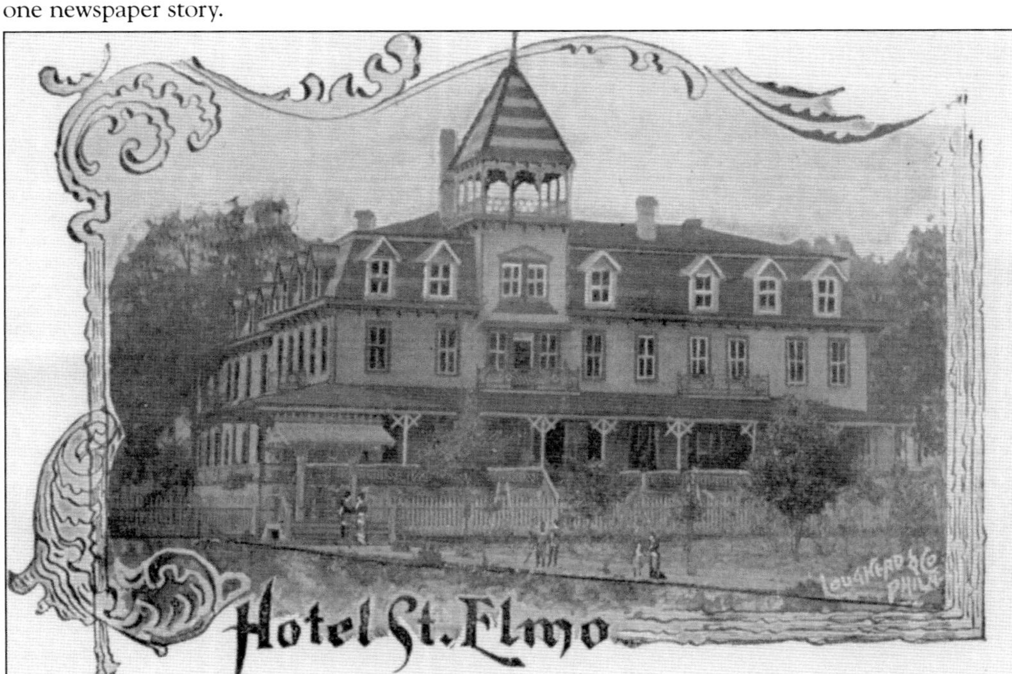

Hotel St. Elmo. The St. Elmo was described as being free from dust and noise and that "everything money and brains can procure has been utilized in fitting up the hotel . . . making it *absolutely a place of rest and comfort.*"

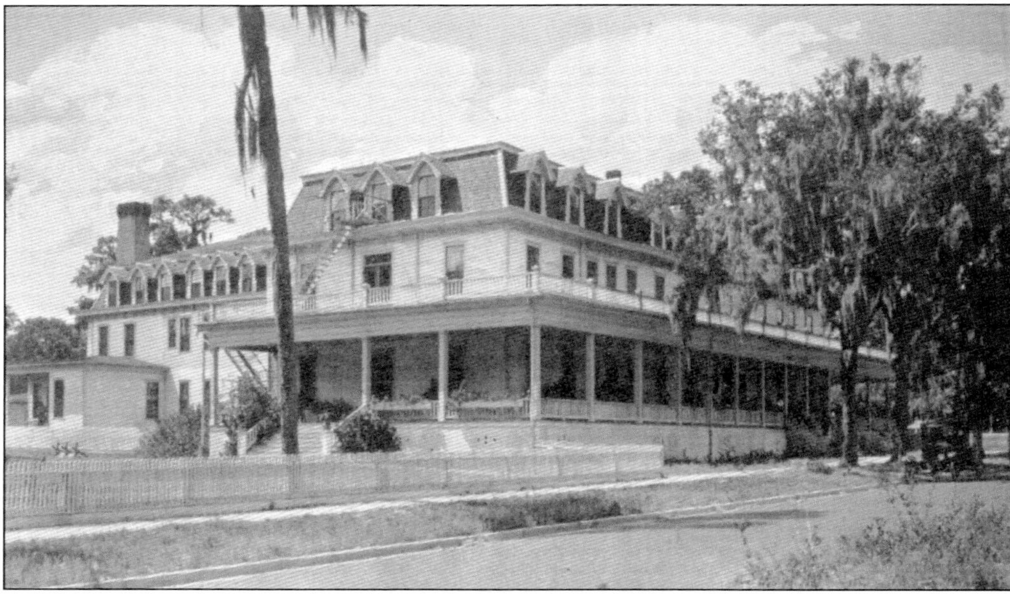

ST. ELMO HOTEL AROUND 1925. The St. Elmo around 1909–1911 was converted into a school by the Florida Military Academy, and by 1917 (with the academy having moved to the Magnolia Springs Hotel) the St. Elmo had been converted into apartments.

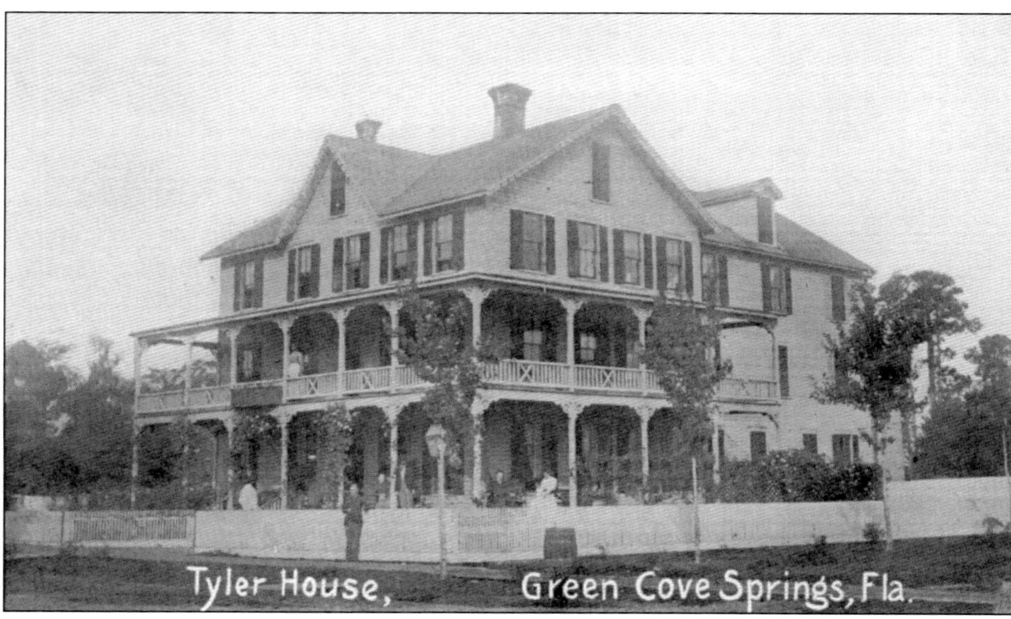

TYLER HOUSE. Originally called the Lochmore, it changed names sometime around the turn of the 20th century. By 1917, it was known as the Seminole Hotel. This postcard is dated May 1, 1911.

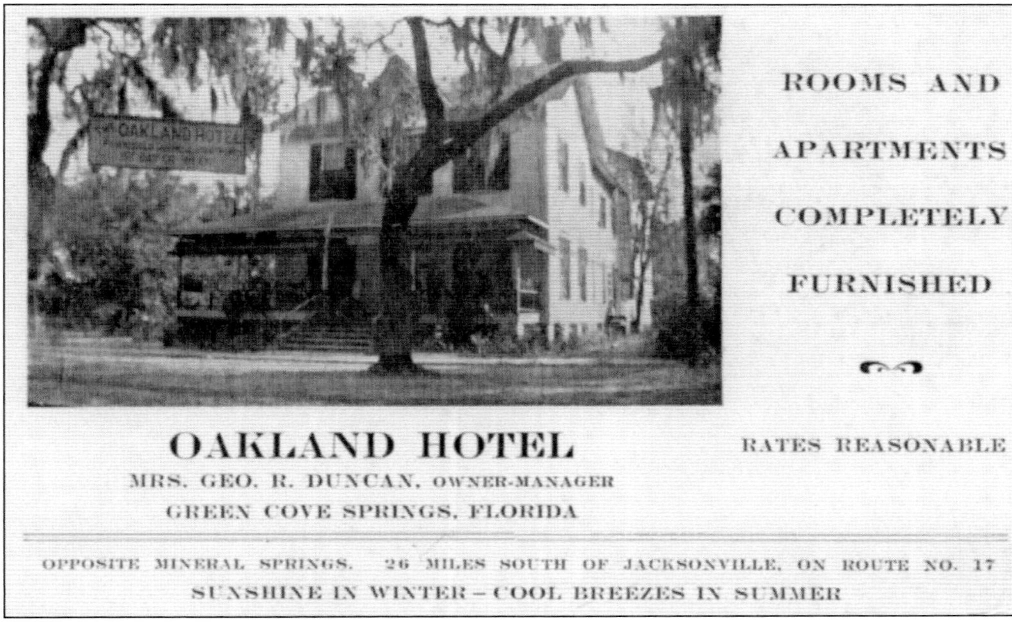

OAKLAND HOTEL. The Oakland Hotel was located near the spring and, in 1896, charged $2.00 to $2.50 per day. By early 20th century, the hotel had converted into an apartment building with 30 furnished rooms that could each be rented for $30 a month. (Courtesy Clay County Archives.)

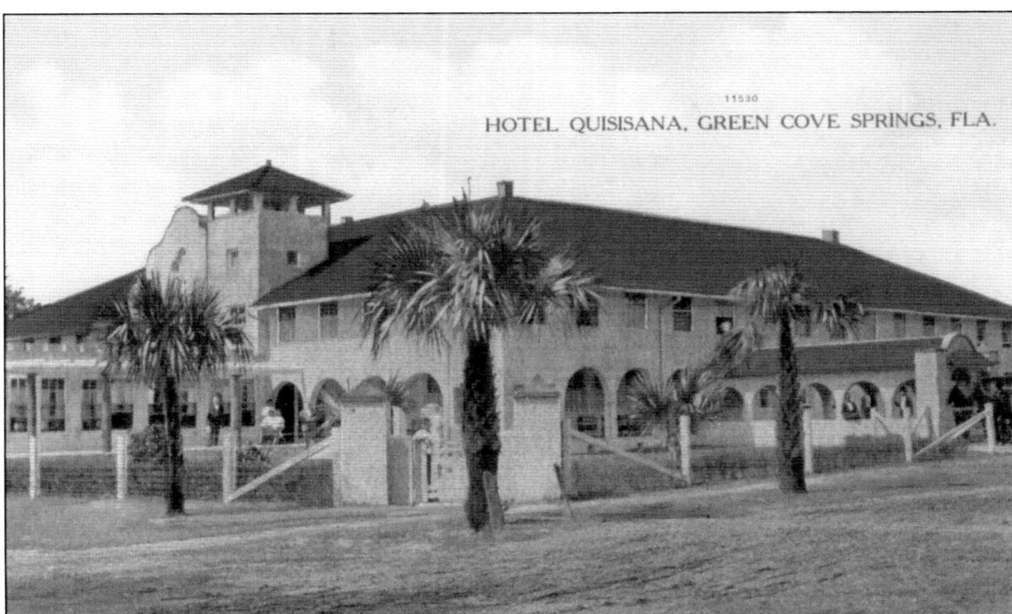

QUI-SI-SANA HOTEL. Built in 1907 on the same lot the Clarendon hotel stood, the Qui-Si-Sana became the major hotel for the town. In 1912, John Barnes, the manager of the hotel, advertised that the Qui-Si-Sana was the "oldest resort in Florida." It had eclectic lights, steam heat, was fireproof, and had a Spanish-mission style throughout.

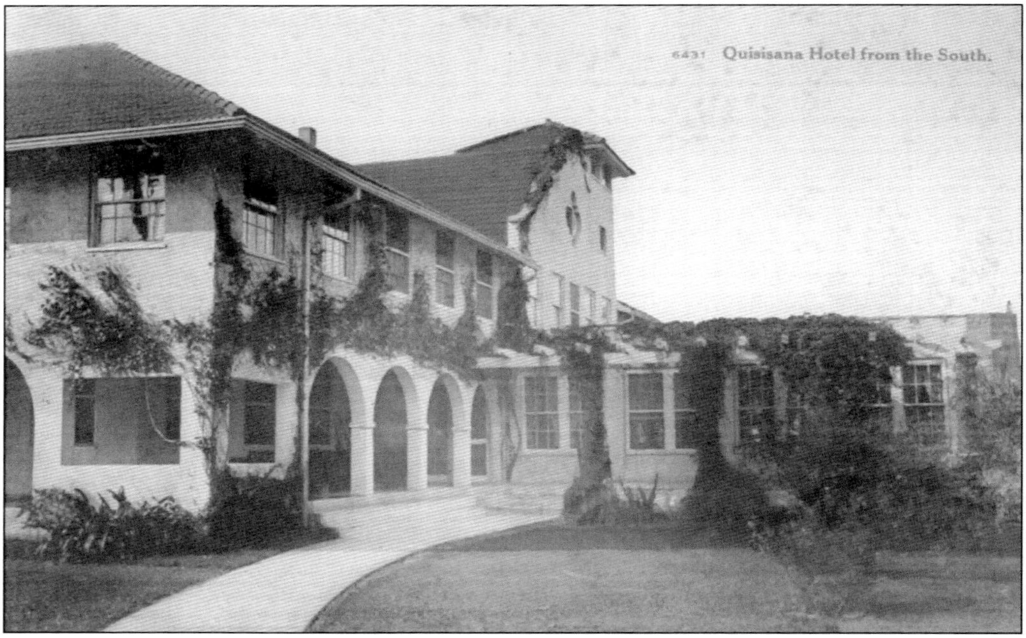

QU-SI-SANA HOTEL FROM THE SOUTH. In 1931, the hotel had 50 rooms with weekly rates from $25 to $30. It advertised for the sportsman that it had golf, tennis, fishing, and boating. The hotel manager was G. J. Maust. (Courtesy Clay County Archives.)

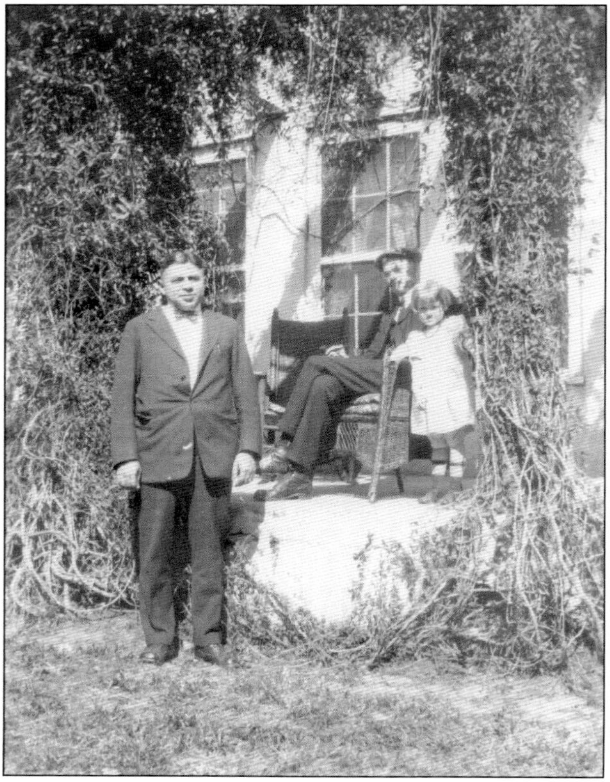

GUESTS AT THE QUYI-SI-SANA. This *c.* 1920s photograph shows three guests on the south side of the Qui-Si-Sana. It was during this decade that the tourist industry greatly diminished in Green Cove Springs.

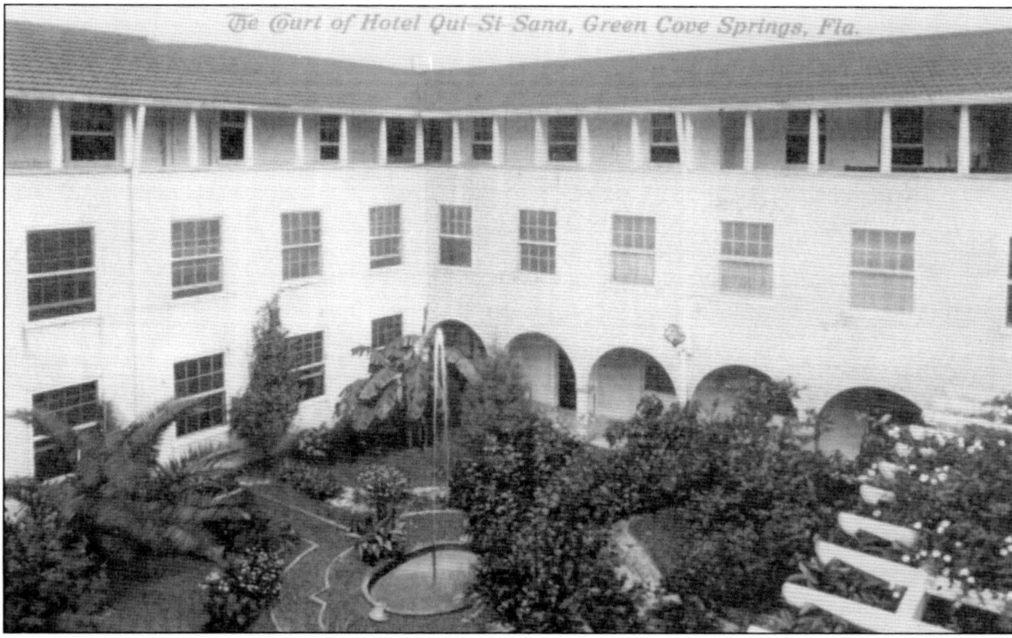

THE COURT OF HOTEL QUI-SI-SANA. The hotel continued to provide accommodations for travelers, although the town had lost its reputation as a winter resort. The casino provided 10 bathing pools, and the hotel's golf course had a clubhouse and a golf professional in charge.

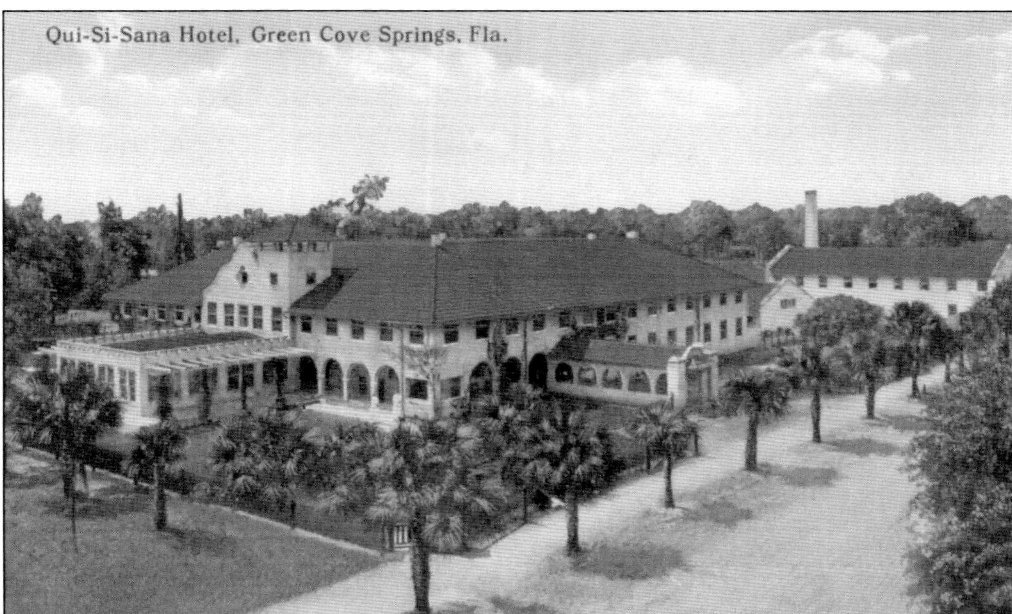

QUI-SI-SANA. The Qui-Si-Sana in later years became known as the Green Cove Motor Inn, and parts of it were Carey's Antique Store. In 2002, the old hotel was demolished for a new city hall whose architecture was consistent with that of the original hotel.

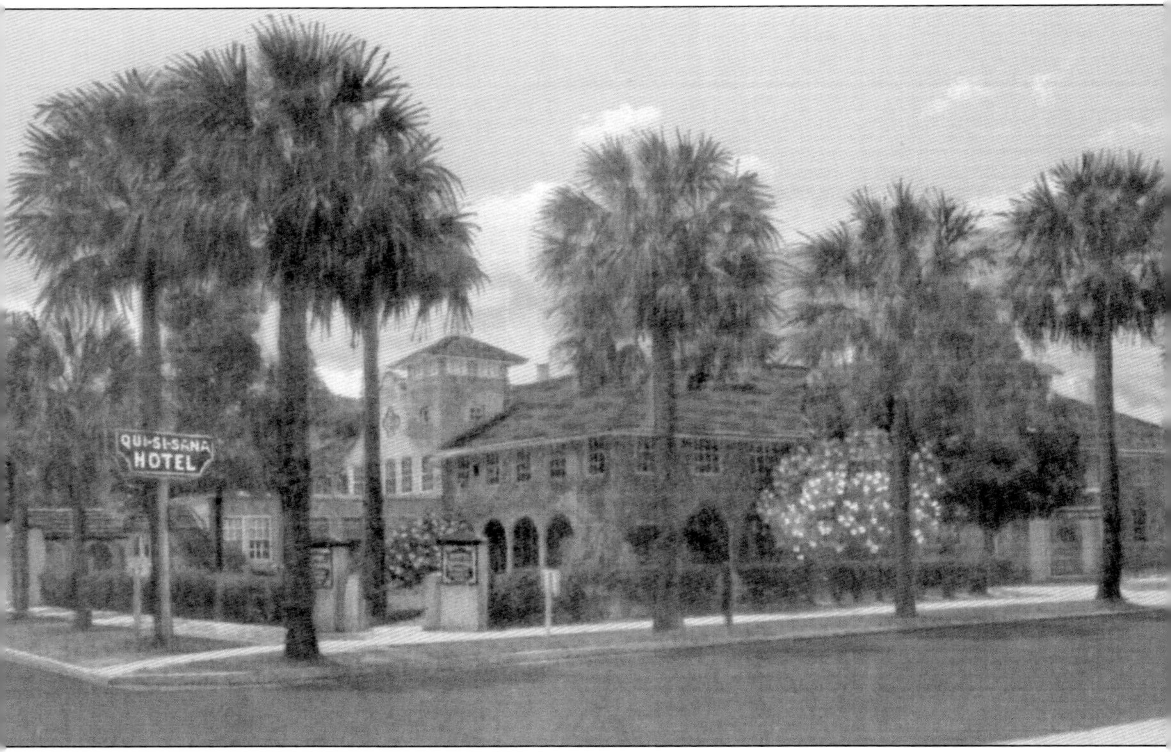

QUI-SI-SANA AROUND 1945. The Qui-Si-Sana became busier when the navy arrived in town. The hotel could accommodate 70 guests, and the rates were $5 per day. In 1945, the hotel was managed by C. C. Thompson. The flagpole to the far right still stands on Walnut Street.

Four

The Green Cove Spring

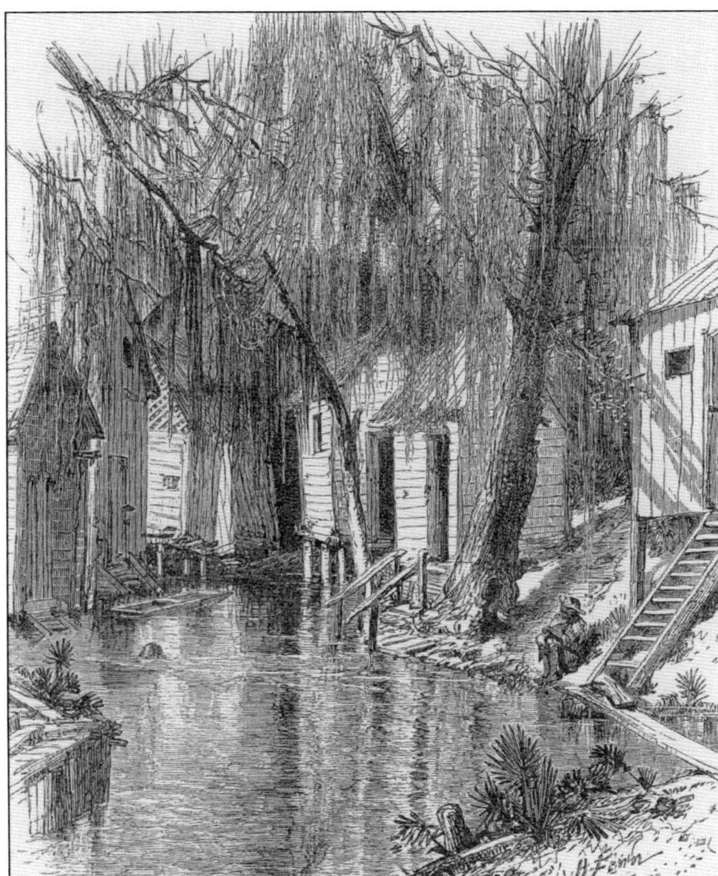

Spring Run. Before the Clarendon Hotel was built, the spring was "almost in a wild state," according to William Long, who helped to make improvements on the spring. Long said there were a "few small bath houses built by private parties," but it was not until John S. Harris and Arthur T. Aldrich took possession of it did the condition of the spring improve.

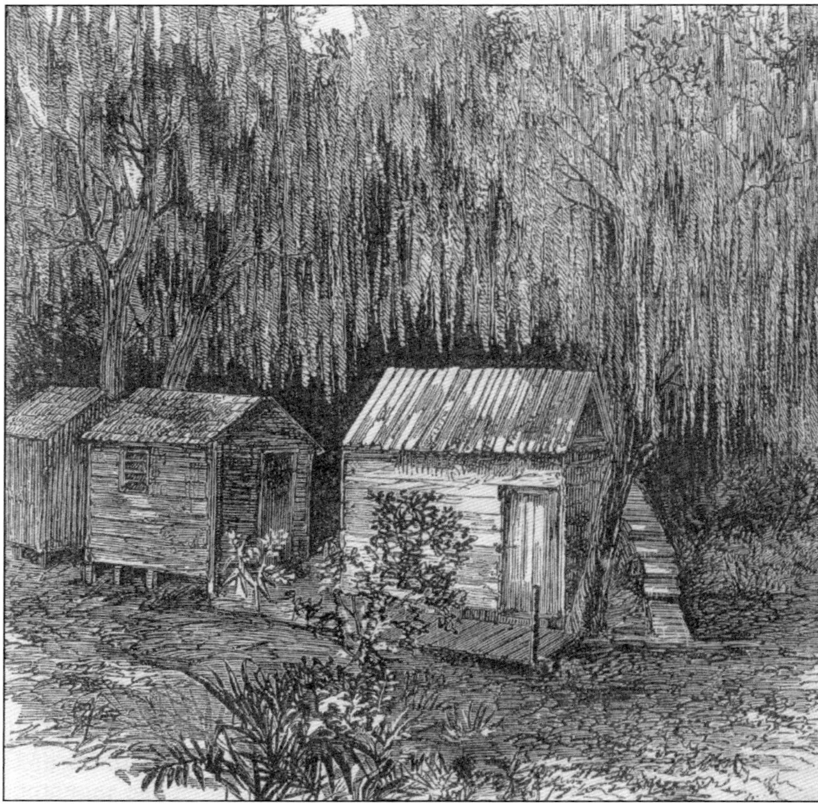

Shanties on Spring Run. Before the spring was developed by John S. Harris and Arthur T. Aldrich, several shacks were built along the spring run. This engraving is based upon a stereoview produced by A. F. Styles around 1868.

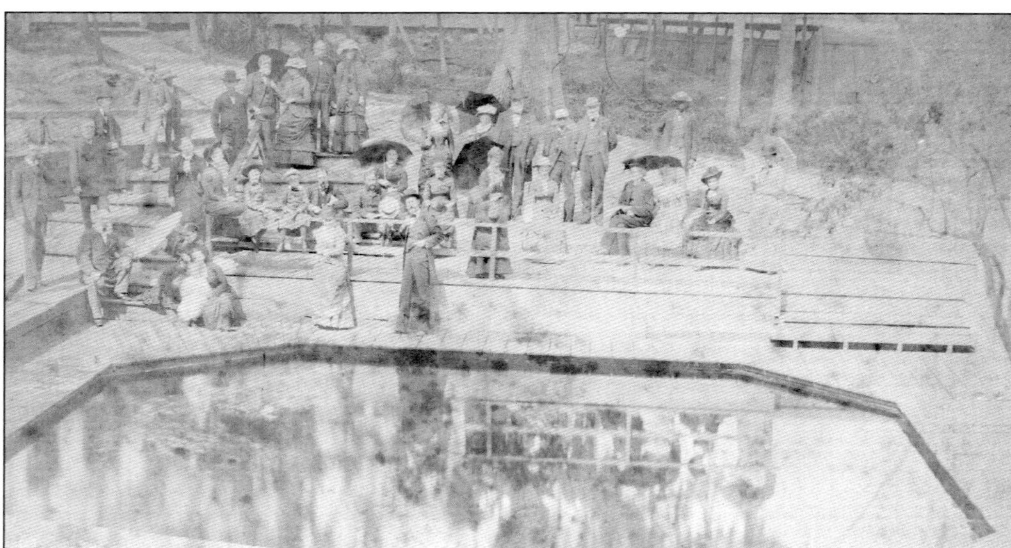

Green Cove Spring by J. S. Mitchell. In 1876, a sporting guide said, "The spring boils up in great lumps from a deep crevice, and fills a pool some twenty feet in diameter with its bright but greenish-hued water, clear as a crystal—a green crystal. Every little speck on the bottom is distinctly visible, even in the deep crevice."

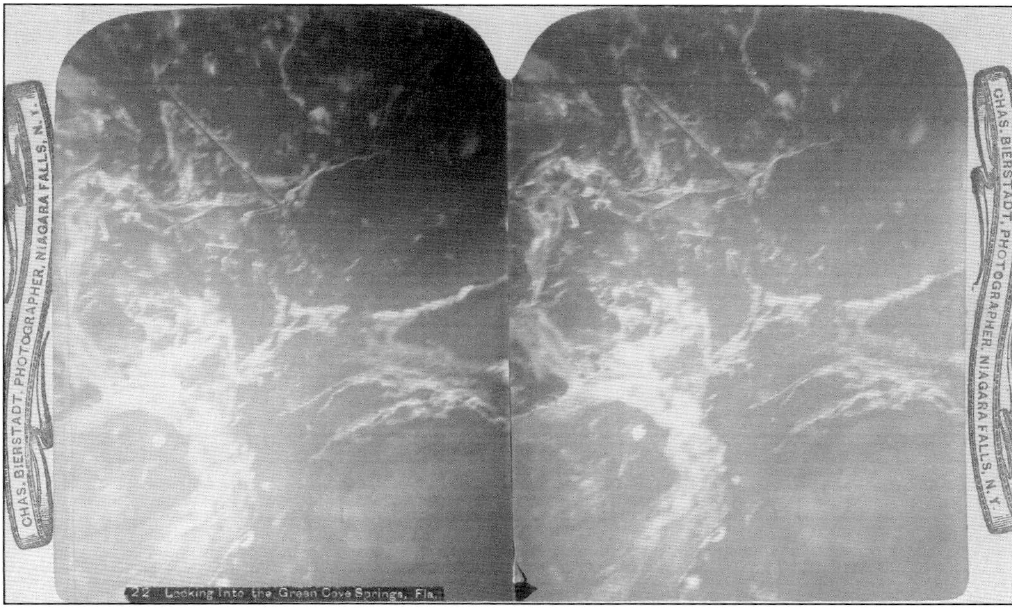

LOOKING DOWN INTO THE SPRING BY CHARLES BIERSTADT. The spring was the most photographed site when the city was a winter tourist destination. The St. Johns River Water Management District classified the spring as a third-magnitude spring, and it has a mean discharge of 3.05 cubic feet a second.

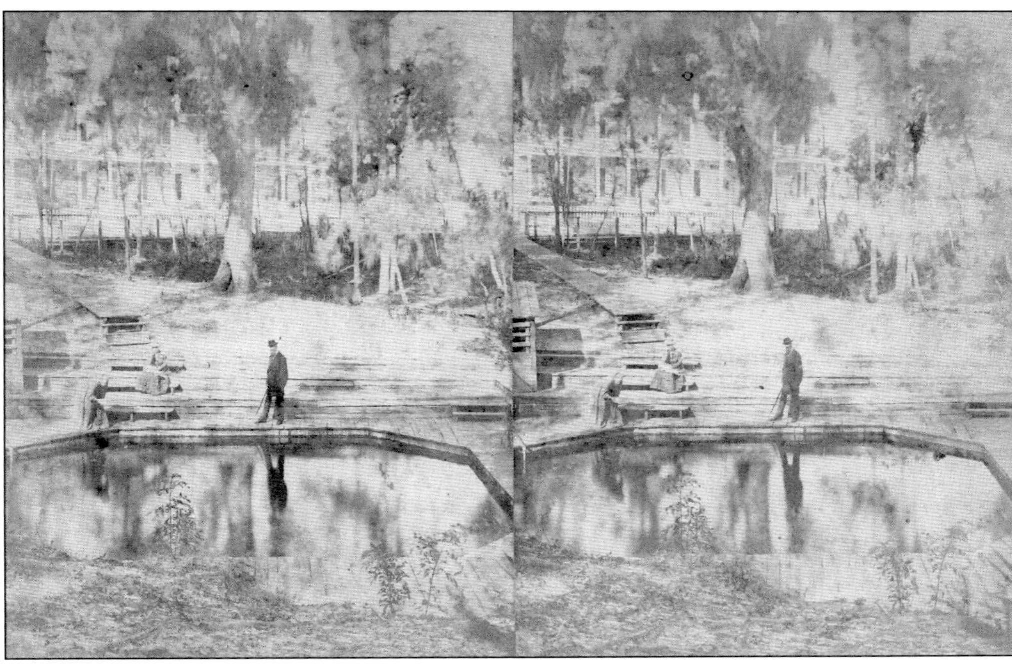

GREEN COVE SPRINGS ON THE ST. JOHNS RIVER BY J. N. WILSON. In March 2001, a test was performed on the water discharging from the spring, and it was determined to be 14,397 years old.

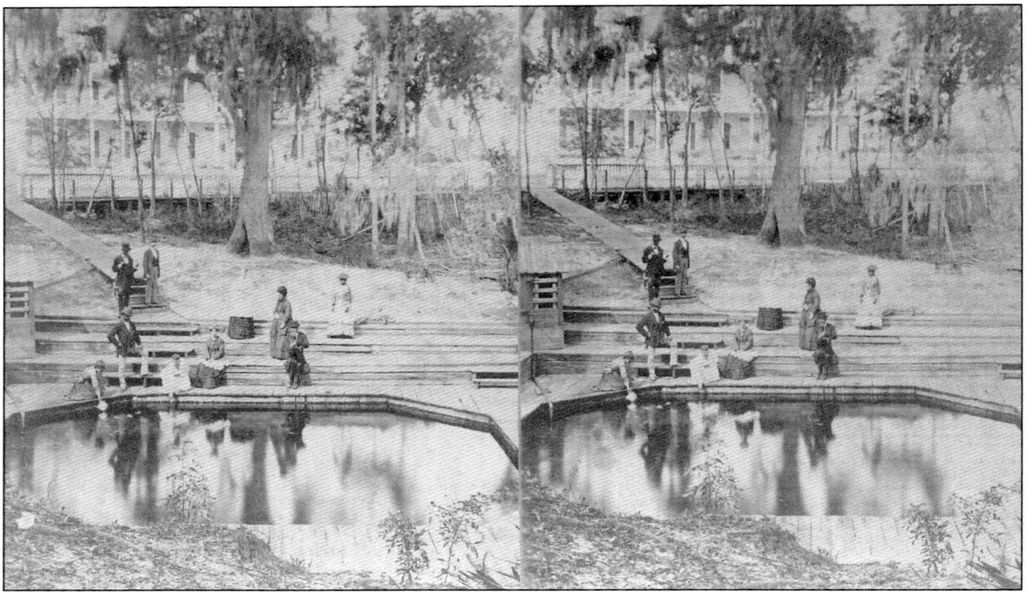

GREEN COVE SPRINGS BY WILSON AND HAVENS, NO. 168. Frederick Adams was a traveling tin smith in Green Cove Springs. He sold tin cups for 5¢, so the visitors could drink directly from the spring. One visitor said that the water was too warm to be refreshing, and it tasted like the "time-honored dishwater." This photograph is dated November 1875.

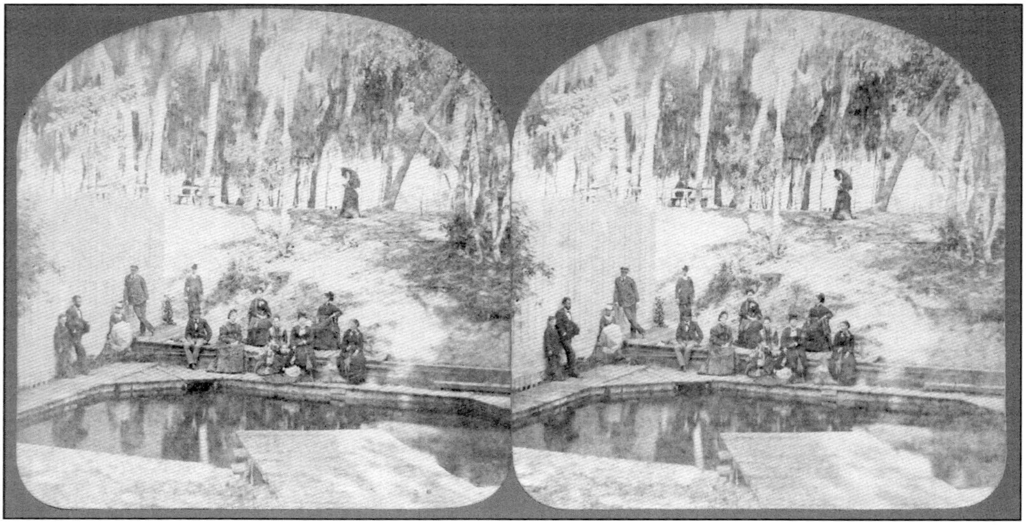

VISITING GREEN COVE SPRING BY ISAAC HAAS. Approximately 30 feet below the spring's surface is a 2-foot opening, from which the spring flows. Behind this small opening is a 25-foot-wide cavern, which heads toward the St. Johns River.

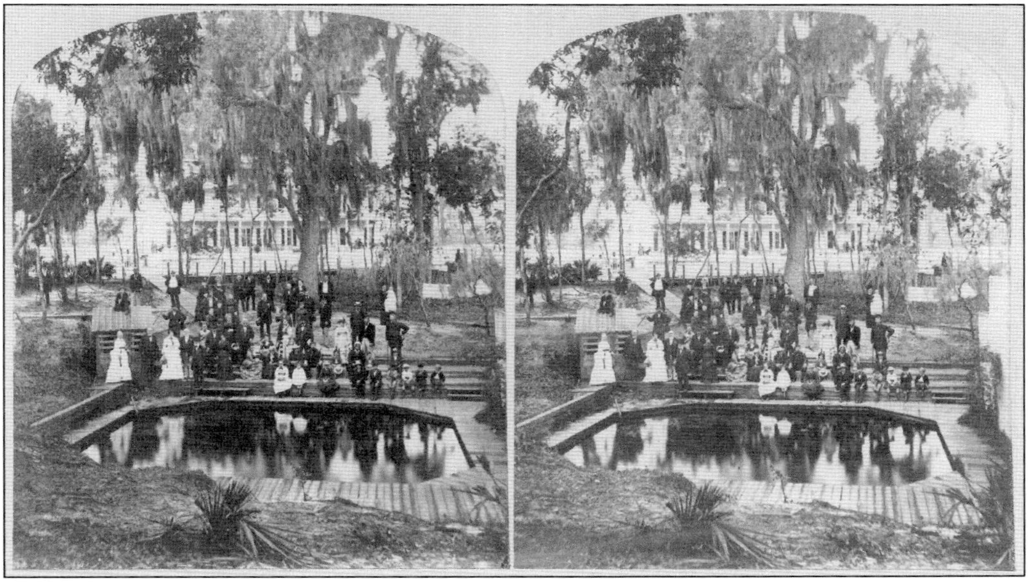

Green Cove Springs (A) by A. G. Grant. To the right can be seen the wall of the ladies swimming area. Miss Smith gave swimming lessons to those who wanted to learn how to swim. John S. Harris paid her $10 a month to manage the spring. She was also responsible for providing clean towels and soap to guests.

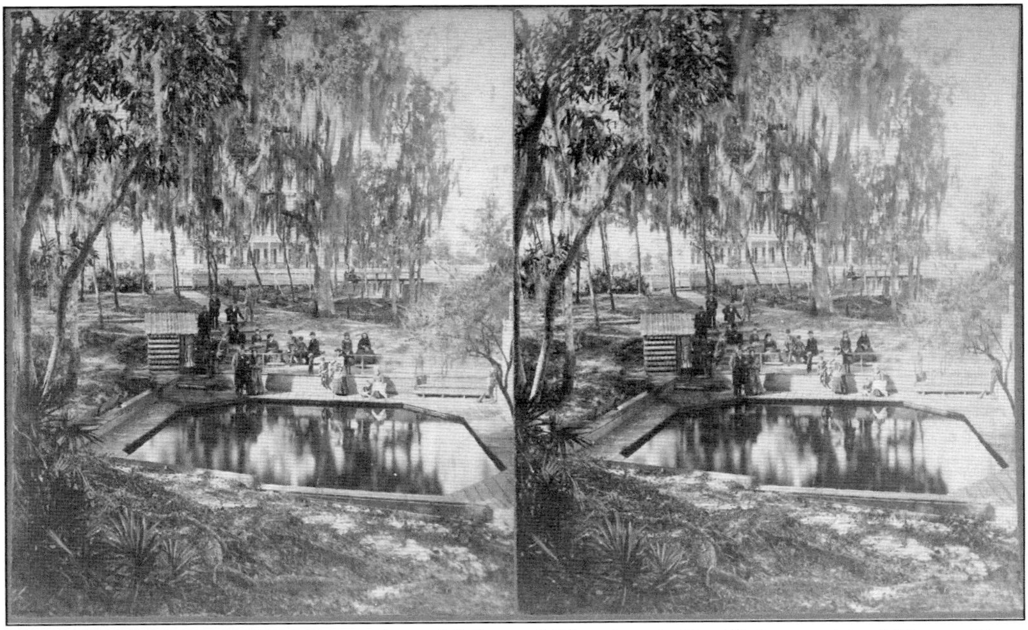

Green Cove Springs. A. I. Root, the publisher of *Gleanings in Bee Culture*, visited Green Cove Springs during his travels to inspect bee culture in Florida. In an 1895 article, Root wrote that the spring was "right out in the open—in a little park . . . in the midst of the town. The water is of such sparkling clearness and crystal brilliancy that it brings forth an involuntary exclamation of delight from every visitor who first sets eyes upon it."

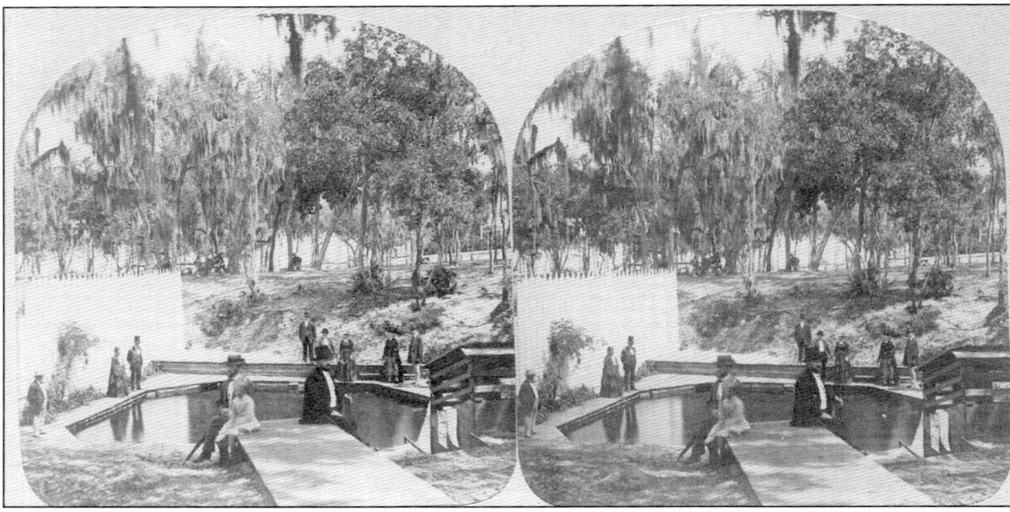

Gathering at Green Cove Springs. Every effort was made to indulge visitors into a tranquil relaxing state of mind. Description such as the following helped to entice the visitors to Green Cove Springs. "No more fascinating scene could well be imagined than the light and shadow effect on water and land as the health-restoring sun sinks down after its faithful day's duty, leaving a wake of golden light on this beautiful resort."

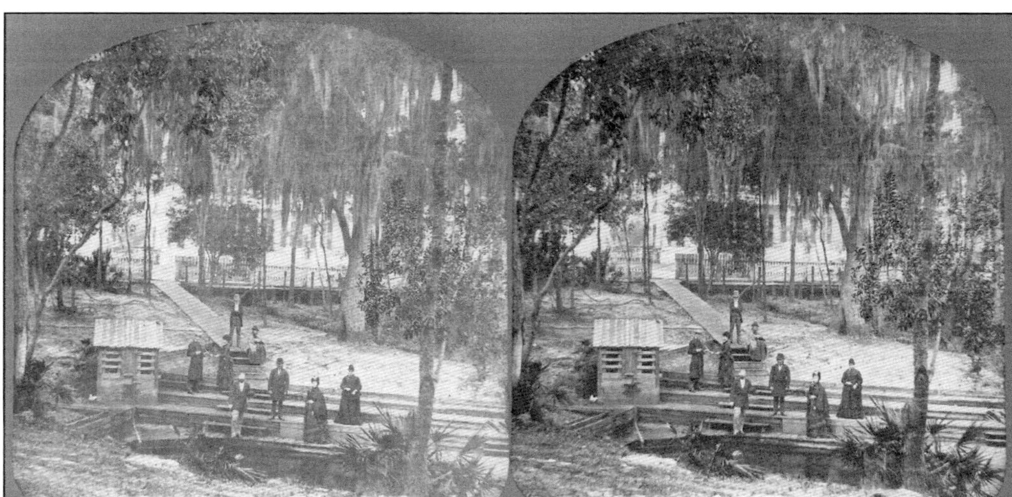

Green Cove Springs by Isaac Haas. When Union troops occupied Magnolia Springs, officers and men would venture to Green Cove Springs to bathe. In 1864, while troops were bathing in the spring, a shot rang out and there was much consternation as officers and men scrambled to put their uniforms back on. This incident was later a much-talked-about event that brought much merriment into the camp.

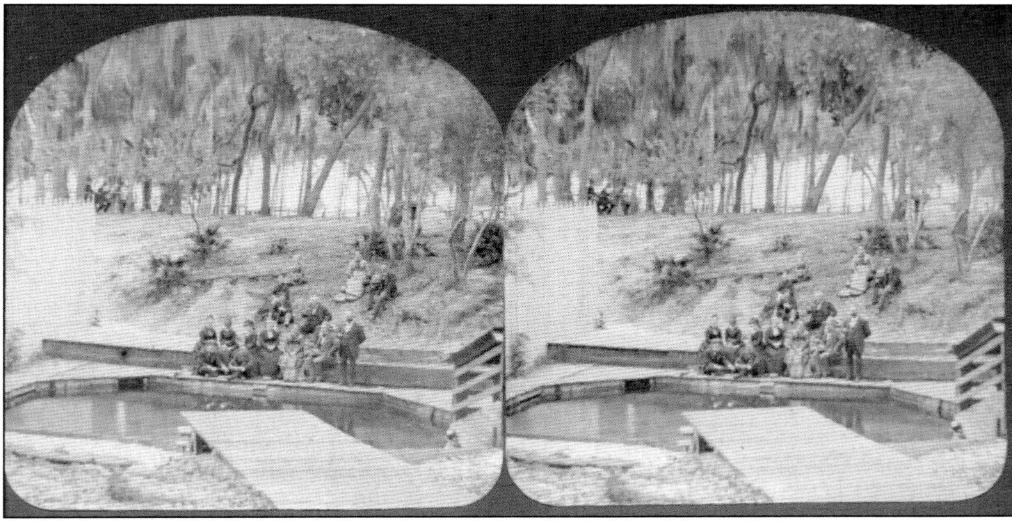

"The Sulphur Boil" by Isaac Haas. Because Florida was advertised as a place to heal, many individuals created remedies for various illnesses. Dr. J. H. Schenck advertised in 1871 that those inflicted with consumption and other lung diseases should "take stock in Schenck's Pulmonic Syrup, Schenck's Seaweed Tonic and Schenck's Mandrake Pills, and go to Florida." Palatka, Hibernia, and Green Cove Springs were the three towns he recommended. This photograph is dated April 3, 1877.

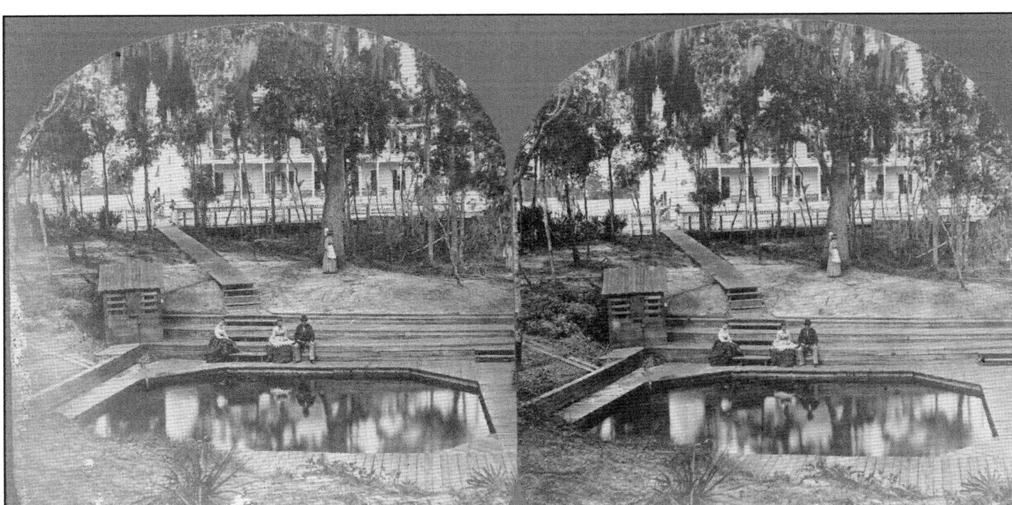

Green Cove Springs. The water discharging from the spring was said to be "clear as a diamond and the effect is most beautiful at noon when the sun shines directly into the spring and objects can be seen at the bottom tinted with prismatic hues."

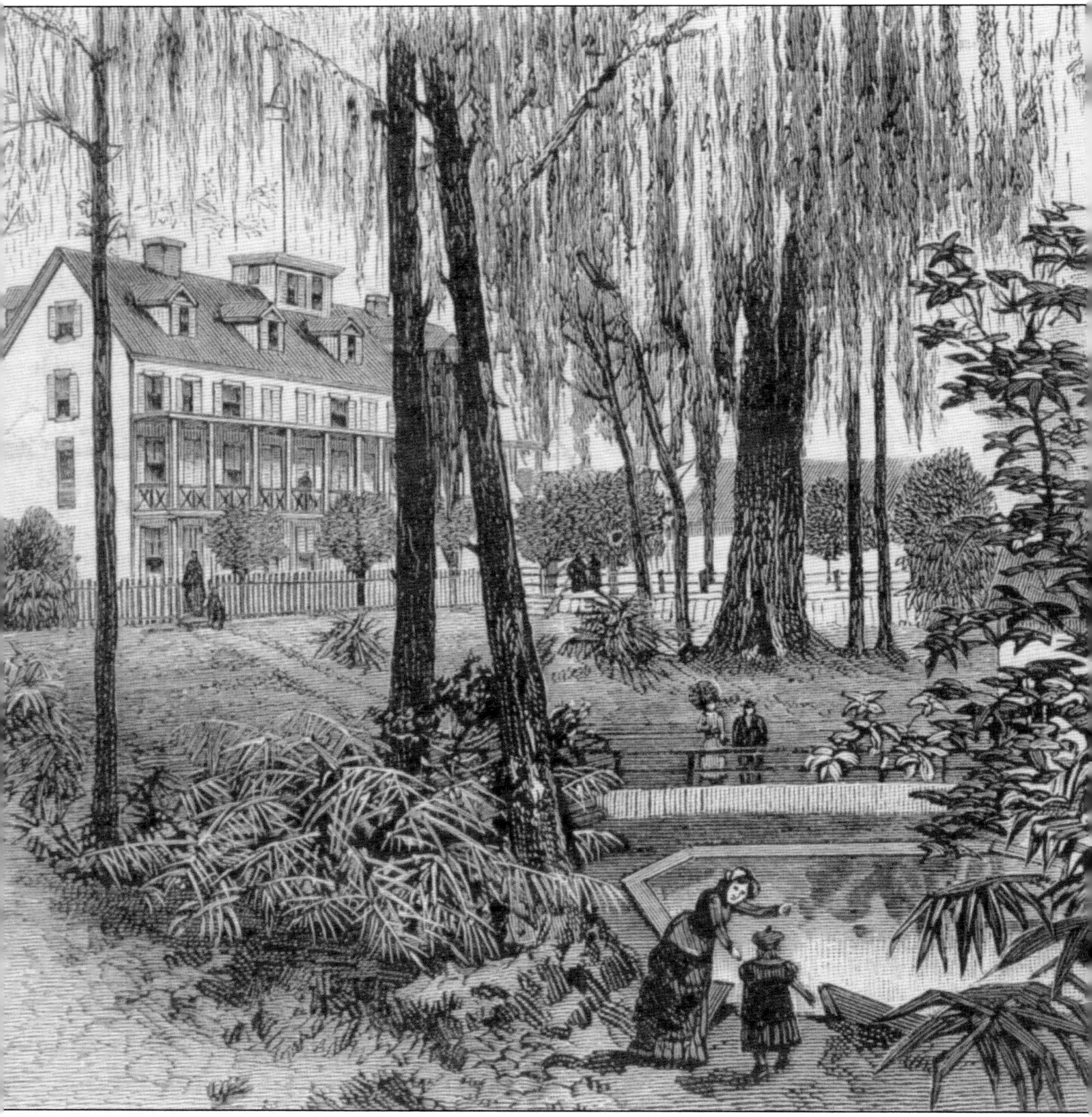

Clarendon Hotel and Spring. In 1891, the scenery around the spring contained "large magnolia trees 30 to 50 feet high, oak, pine from whose branches hang the ever present moss clinging in large festoons from 3 to 6 feet long . . . looking weird and ghost-like."

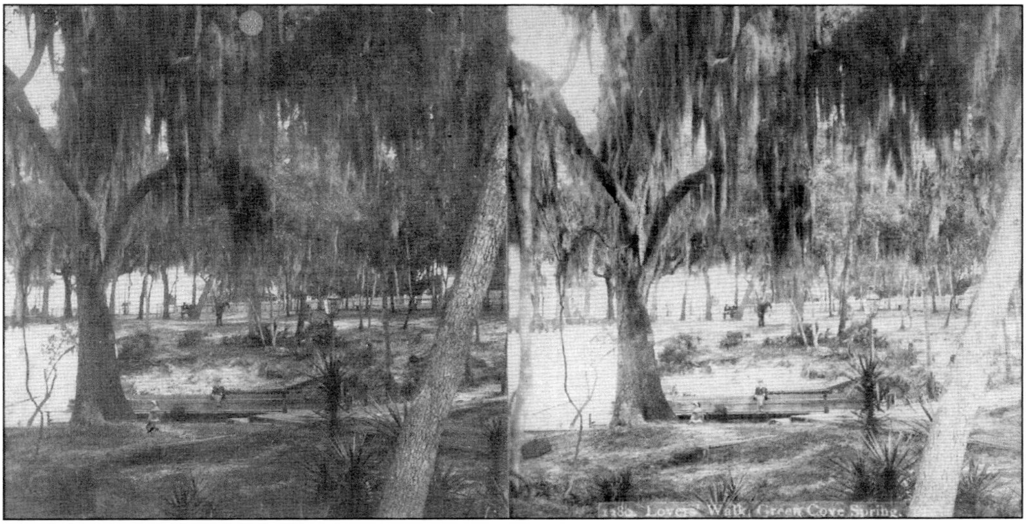

Lover's Walk at Green Cove Springs. St. David's path, or Lover's Walk, originated at the spring. It provided a relaxing area for a stroll where "the singing of the wind overhead, the murmur of waves on the shore, the soft notes of the mocking bird . . . and fragrant jasmine . . . make for the tourists one of the most delightful of strolls."

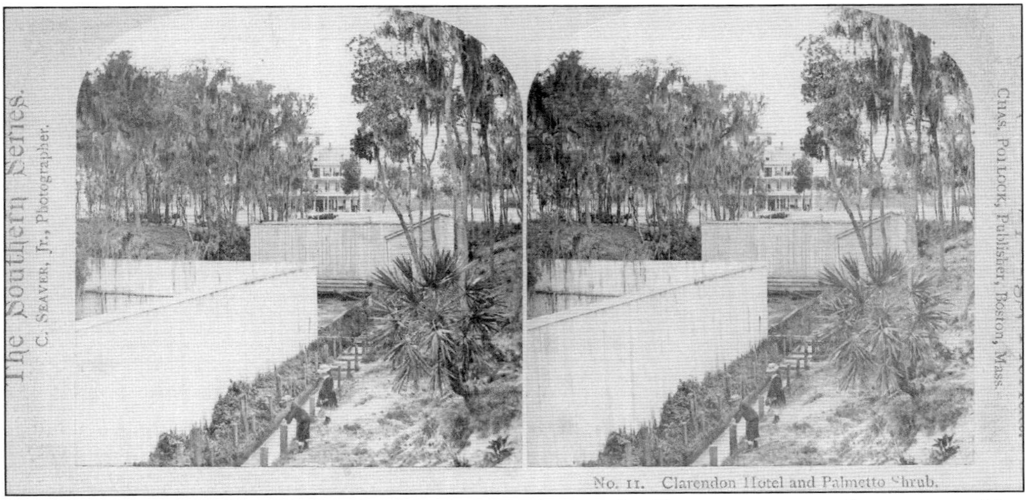

Clarendon Hotel and Palmetto Scrub by C. Seaver Jr. To attract guests, the owners of the Clarendon built swimming pools around the spring. In 1876, the water from the spring "forms quite a little river, and over it a bathing house has been built; and here those suffering with rheumatic or kindred complaints luxuriate in its warm embrace. Seventy-six degrees is the average temperature summer and winter, seldom varying from this point more than a degree or two."

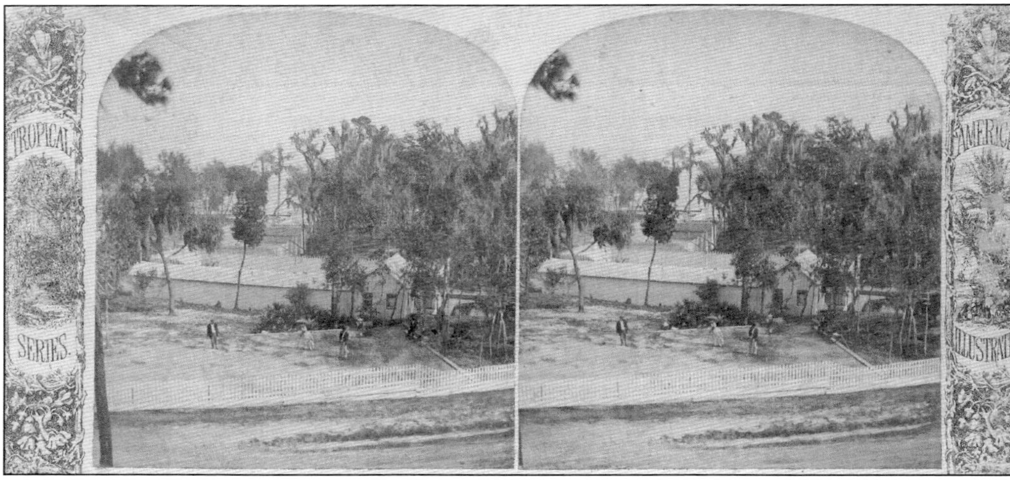

Green Cove Springs from Clarendon House. Arthur T. Aldrich spent a considerable amount of money to improve the spring. He said he "cleared up the spring, fenced it in, cleared off the run-way dam to the river, spiled and planked in the spring, curbed and platformed it, excavated and sunk four timber bathing curbs for bathing pools, timbered and floored the bottom of them, constructed flumes for conducting water to each pool, built and sunk drains for pools to the river, built buildings for the keeper's office and for washing towels, constructed dressing rooms in two continuous lines of one hundred and fifty feet . . . constructed flumes and waterways for taking in and letter out the water, enclosed all of the bathing pools, enclosed all the bathing pools with a high fence, and the entire spring grounds were enclosed with a picket fence."

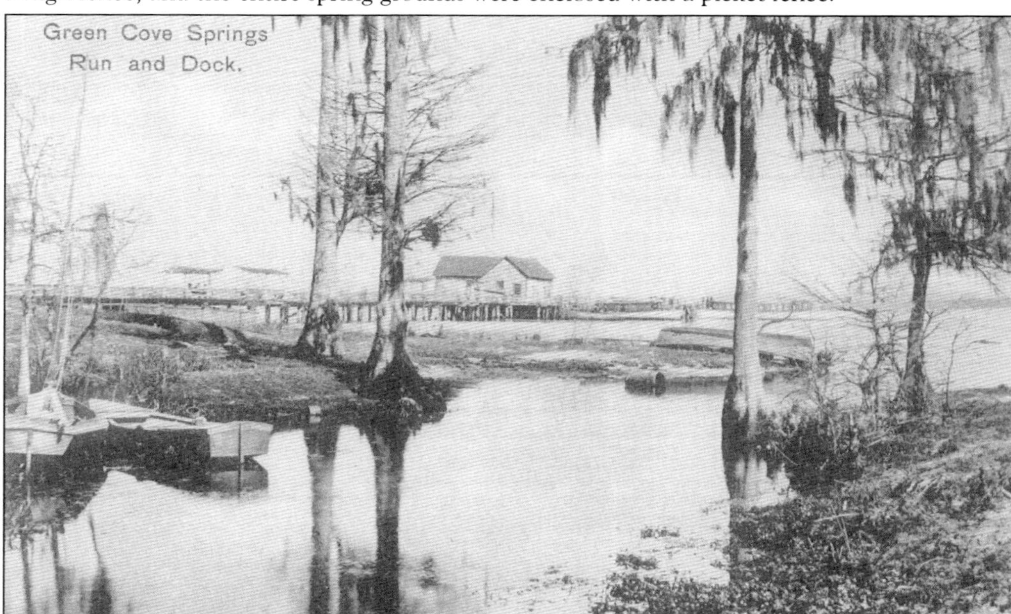

Green Cove Springs Run and Dock. The water from the spring was said to be "slightly sulphurous; more perceptibly so in the order than in the taste, but sufficiently to banish any form of animal or reptile like from its proximity." One hotel brochure claimed that a "native" said that "there was a right smart chance of moccasins." But wherever else they may locate, the Green Cove Springs is exempt, and the invalid may enjoy his bath without a nervous tremor.

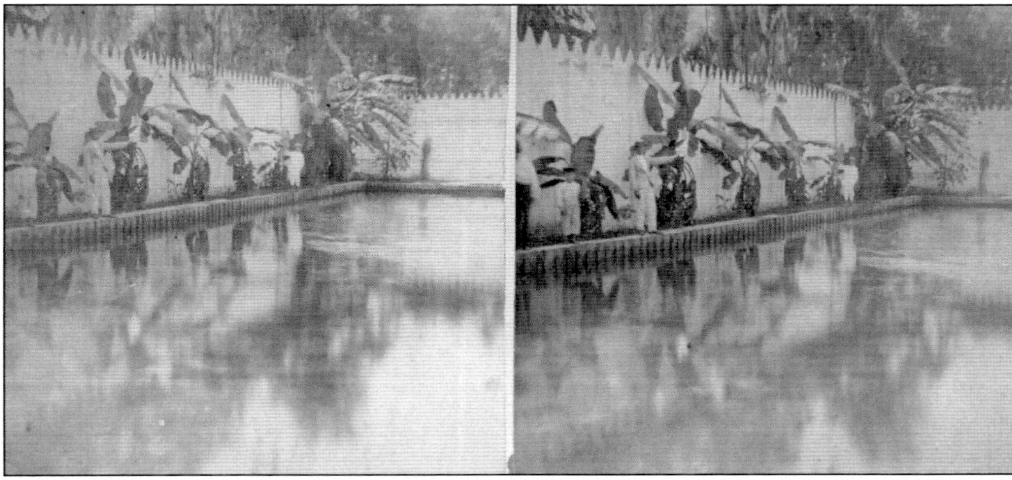

BATH, GREEN COVE BY WOOD AND BICKEL. In 1899, a newspaper advertisement stated that "the bathing pools are extensive and the baths are recommended not only to invalids, but to all who enjoy a plunge into limpid waters. Bathing in the open air in December is a common enjoyment."

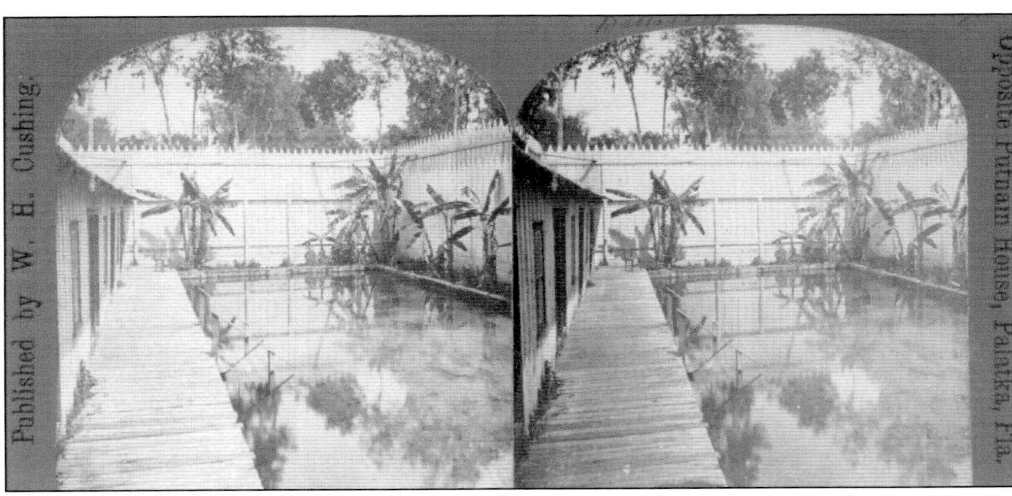

BATHING POOL, GREEN COVE SPRINGS BY W. H. CUSHING. The swimming pools were a few feet from the base of the springs. The women had a separate pool, which measured 30 feet across and about 3 feet deep. The men also had private baths, which were a little larger and deeper.

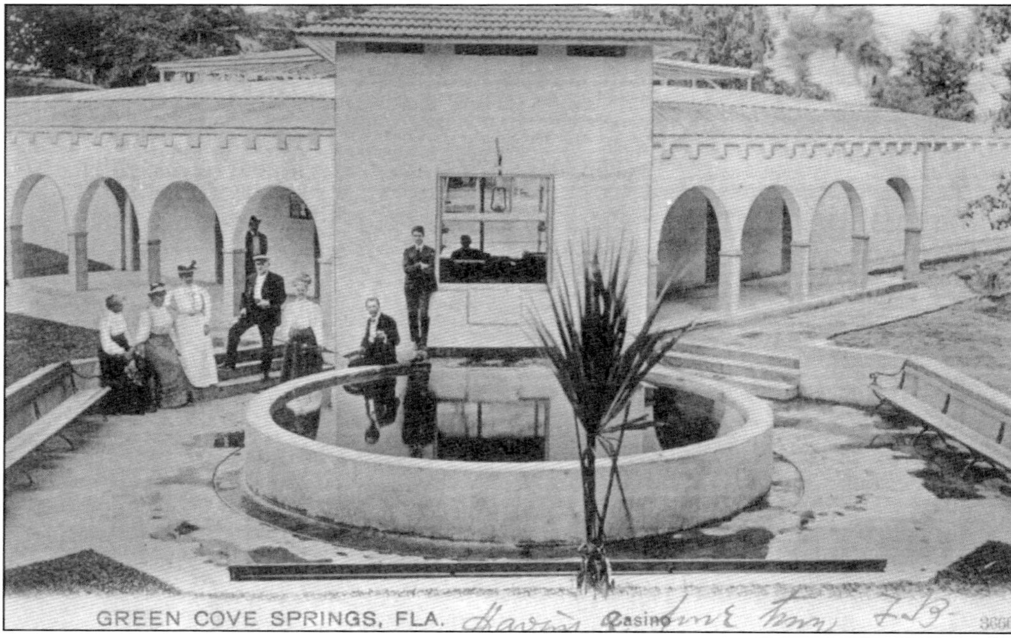

CASINO. In 1907, the *Chicago Clinic and Pure Water Journal* wrote that Green Cove Springs "in striking contrast to other southern resorts, which have passed through a period of prosperity and then assume a condition of decay . . . retained its popularity for generations and is today, as highly esteemed by visitors from both north and south." This postcard was mailed on January 18, 1907.

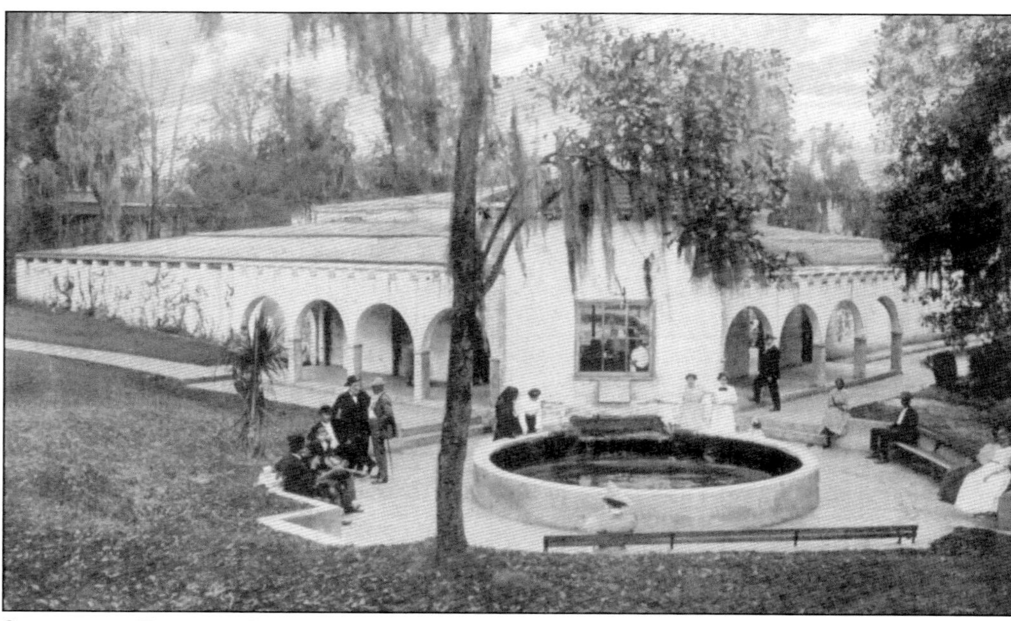

SPRING AND BATHING PAVILION. As early as 1897, there were plans to rebuild the baths around the spring. The casino that was built was expanded around 1917 to include a dance hall. The archways on the right were enclosed in glass to accommodate part of the expansion.

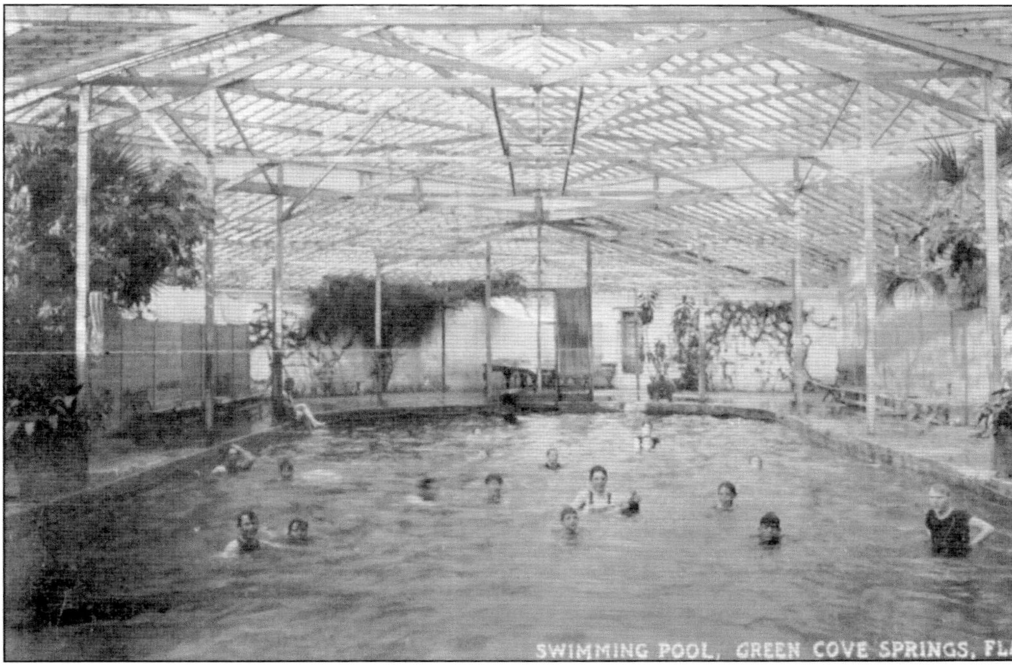

SWIMMING POOL. In 1909, the U.S. government reported that mineral water sales were down that year for the 12 Florida springs. Total sales for the year were $16,534, selling 113,944 gallons of water. Of these 12 springs, 7 had resorts and the water at 6 was still used for baths. This included the spring at Green Cove. This postcard is dated April 15, 1914.

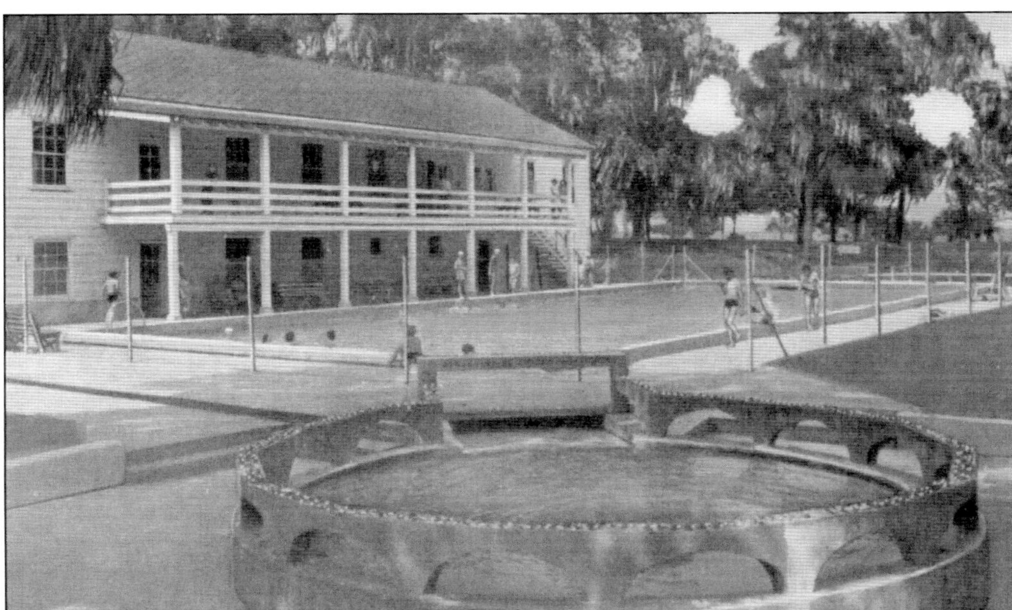

SPRING AND BATHING POOL. Today the city runs the pool during the warmer months of the year. Spring Park offers facilities for picnics, and there is a new playground.

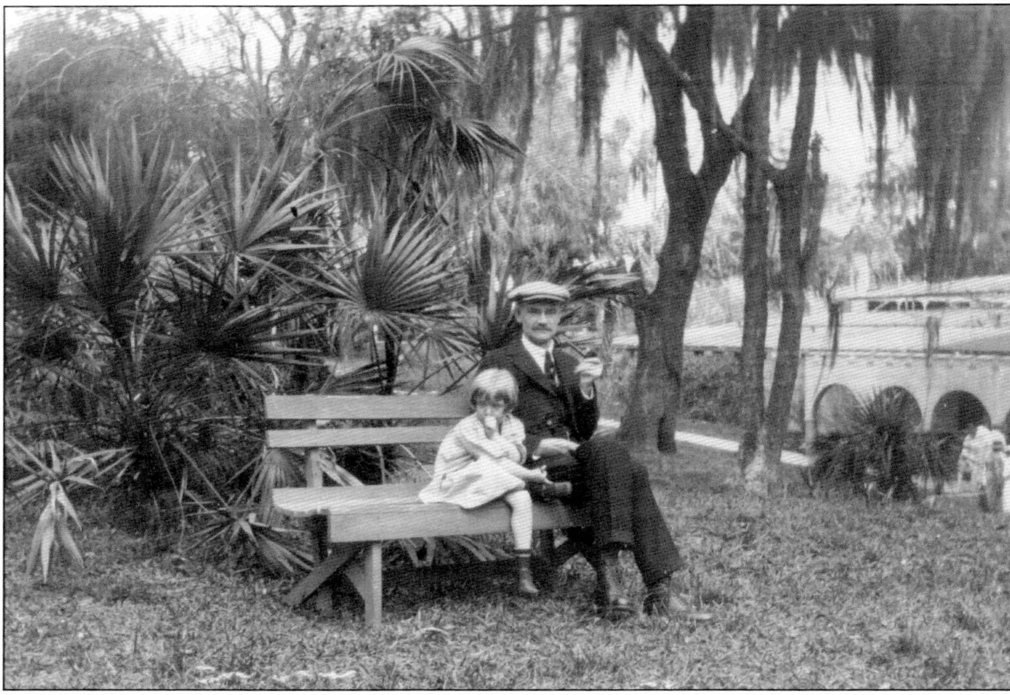

SPRING PARK C. 1920S. Like yesteryear, the spring continues to draw visitors year-round. The park is the site of the city's Memorial Day festival, and during the winter, dozens of Christmas trees are decorated by many of the city's charitable organizations.

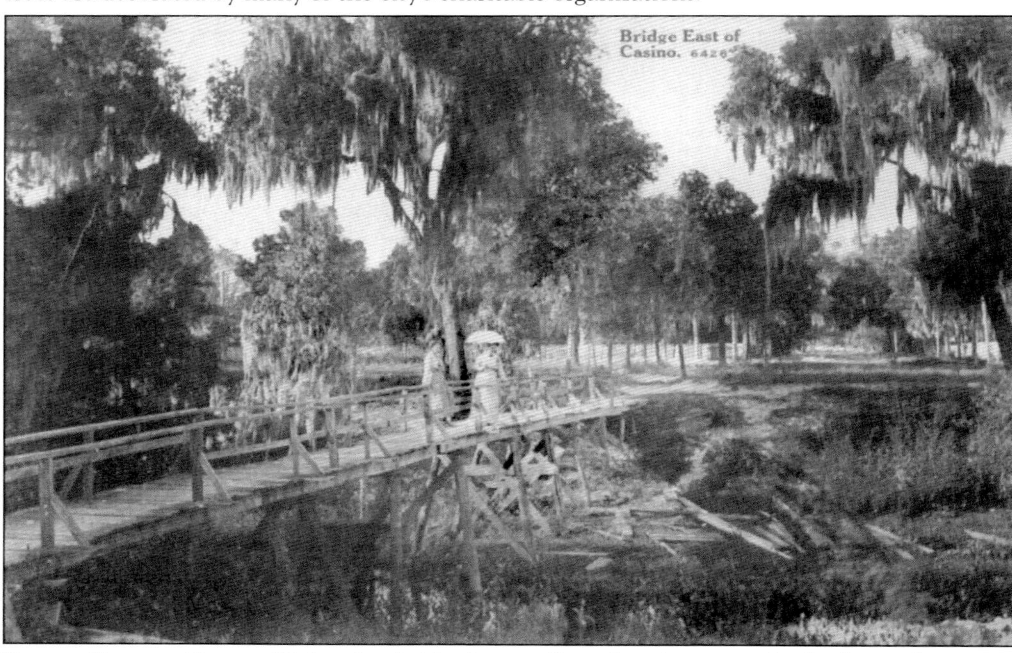

BRIDGE EAST OF CASINO. Today this bridge is a small steel and concrete bridge located in spring park. The message on the back of this postcard says it was related to the Oakland Hotel, which was located off Spring Street.

Five

Tourist Recreation

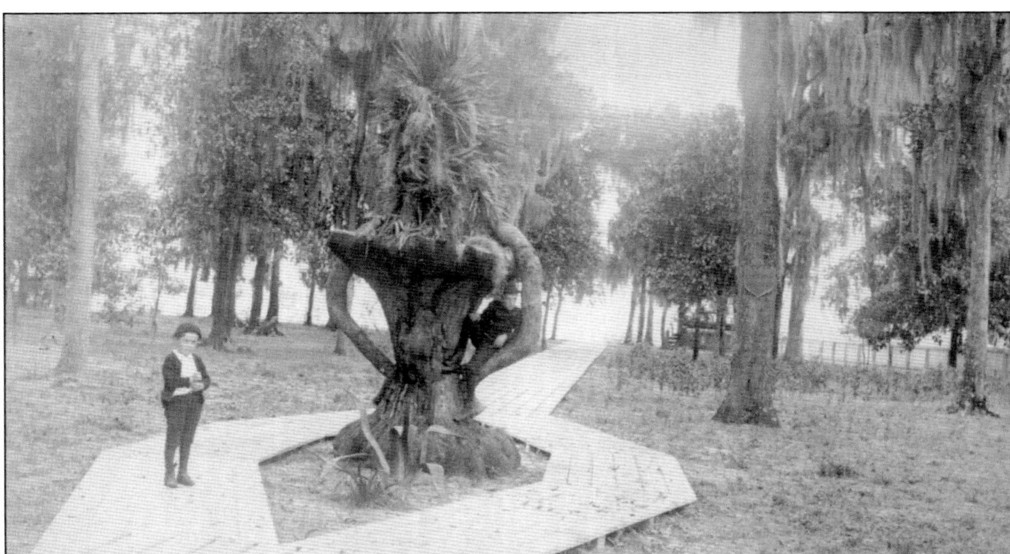

MARION BORDEN PARK. The park was established in 1885 by John Borden, and it encompassed 3 acres and bordered the property of Thaddeus Davids. Gnarled old live oaks, fragrant magnolias, and stately pines were left standing in the park. In the middle of the park along the wide walkways stood a large urn made from a tree that was filled with plants. This urn was much more elaborate than the one at the entrance, which stood nearly 7 feet tall.

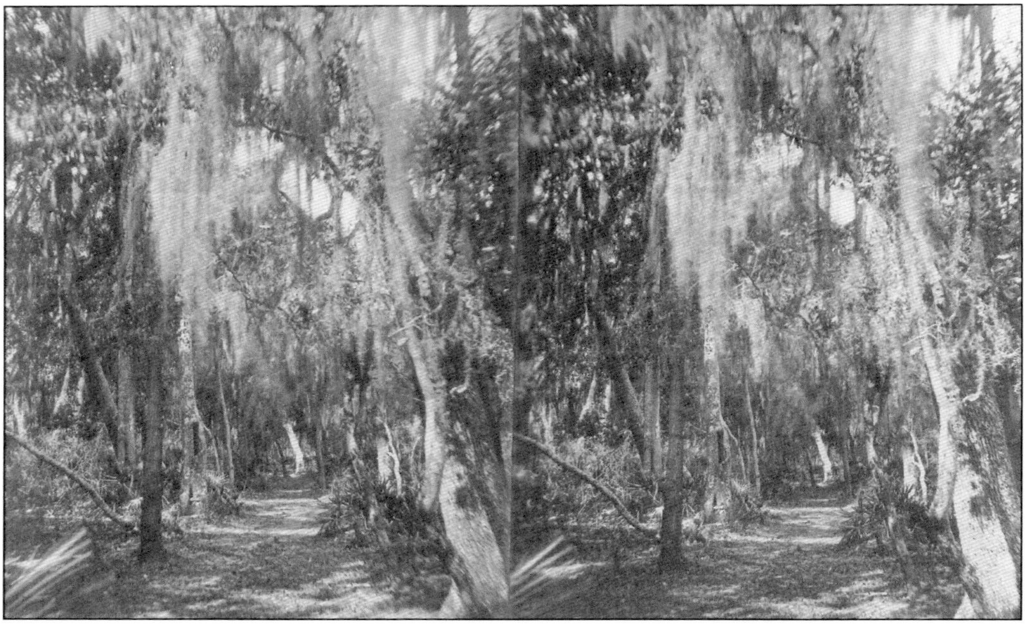

Lover's Walk. For the tourist's enjoyment, a path ran between Magnolia Springs and Green Cove Springs, and it ran along the banks of the St. Johns. This 1.5-mile path was very popular. Deep within the woods, many young enrapturing boys hunted for chameleons. They would catch the lizards and sell them to dealers who would then sell them as pets to tourists.

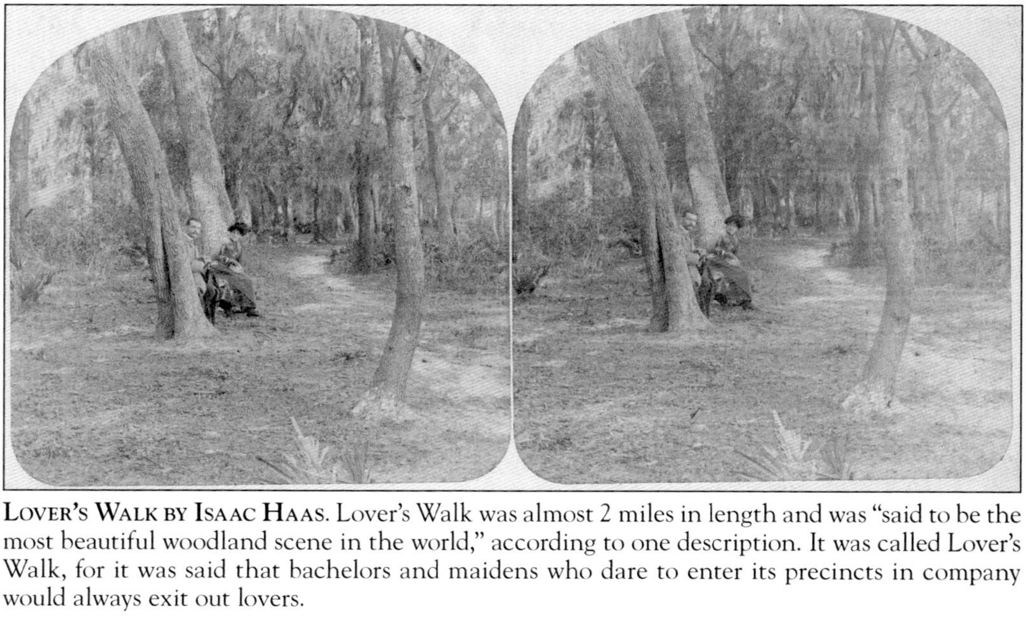

Lover's Walk by Isaac Haas. Lover's Walk was almost 2 miles in length and was "said to be the most beautiful woodland scene in the world," according to one description. It was called Lover's Walk, for it was said that bachelors and maidens who dare to enter its precincts in company would always exit out lovers.

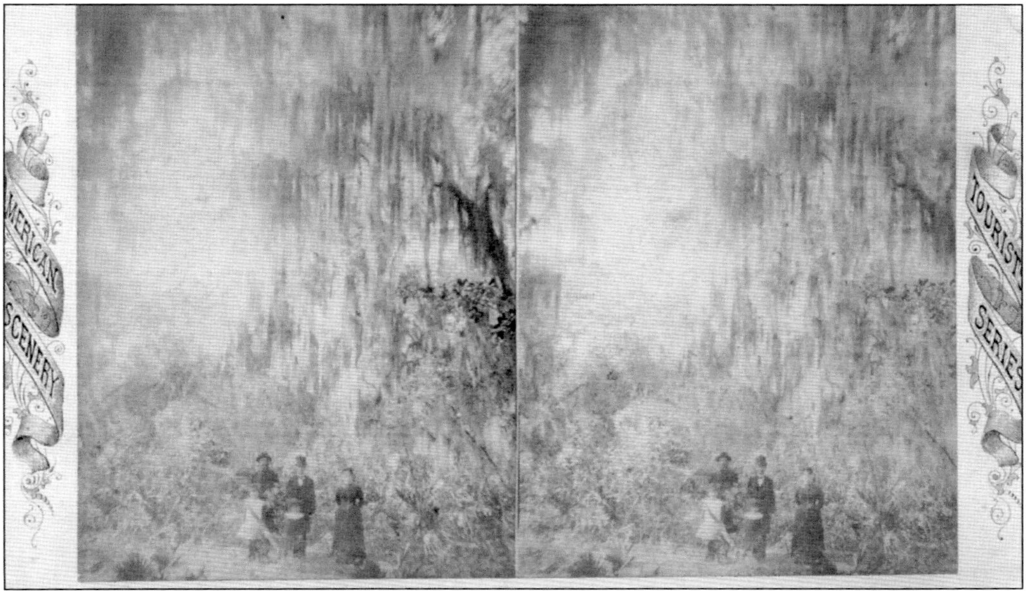

St. David's Path. A part of St. David's Path, or Lover's Walk, meandered through Marion Borden Park. The path roughly followed the St. Johns River, and it was filled with live oaks, palmetto, and magnolia trees, "festooned with gray Spanish moss," with no attempt to clear the native wilderness.

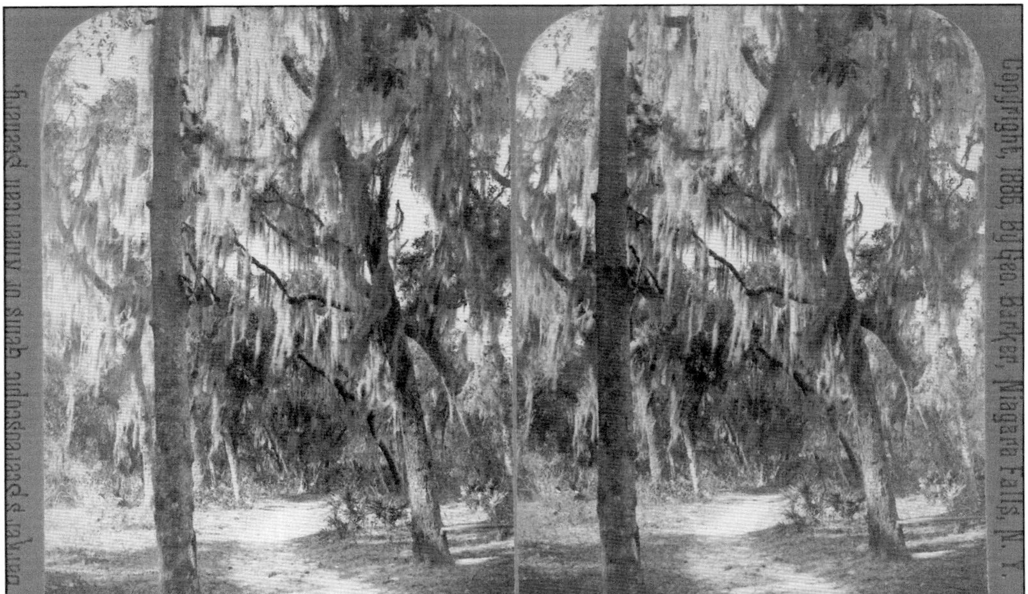

Florida—The Lover's Walk by George Barker. St. David's Path extended from Riverside Cottage and ended at Governor's Creek. It was said that the oldest inhabitants would not recognize the spot had they not been eyewitness to its transformation.

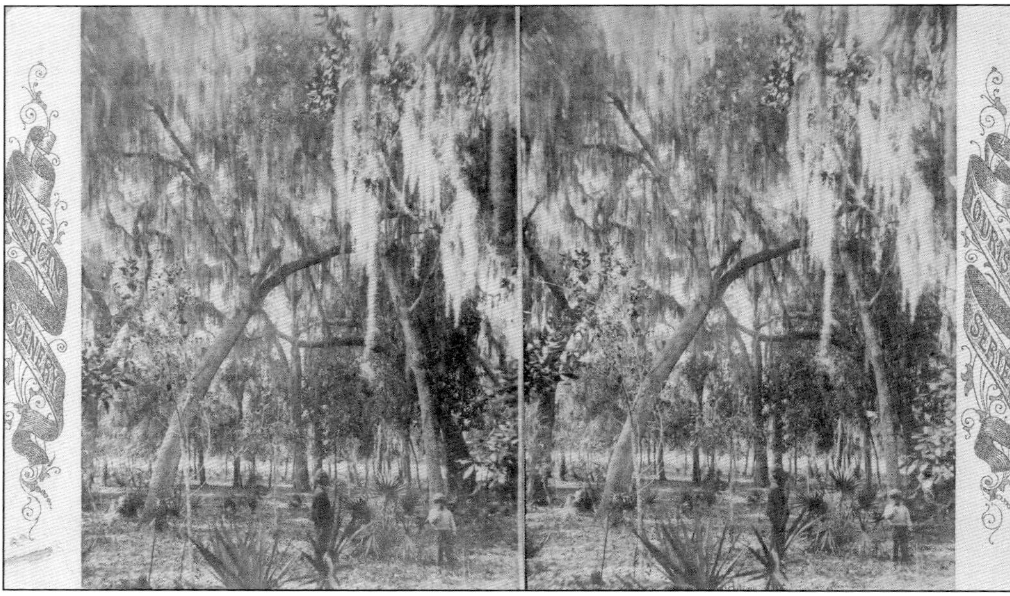

View from St. David's Path. Not all strolls through the area were for lovers. Several new discoveries of fungi were reported in Green Cove Springs. *Isariopsis Clavata* was reported to have been discovered by Dr. George Martin during the winter of 1882–1883.

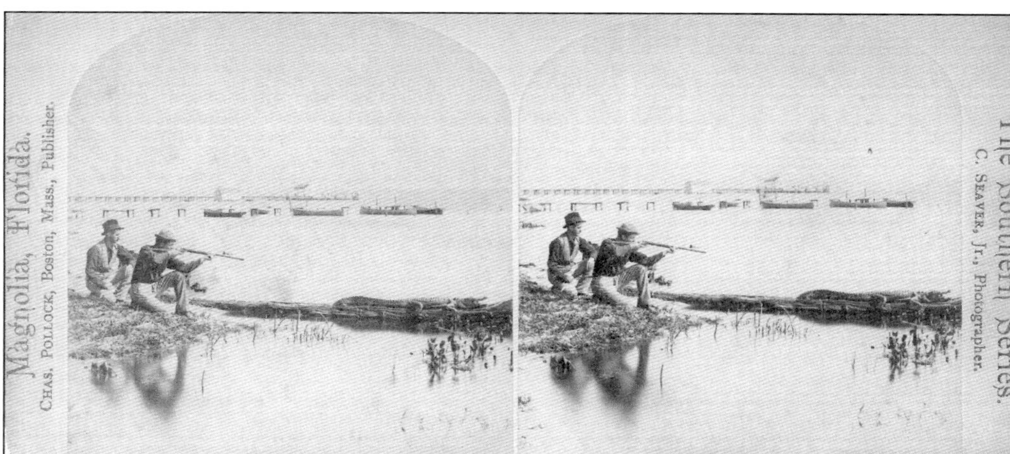

Shooting the Alligators. Charles Seaver Jr. traveled to the south in the early 1870s to photograph the area. He produced several series of photographs from Jacksonville, Mandarin, Magnolia Springs, and Green Cove Springs approximately between 1870 and 1875. He also photographed in St. Augustine and helped to form the Florida Club for photographers working in that city.

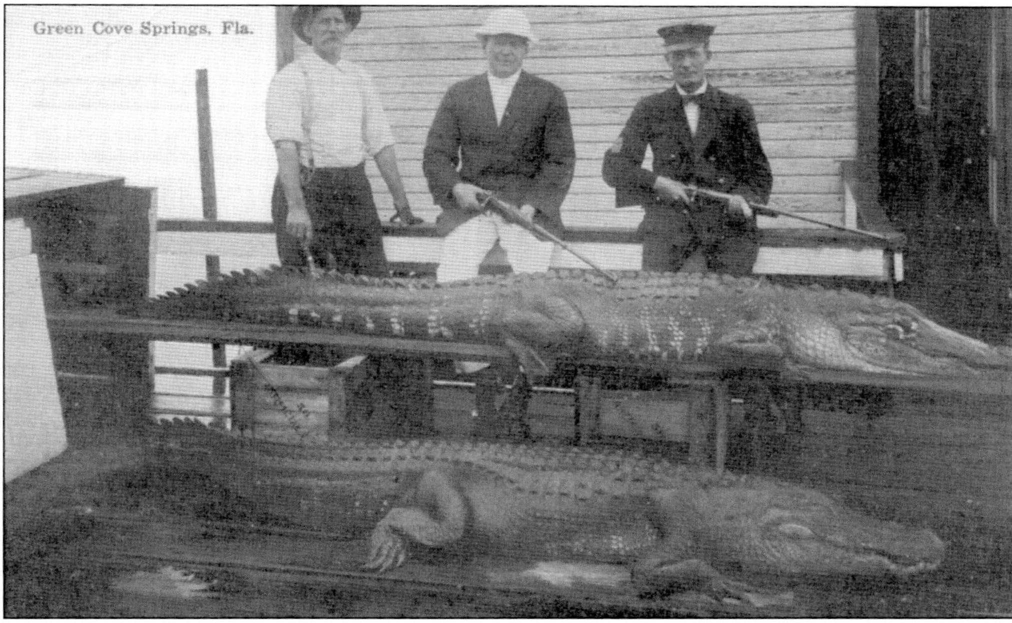

Hunting at Green Cove Springs. Hunting alligators was very popular. Trips up Black Creek would allow hunters to take shots from small steamboats. Other game such as quail and deer were popular and competent guides with good dogs would be furnished by many of the hotels. During the early 20th century, Alfred Thomas was the sportsman's guide. This postcard was mailed in 1912.

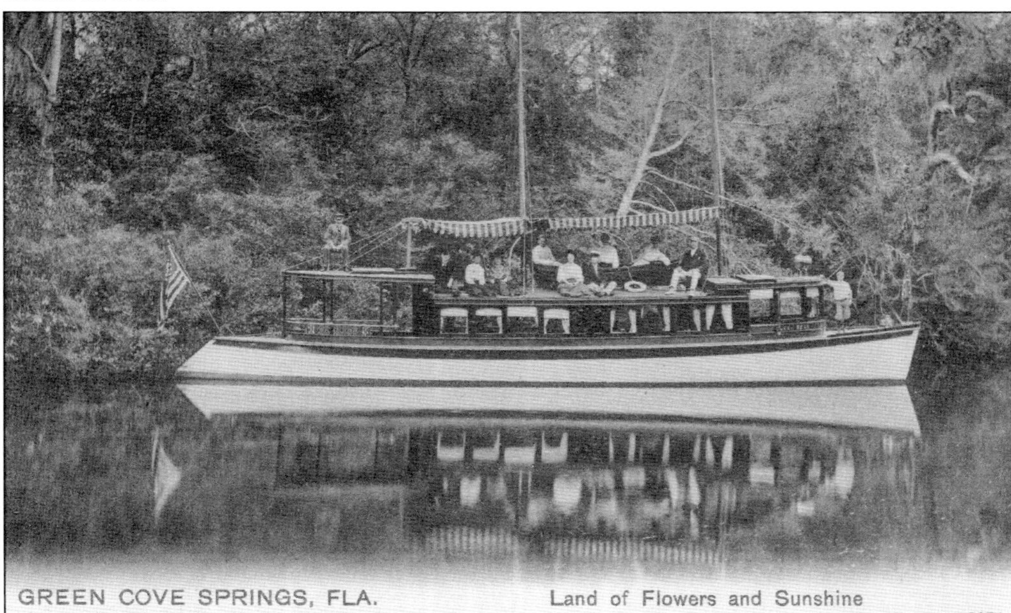

The *Queen Bess* at Green Cove Springs. The *Queen Bess* sits anchored in tranquil waters of Governor's Creek. Larger boats from Jacksonville and Palatka would take short excursions on the weekends to explore the waters and natural wonders the area had to offer. (Courtesy Clay County Archives.)

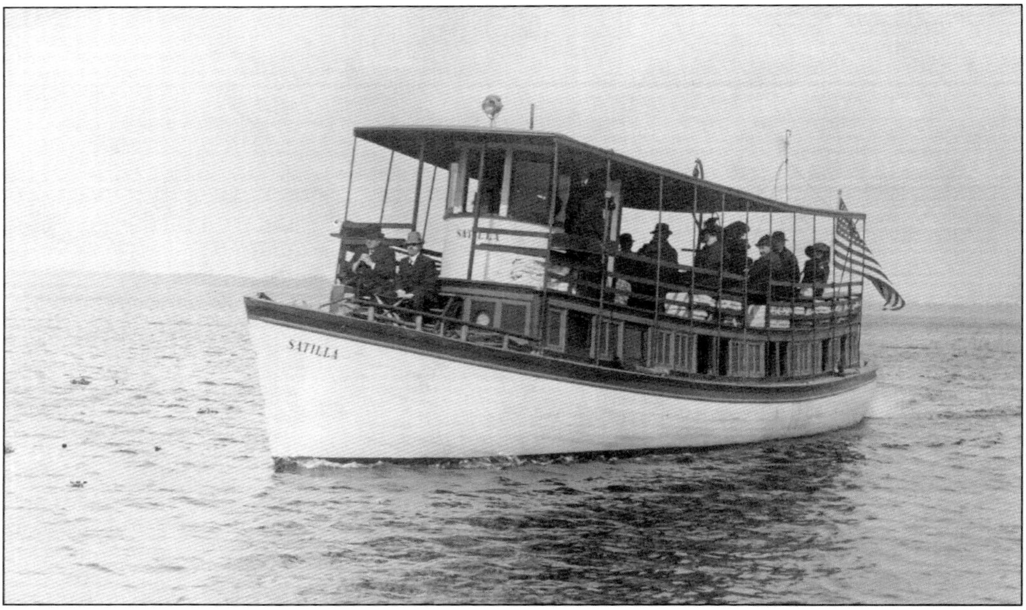

THE *SATILLA*. Although the railroad became the more popular means of vacation travel, smaller personal boats were still a popular means of transportation. A note scrawled across the back of this image indicates these tourists were from Jacksonville.

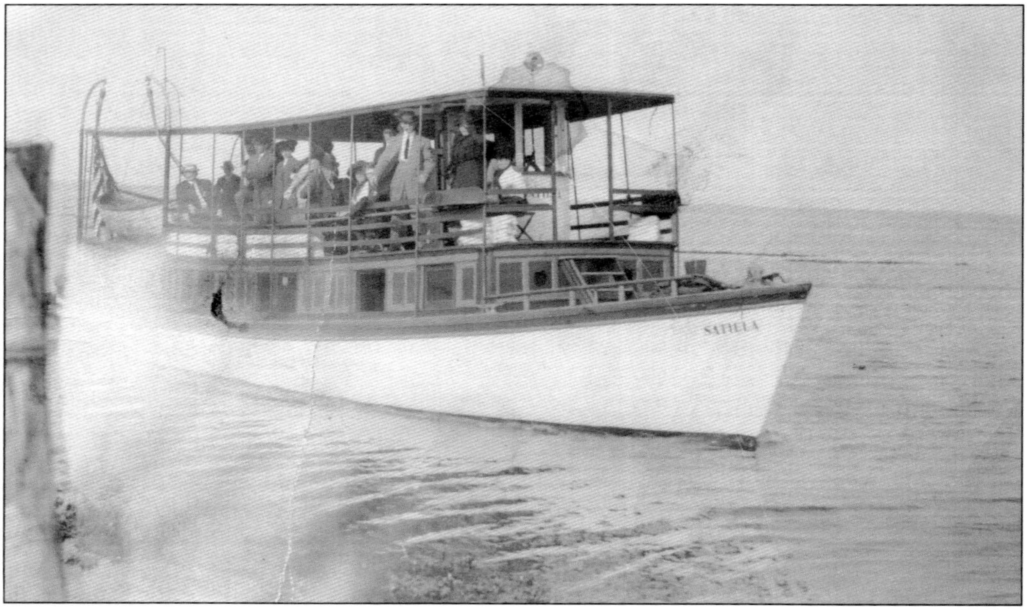

THE *SATILLA* NEAR THE DOCK. With smaller craft like this, visitors could easily explore the waters of Governor's Creek and Black Creek to the north. Black Creek was popular for those wishing to see alligators.

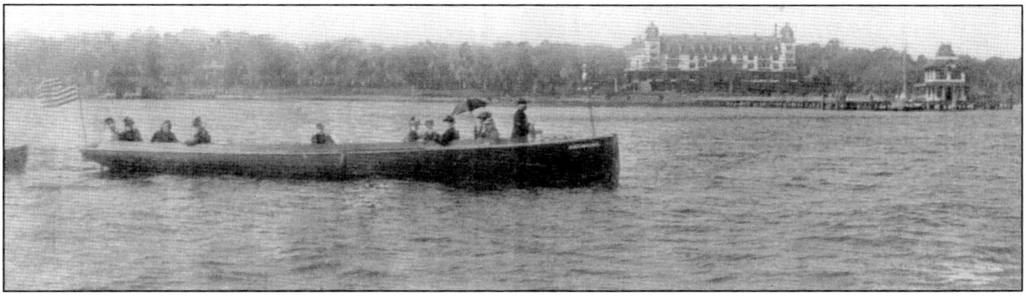

STEAM LAUNCH *ANEMONE*. Boating was very popular with the guests. Rowboats were available to rent, and the Magnolia Springs Hotel employed the steam launch *Anemone*. The launch was used for larger groups wishing for "more extended excursions, where the beautiful scenery and reflections in the quiet waters are of never-ceasing interest."

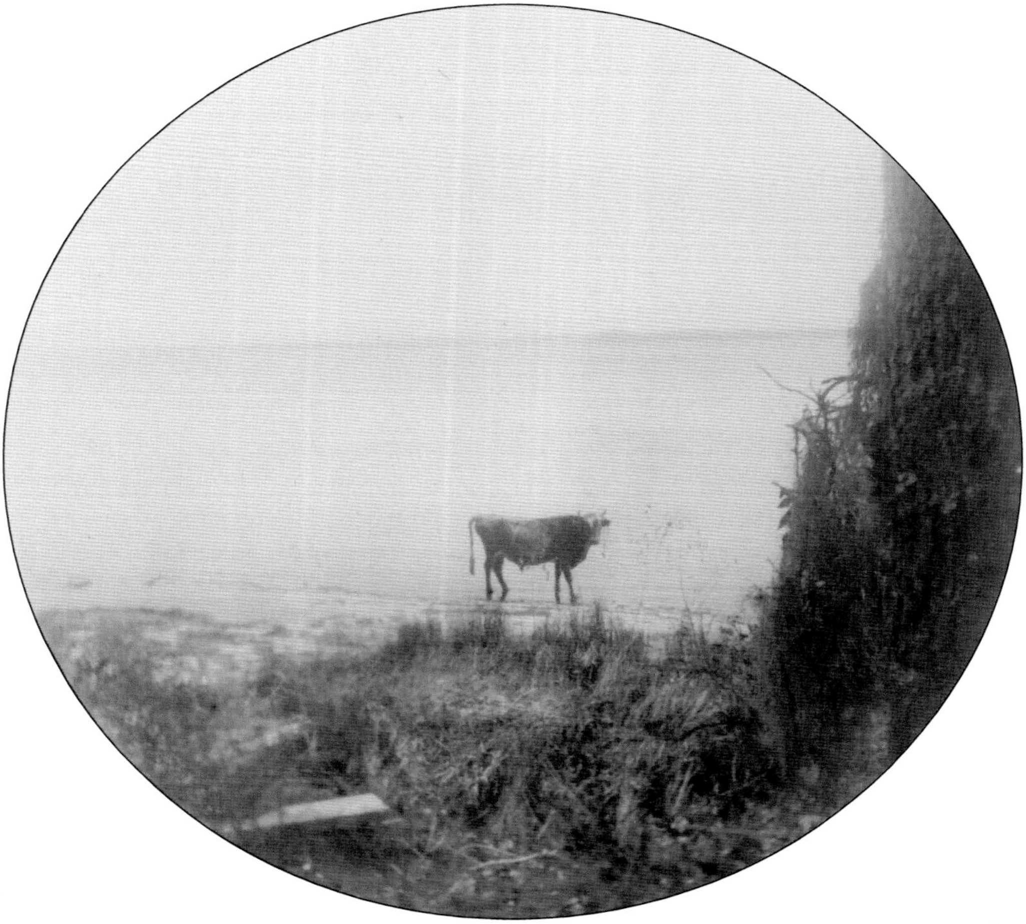

COW IN THE ST. JOHNS RIVER. The Florida cow intrigued the northern tourist. In December 1879, one New York newspaper wrote, "the Florida cow is a peculiar animal. She is not in the milk business to any alarming extent, and even when the trials and tribulation of its life are over she doesn't cut up well. Her principal occupation in connection with the river St. Johns, is eating grass which grown upon the bottom. I had never seen cattle grazing with their heads under water, and keeping them there for a minute or so."

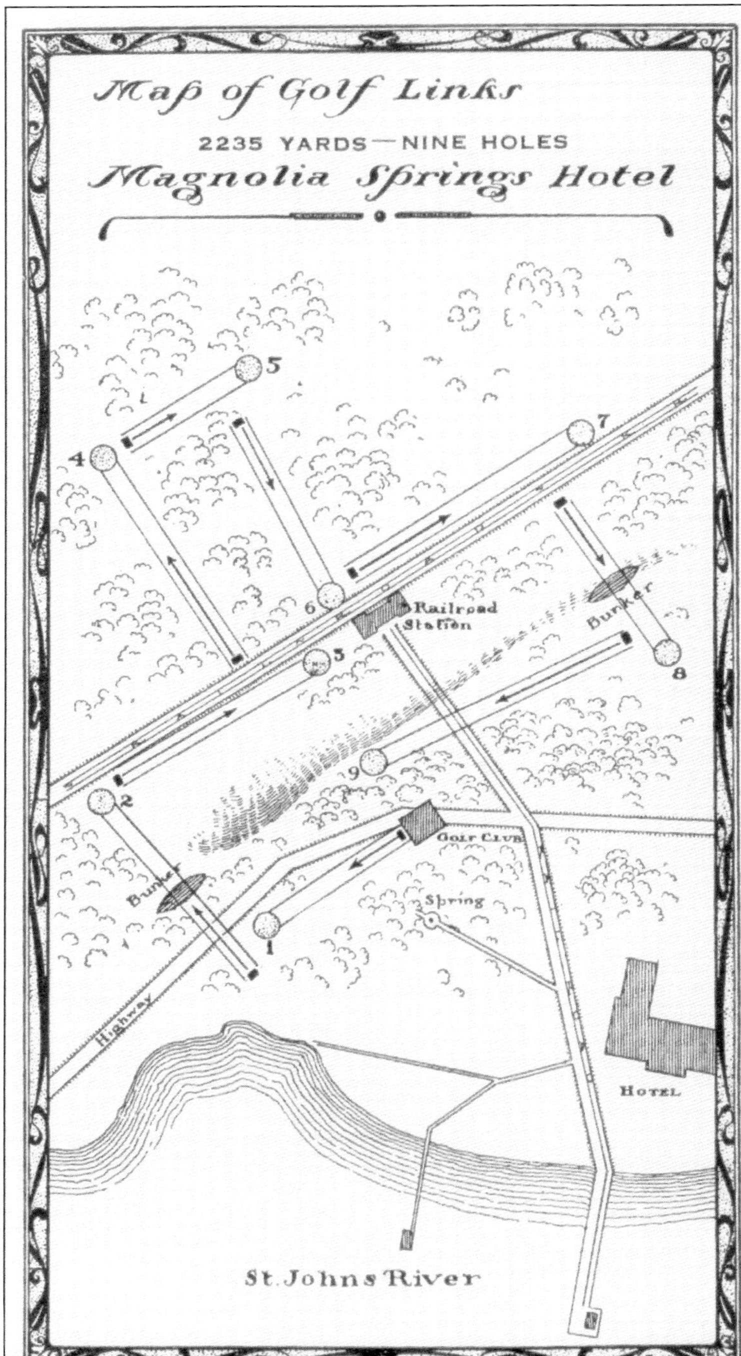

Magnolia Springs Hotel Golf Course. With a total length of 2,235 yards, the Magnolia Springs course offered nine holes. The initial length of each fairway was as follows: one, 197 yards; two, 248 yards; three, 232 yards; four, 270 yards; five, 154 yards; six, 256 yards; seven, 255 yards; eight, 245 yards; and nine, 269 yards.

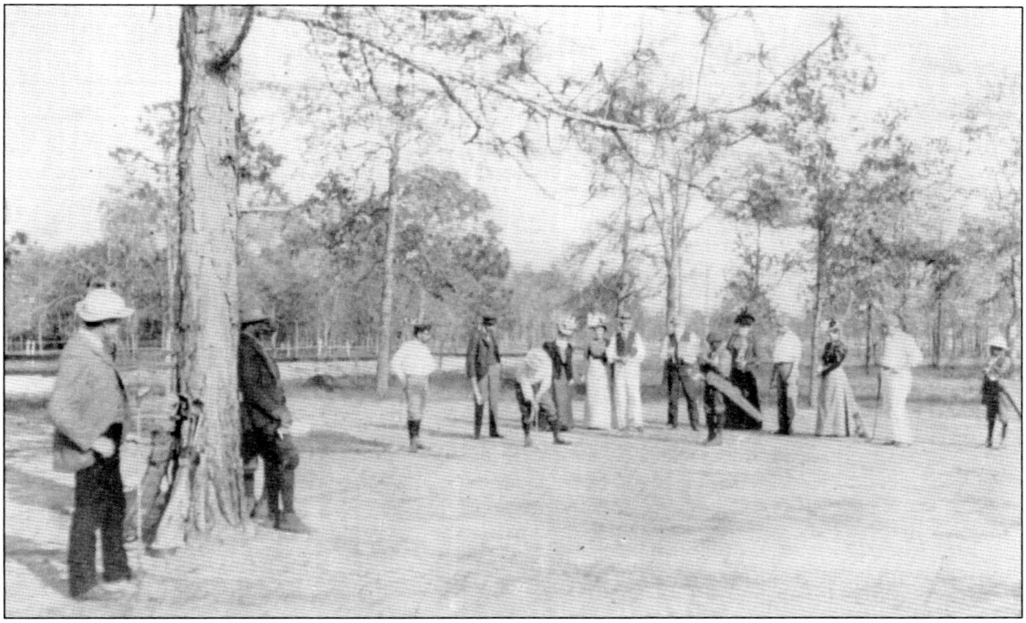

PUTTING OUT ON NO. 6. On January 22, 1900, a golf tournament was held at Magnolia Springs. The tournament drew 11 men and included the current U.S. Open champion, Willie Smith of Chicago, and runner-up George Low. At the end of the first nine holes, Willie Smith was leading with 41 followed by Low's 43. After the second round of nine, the order was reversed, with Low shooting 37 to Smith's 41. Smith was rewarded with $25 for his effort, and his play was characterized by long, steady drives. On the following day, the golfers were to play match play to determine which two players would play for the $100 prize.

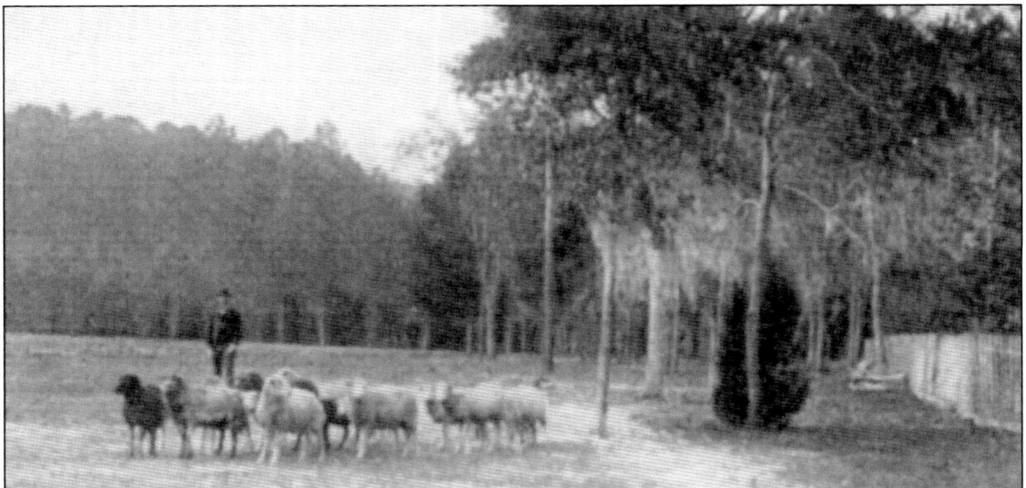

NINTH GREEN GOLF LINKS. On the morning of January 24, 1900, a long driving contest was held at Magnolia Springs. Driving into a strong wind, Willie Smith won the contest with a drive of 189 yards. Placing second was George Low with a shot of 187 yards followed by Launcelot Servos who was one yard behind Low. The contest was held on the sixth hole since there are no bunkers on the fairway. It was said that Servos could drive the ball well, but in tournaments, he could not approach the greens very well when hitting out of the bunkers.

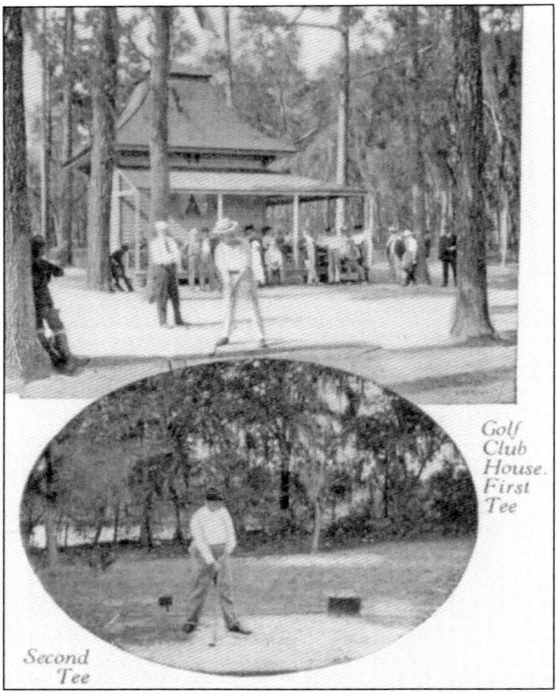

Clubjouse and First and Second Tee. Around the same time that O. D. Seavey purchased the Magnolia Springs Hotel, a nine-hole golf course was built. The course took advantage of some land features that had been manmade from previous years. The course was 2,235 yards in length, and Tom Dunn, who had recently been managing the links at Bournemouth, England, was employed to be the superintendent of the grounds and the East Coast Tournament that was to be held in Florida at the turn of the 20th century.

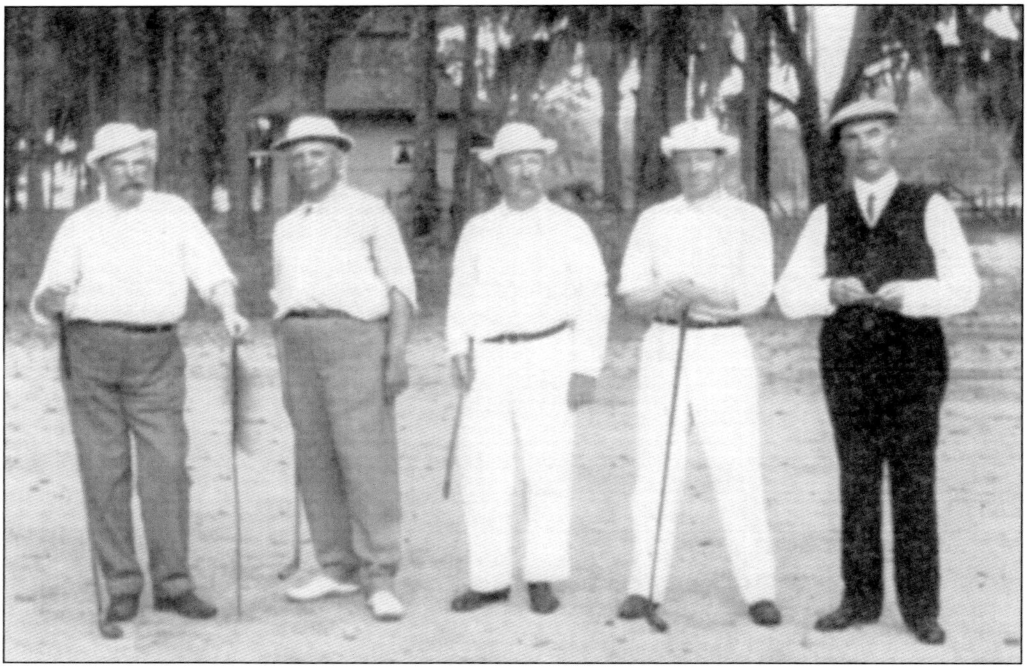

A "Four-some" and Scorer. Osborn Dunlap Seavey, proprietor of the Magnolia Springs Hotel, helped to promote golf in Florida. Seavey, a savvy golfer himself, would participate in tournaments. In September 1912, at Maplewood, New Hampshire, he made it to the first semifinal round loosing by three strokes. Seavey when playing golf stated that he had to remain "looking young and confidant at 41" so he could entertain "Colonel Bogey."

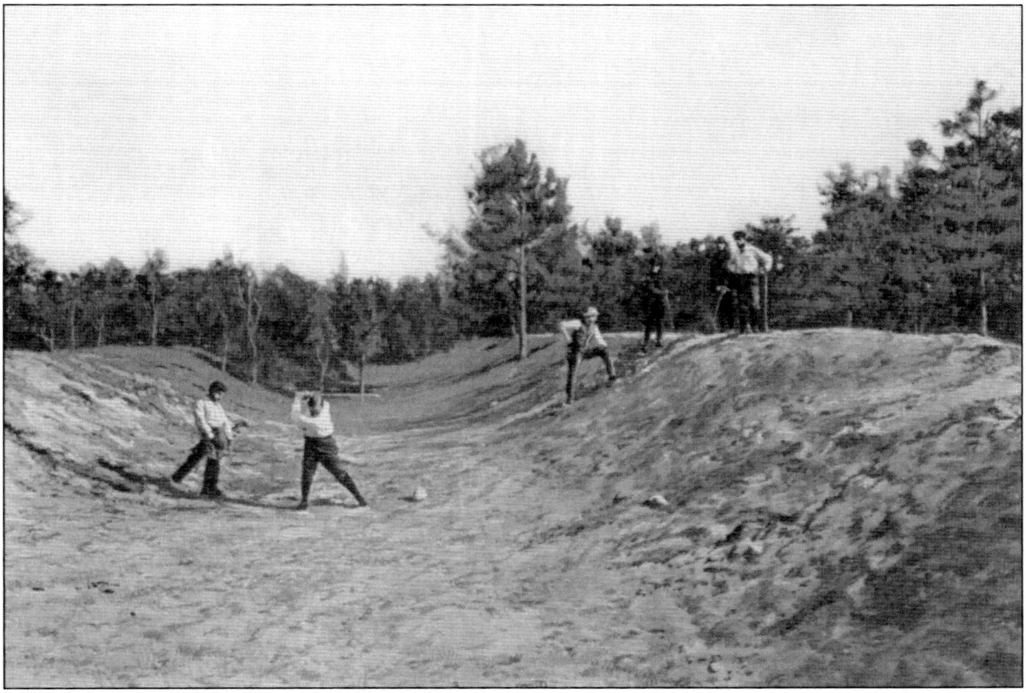

THE BIG BUNKER. The course at Magnolia incorporated several manmade earthen features that remained from past years. Pictured here are some of the defensive works left behind by Union troops from their failed occupation in late 1864.

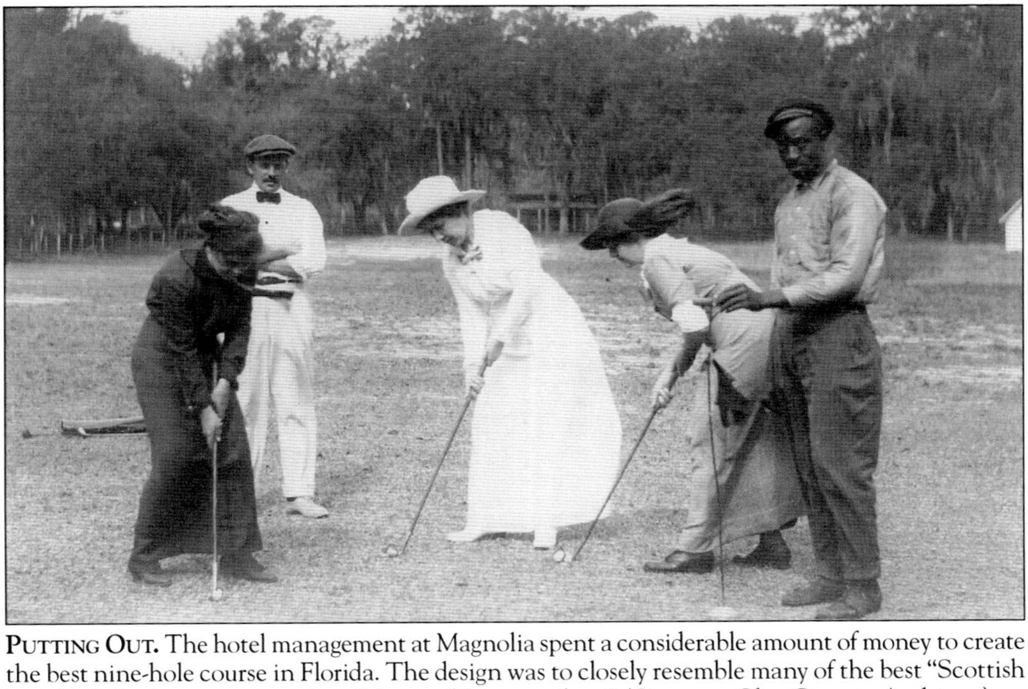

PUTTING OUT. The hotel management at Magnolia spent a considerable amount of money to create the best nine-hole course in Florida. The design was to closely resemble many of the best "Scottish links" while the course was kept "thoroughly up-to-date." (Courtesy Clay County Archives.)

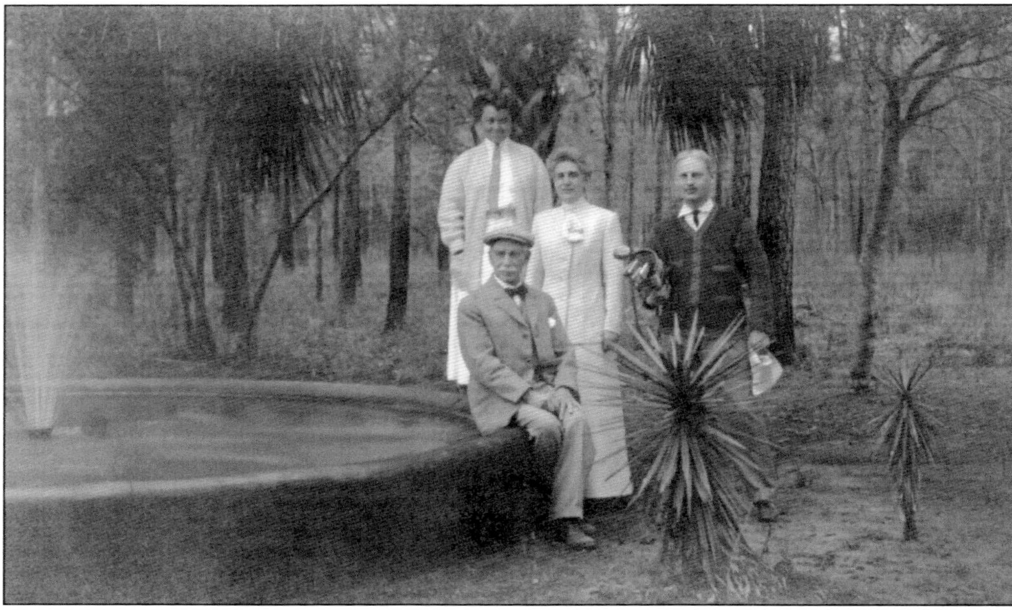

Golfers at Magnolia Springs. Golfers poise at the fountain near the railroad station. The golf course crossed the railroad line with the train depot at the green for tee No. 3. It appears that there are three irons, one wood, and one putter in the golf bag. (Courtesy Clay County Archives.)

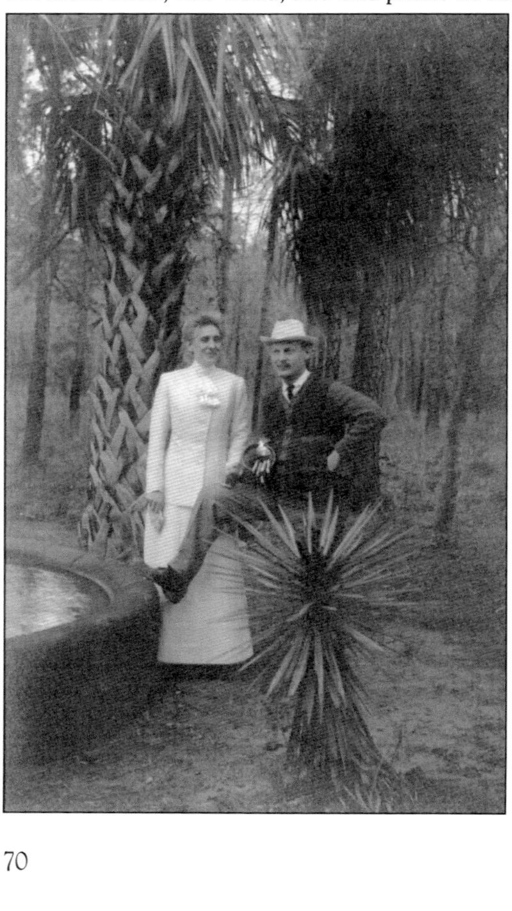

Golf Couple at Magnolia Springs. The Magnolia Golf Club was organized in 1898 with annual dues of $8. During the summer months, it moved to Plattsburg, New York. O. D. Seavey was the president, and Dr. C. C. Schuyler was the secretary. Nonmembers could play the nine holes for 50¢ a day. (Courtesy Clay County Archives.)

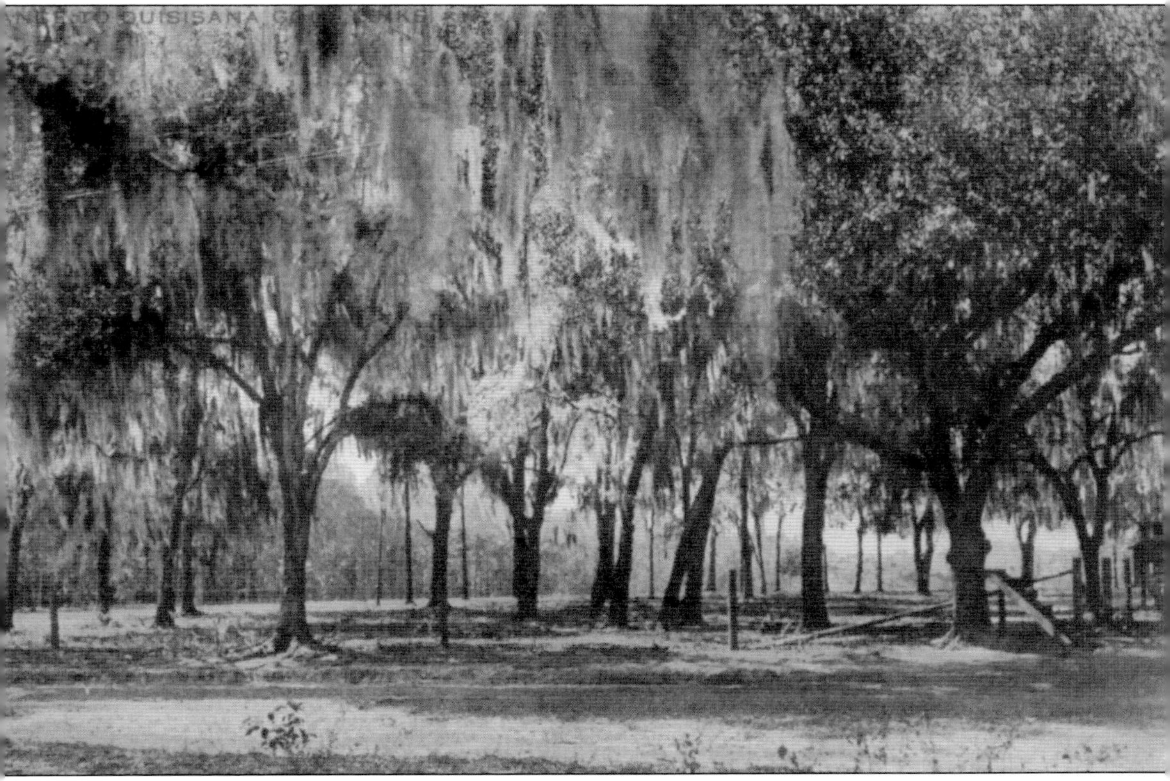

ENTRANCE TO QUI-SI-SANA GOLF COURSE. After the Clarendon Hotel burned down in 1900, the Qui-Si-Sana emerged and was opened in 1907 on the same site. Like the Magnolia Hotel before, the Qui-Si-Sana also had a golf course. It was 2,780 yards with a par of 42. Pictured here is the entrance to the golf course. This postcard is dated February 9, 1917.

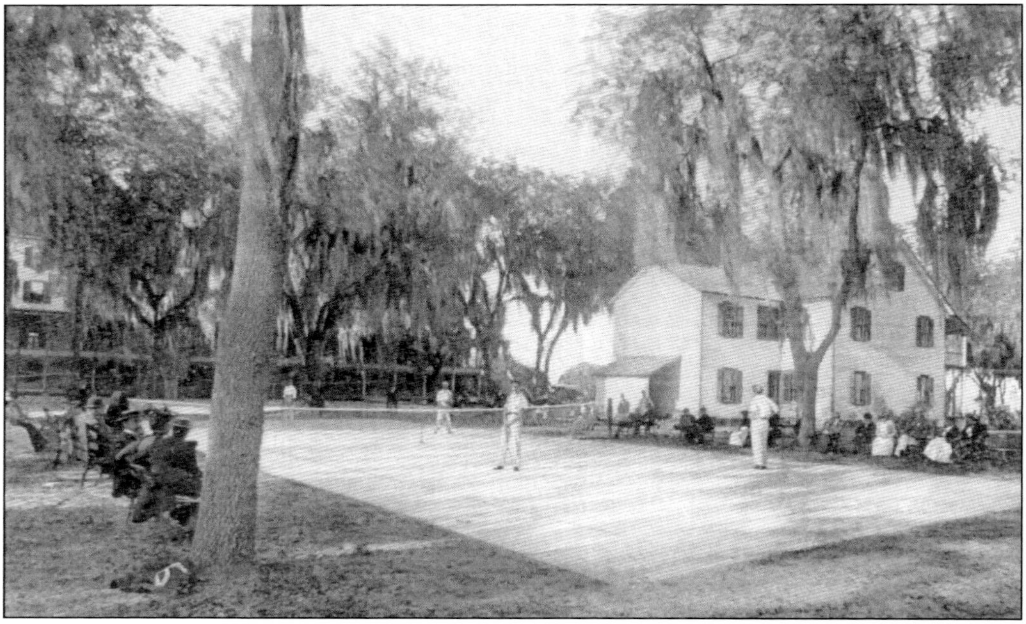

Tennis Court of the Magnolia. Lawn tennis was introduced at Magnolia around 1890 or 1891. Smaller tournaments were held in the south during the winter months. These southern tournaments were of "little importance so far as the determining of relatively ability" as Clarence Hobart wrote in 1894. "The players are rusty and out of training [but] are very enjoyable." In the early 1890s, U.S. champion Richard Sears participated in tournaments held at Magnolia. In later years, two concrete tennis courts were established.

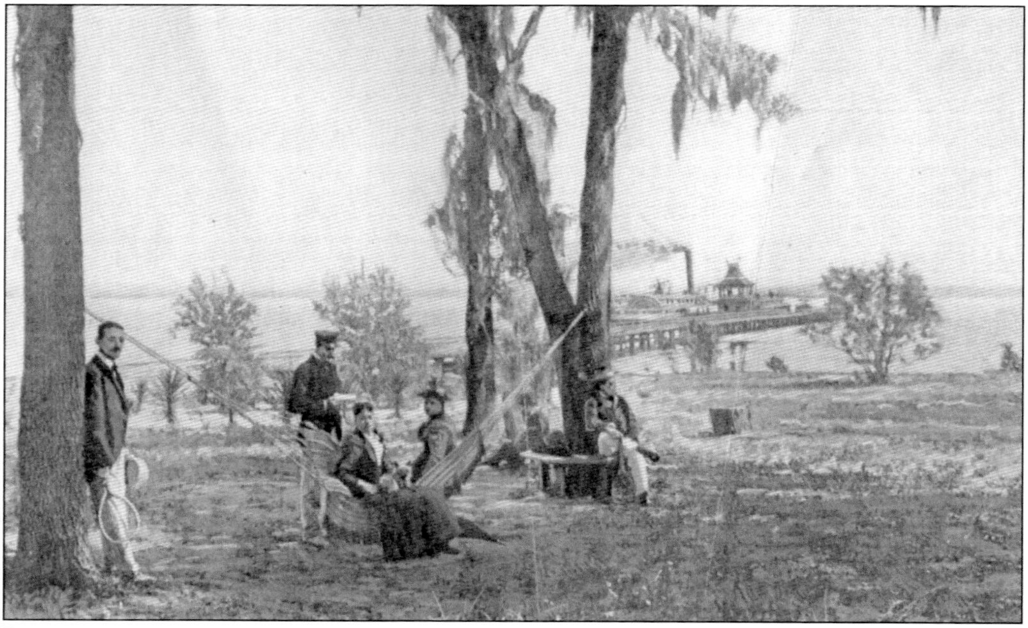

River View from Lawn at Magnolia. The hotels offered guests many activities so they could enjoy their visits. The Magnolia Springs Hotel boasted that it "caters to the lover of sports." Amongst this group of relaxing visitors. the two men nearest the trees each hold tennis rackets.

Six

City of Green Cove Springs

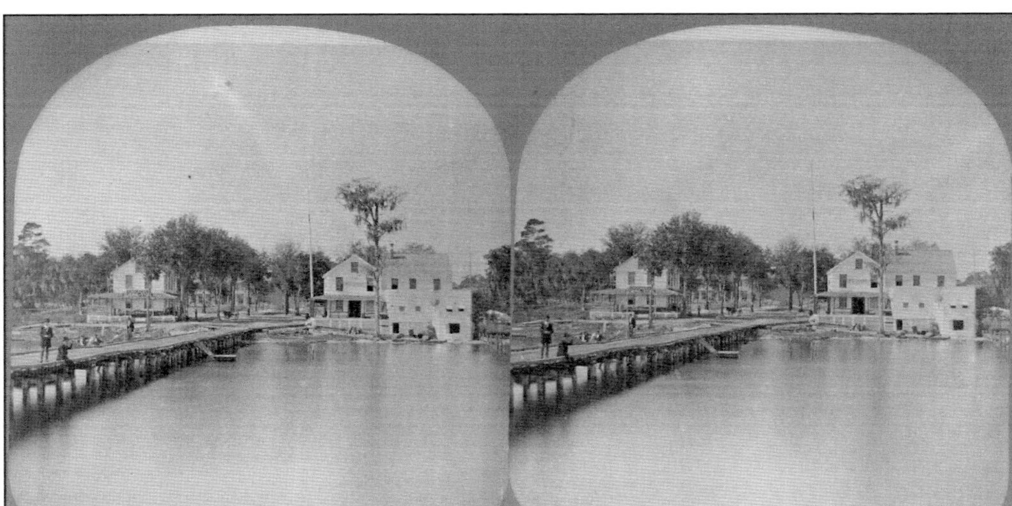

Landing at Green Cove Springs by Isaac Haas. In April 1883, Pres. Chester A. Arthur made a brief stop at Green Cove. Daniel G. Tyler, who had served as the general's private secretary during the Civil War, greeted the president. President Arthur was on his way to Sanford for a spring vacation. Bonfire and fireworks were lit to welcome the president. The building on the left is Crocker's General Store, and on the second floor of the building on the right was a saloon and billiards.

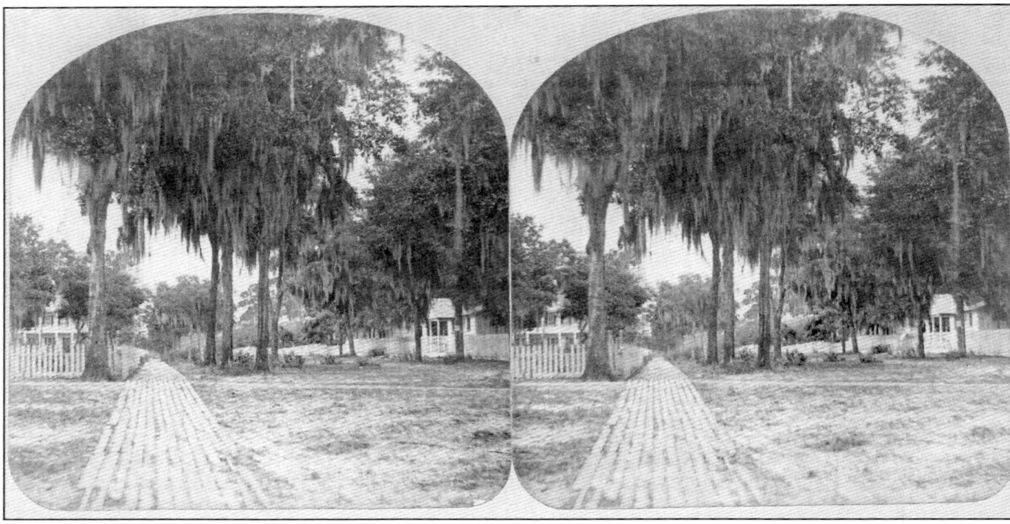

Walnut Street 1882. Walnut Street was the main business road and during the winter months when the tourists were invading the town, the street would have been teaming with tourists trying to find that special curiosity to take back home.

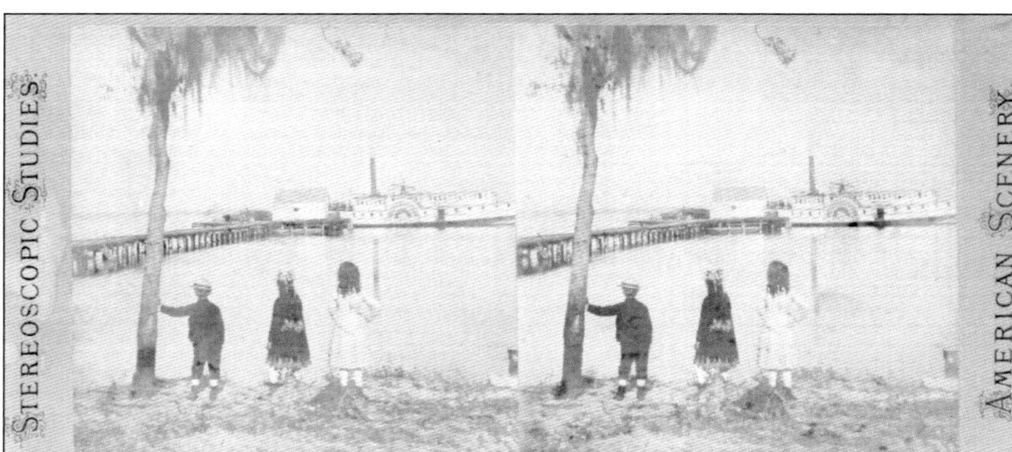

Steamer *Florence* at Green Cove Springs. Although steamers such as the *Florence* did not ply Black Creek, Governor's Creek, or the Ocklawaha, smaller craft did. Many sportsmen took aim at birds and alligators only to leave them decaying on the water's edge. Some citizens were calling for the Florida legislator to prohibit sportsmen from shooting off the deck of steamboats.

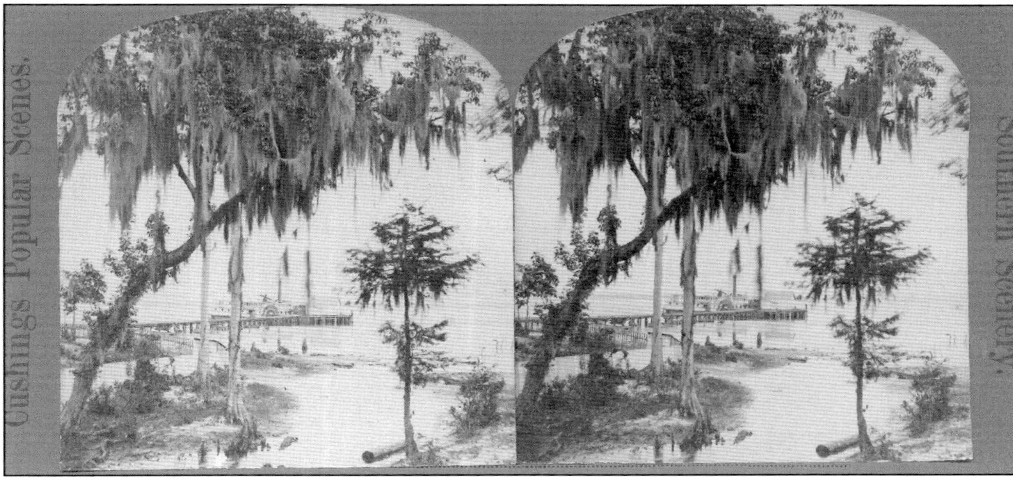

Steamer at Green Cove Springs. Traveling via steamboats was the best way to reach Green Cove Springs before the railroads arrived. Several of the boating lines were in fierce competition with one another, and on April 24, 1886, a race ensued between the *Captain Miller* and the *Manatee* after the *Captain Miller* left the dock at Green Cove Springs 10 minutes early. The two steamboats collided within a few minutes, causing the *Manatee* just over $1,000 in damage.

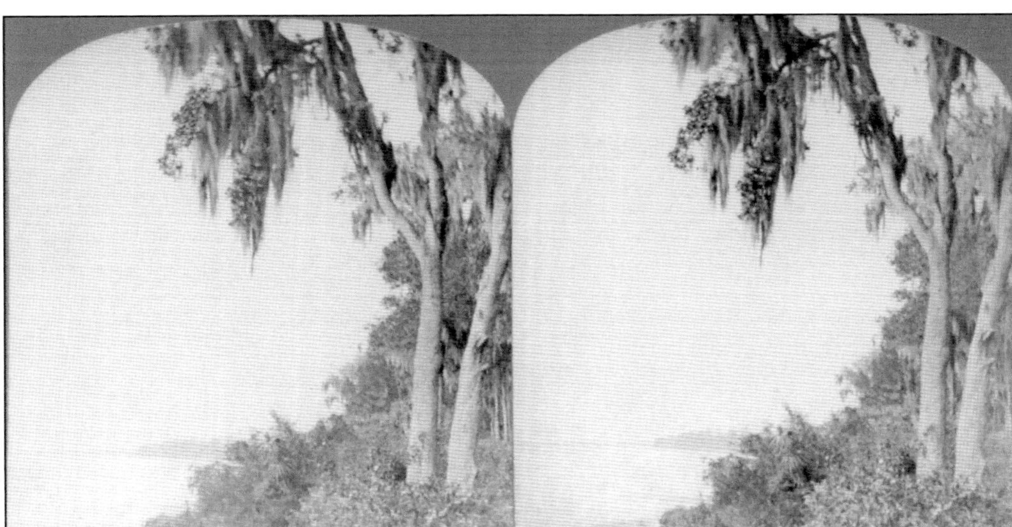

On the St. Johns River. Throughout time, most governments saw the St. Johns River as a natural highway. During the Civil War, Confederate troops placed torpedoes in the river in hopes of stopping the Union transports and gunboats from gaining control of the highway. In 1881, it was called "the great central artery of the state."

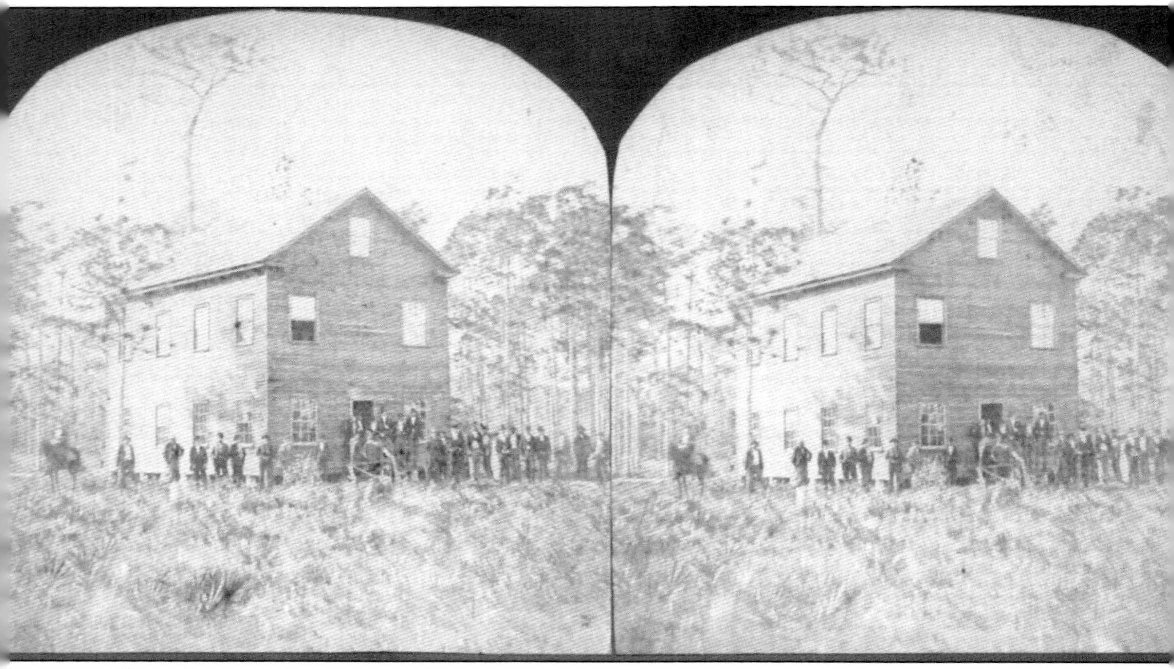

CLAY COUNTY COURT AND COURTHOUSE, JANUARY 31, 1875. Green Cove Springs became the county seat in 1871. The town was rapidly growing due to the post-war tourism, and the local citizens wanted "honest, industrious and peace loving" residents. "Lazy and shiftless persons had better stay away," they warned.

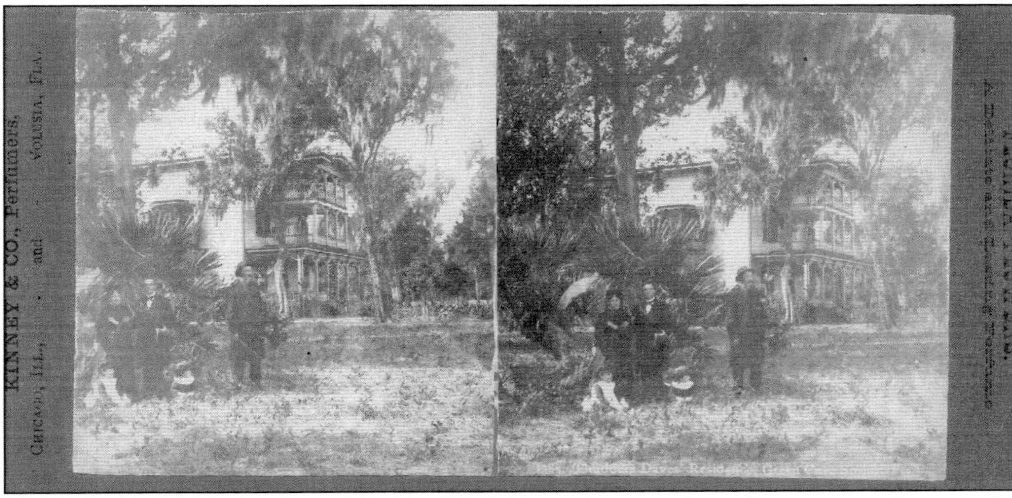

Thaddeus Davids Residence. Thaddeus Davids was the typical northern visitor who spent his winters in Green Cove Springs. He owned a large ink-manufacturing company and would later become mayor of the town and donate land to help build St. Mary's Episcopal Church.

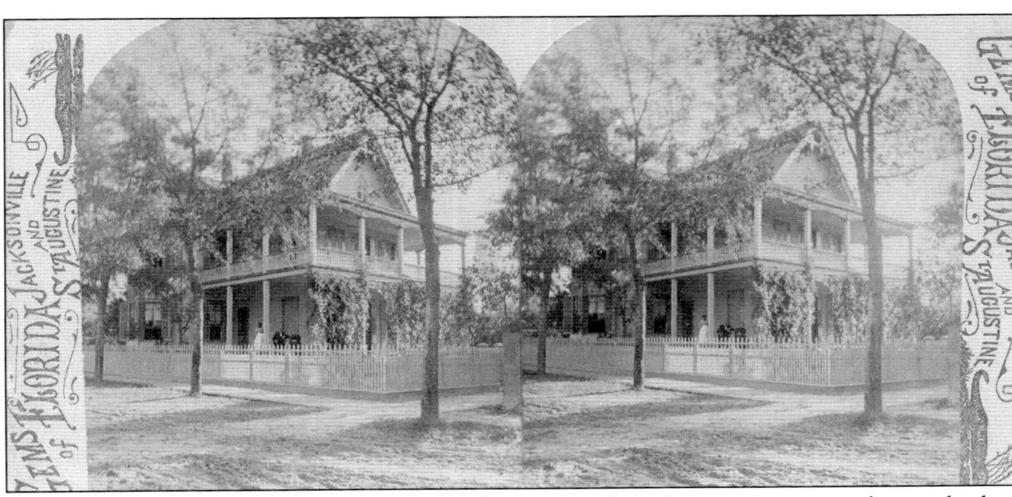

Unknown House, Green Cove Springs. This is one of the large, more ornate houses built in the late 19th century. In 1883, one resident wrote that "houses are hard to rent, about all occupied from $5 to $15 a month, for a one story house, according to location and the finish."

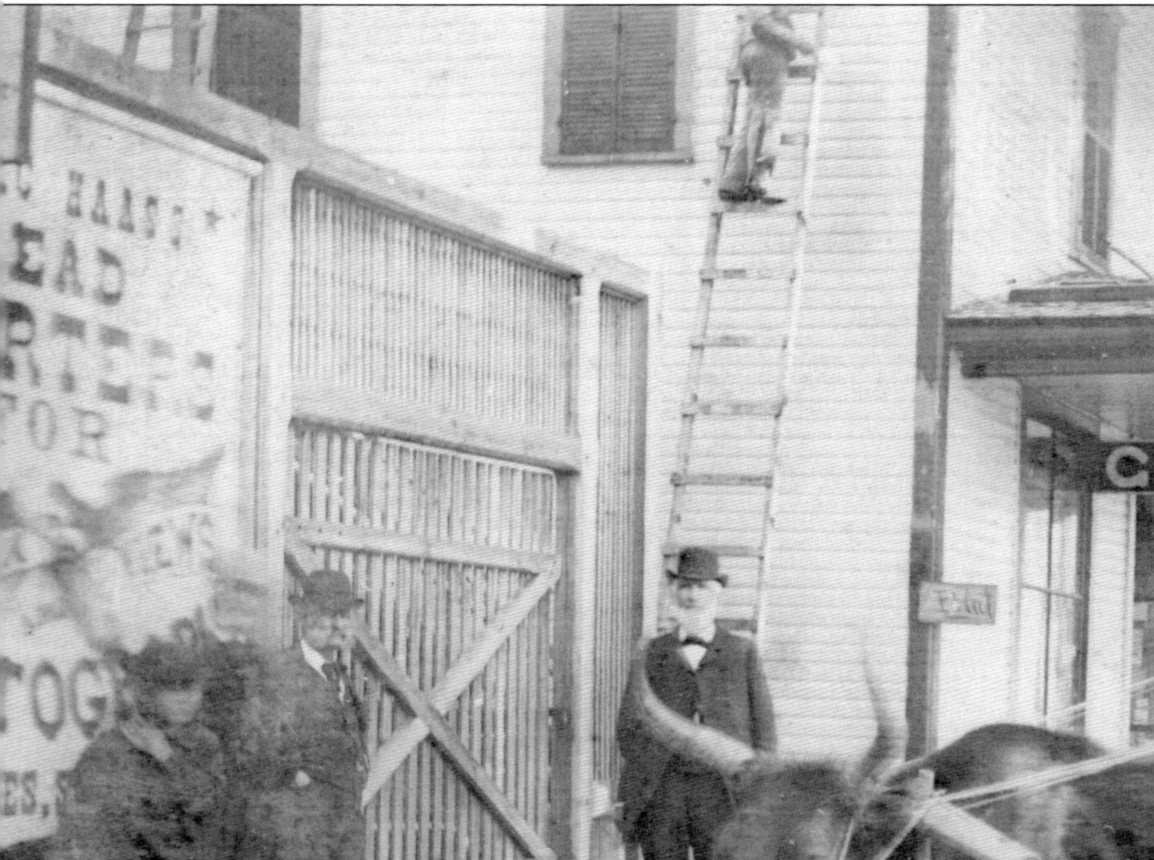

Isaac Haas Studio. The studio of Isaac Haas was located off Walnut Street across from the swimming pools. Notice the large sign to the left that reads, "Isaac Haas Head Quarters For Florida Views Photography." Haas was conscripted into the local Confederate infantry in 1864. He stayed in Florida and mostly likely served around Camp Milton, located about 9 miles west

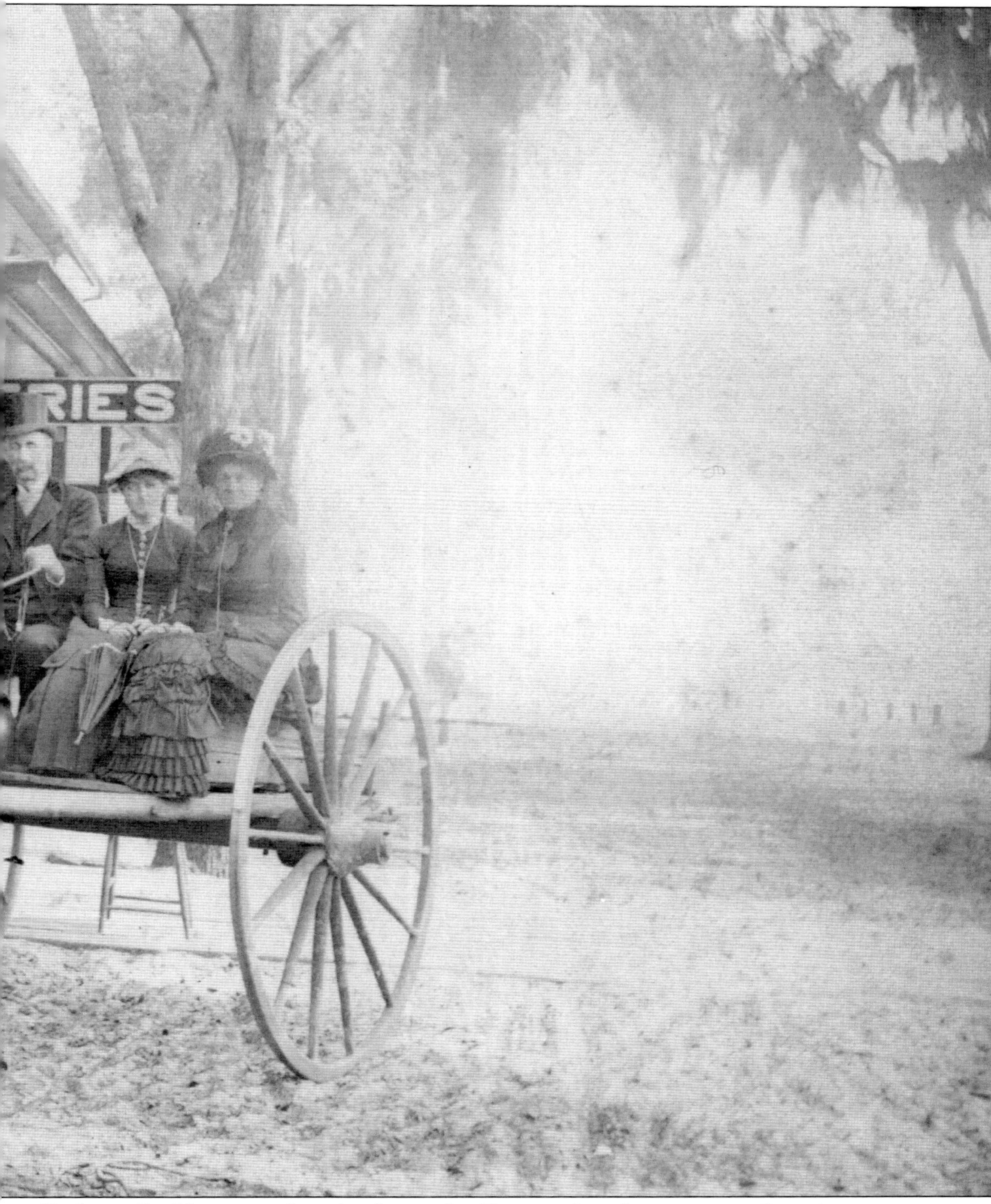

of Jacksonville. This image shows his first studio. Haas was forced to move away from the spring after a few years when the Crocker Block opened forcing Haas to begin a new studio at Palmetto and Spring Streets.

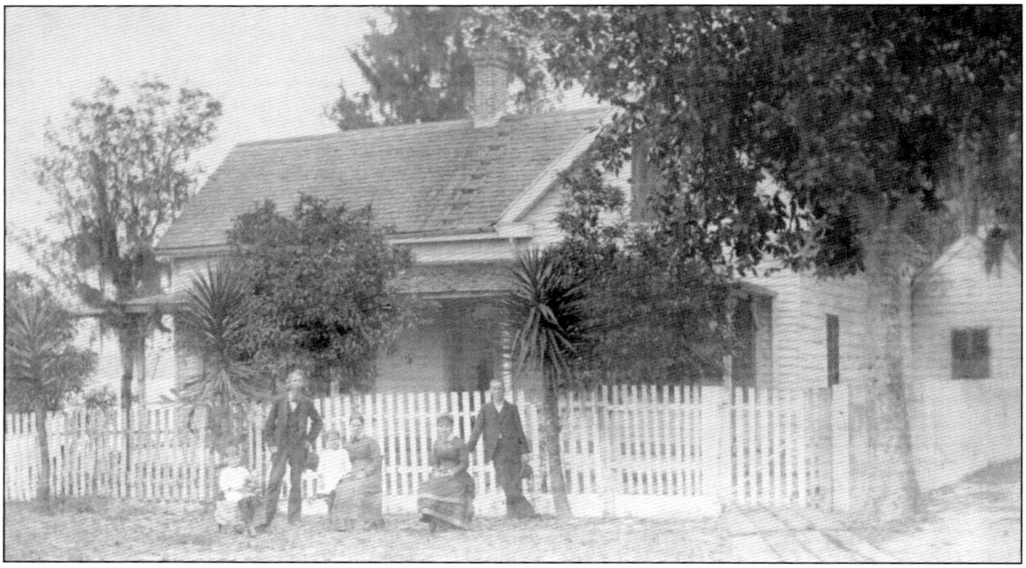

Reed Cottage by J. S. Mitchell. The house of Rufus C. Reed was described in 1881 as "a cozy little house on the cove . . . with some fine orange trees." Rufus C. Reed was one of the many individuals from the north who had a winter home in Green Cove. The family was from New York.

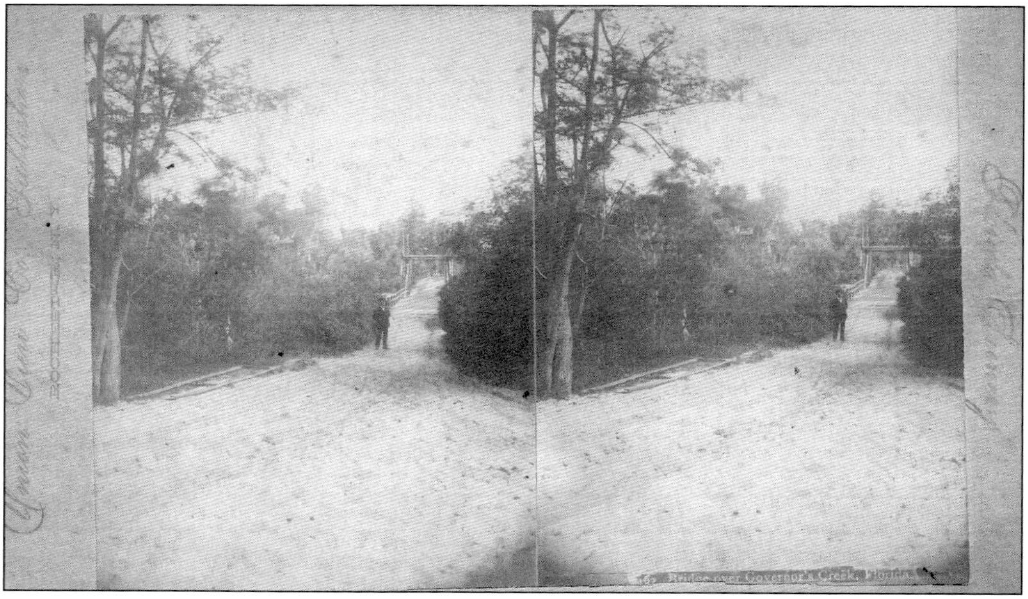

Bridge over Governor's Creek. This image shows the "new" bridge that was built over Governor's Creek sometime after 1872. With the increase of tourism, a new bridge was in much need, since visitors from Magnolia Springs enjoyed shopping in Green Cove Springs.

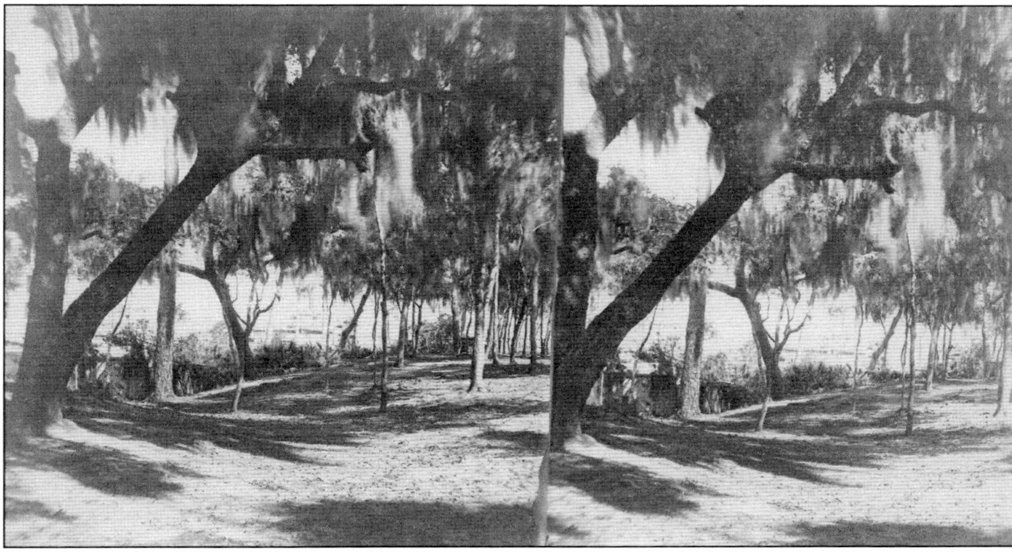

Park and Wharf. In the winter, the town's northern residents returned, including Thaddeus Davids, Rufus C. Reed, Daniel F. Tyler, and Gould Butler, all of New York. Dr. Cary A. Trimble came from Columbus, Ohio, and G. R. Kelsey came from West Haven, Connecticut.

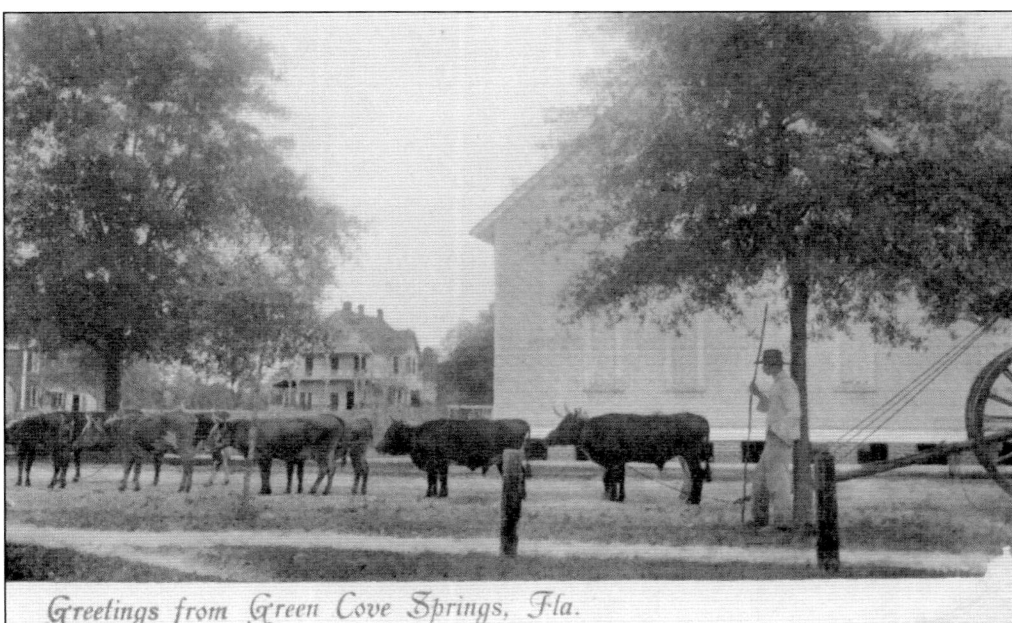

Greetings from Green Cove Springs. In 1886, a disastrous freeze hit Florida. A correspondent to the *Times-Union* reported that "all the crop on the trees was wholly destroyed [and] all the nursery stock, young budded trees and young seedlings were killed. All the berries . . . destroyed. Many domestic animals were killed outright by the cold . . . [and] three persons were frozen to death within 50 miles of Green Cove Springs." This postcard was dated December 31, 1905.

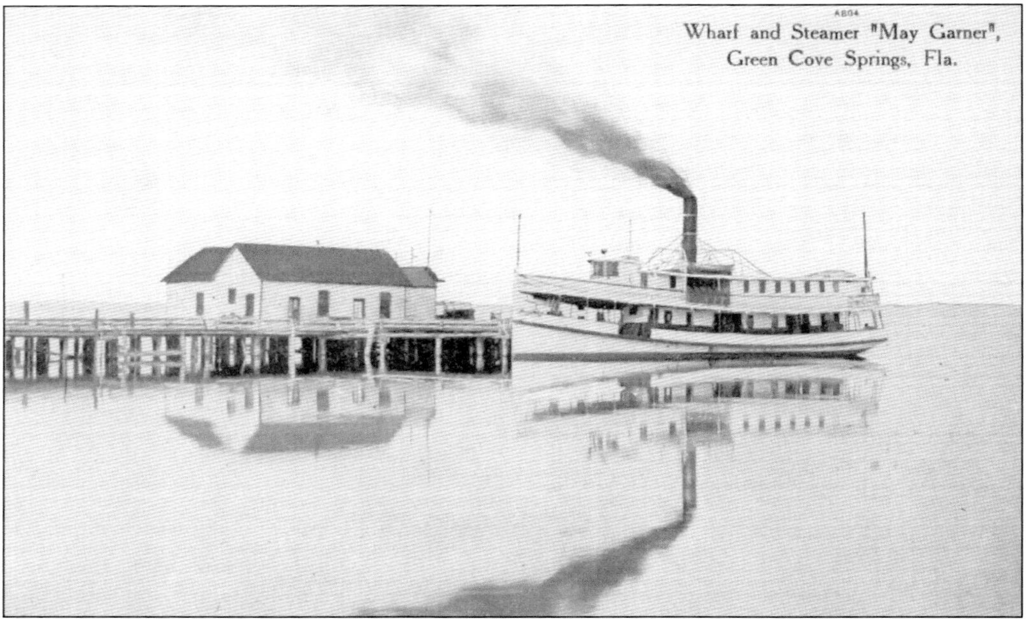

WHARF AND STEAMER *MAY GARNER*. In 1894, a strong hurricane swept through Florida from the Gulf of Mexico. The storm hit Tampa and worked its way east and between Green Cove Springs and Palatka; 12 wharfs were destroyed, and several riverboats were sunk at Palatka. (Courtesy Clay County Archives.)

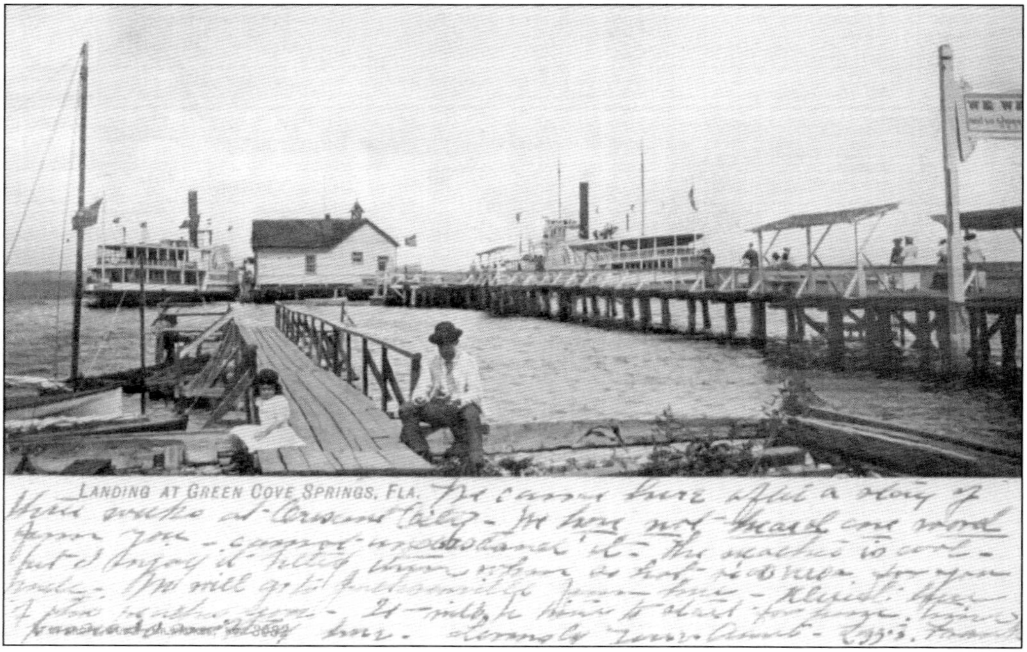

LANDING AT GREEN COVE SPRINGS. The price to travel from New York to Green Cove Springs in 1886 was $26 by boat and $35 by rail. This postcard is dated March 27, 1911.

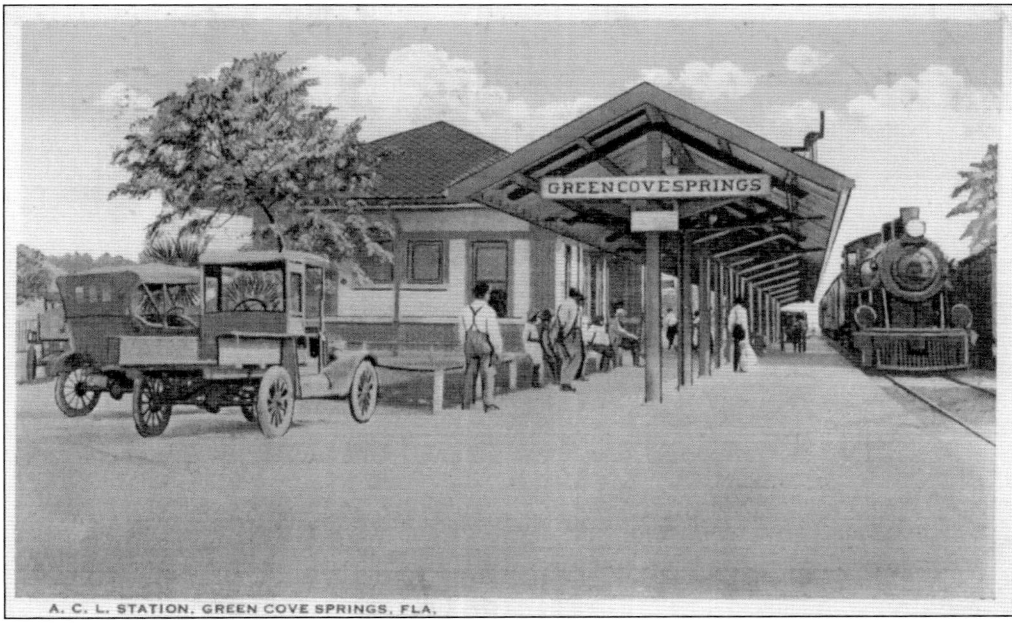

ACL Station. The Atlantic Coast Line Railroad advertised in 1908 that Pullman cars were in service to Magnolia and Green Cove. This postcard was mailed in 1930, and the sender noted that "this is a good picture of the station."

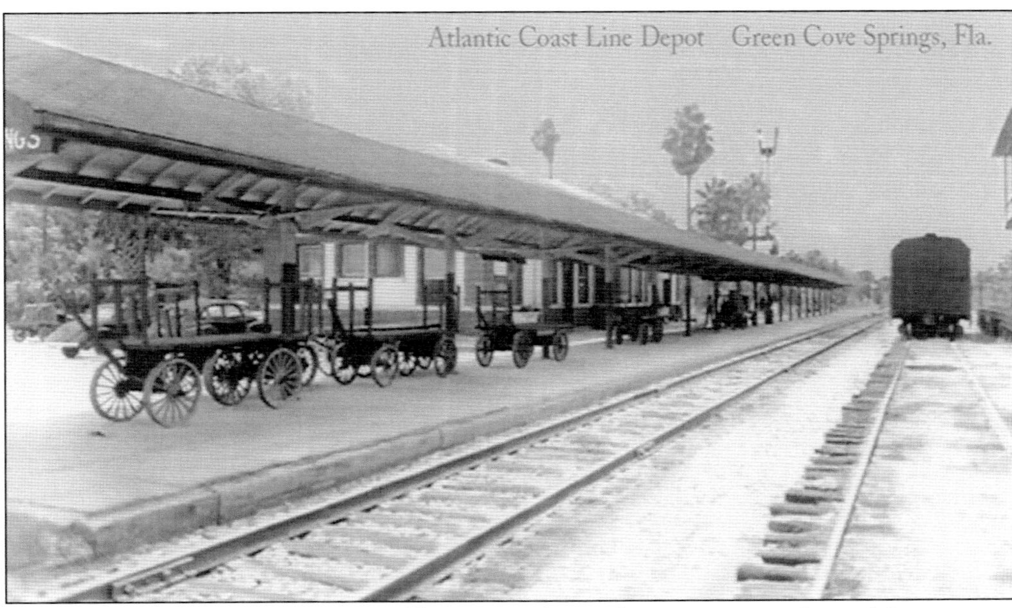

Atlantic Coast Line Depot. In addition to railways that were primarily used for passenger transportation, several smaller railroads existed. The Western Railway Company was organized on July 26, 1886, and leased the Green Cove and Midland Railway, and the company intended to extend the line to Melrose and construct a branch line to Starke. The rolling stock consisted of 1 locomotive engine, 1 passenger car, and 30 freight cars. It was primarily used for moving logs and lumber to Green Cove Springs. (Courtesy Clay County Archives.)

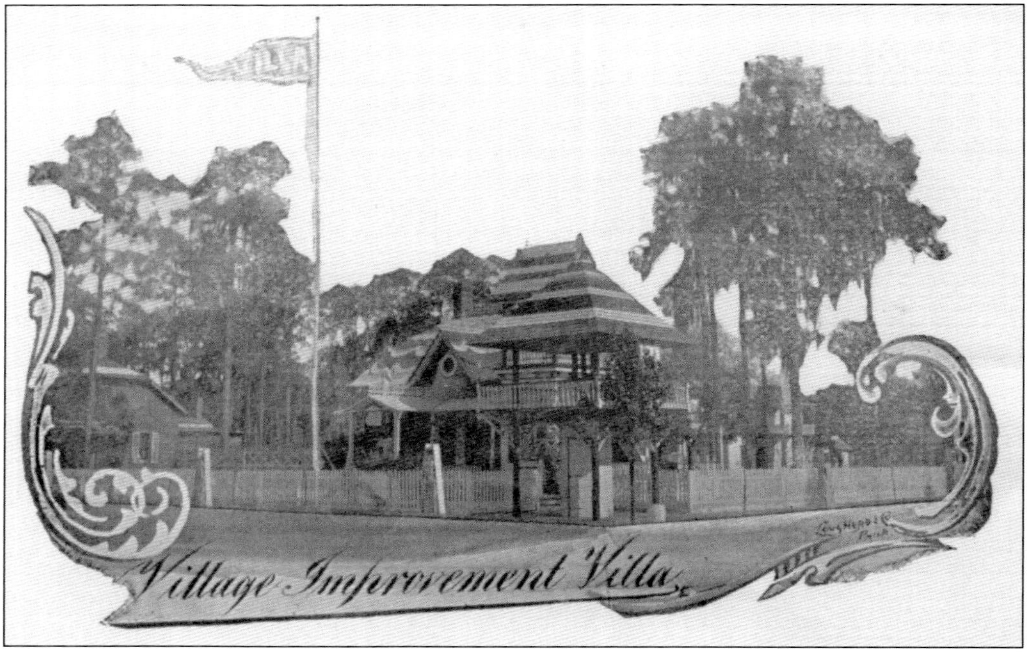

Village Improvement Villa. In 1898, the Village Improvement Association's property was said to include "cozy sitting-rooms, a library and reading-room; also a dinning-room, where a sandwich and a cup of coffee are gratuitously served to visitors. Stationary is provided at the desk for the use of guests; also a small mail-box from which all letters are promptly conveyed to the post office." A maid kept the area clean and attended to the comfort of visitors.

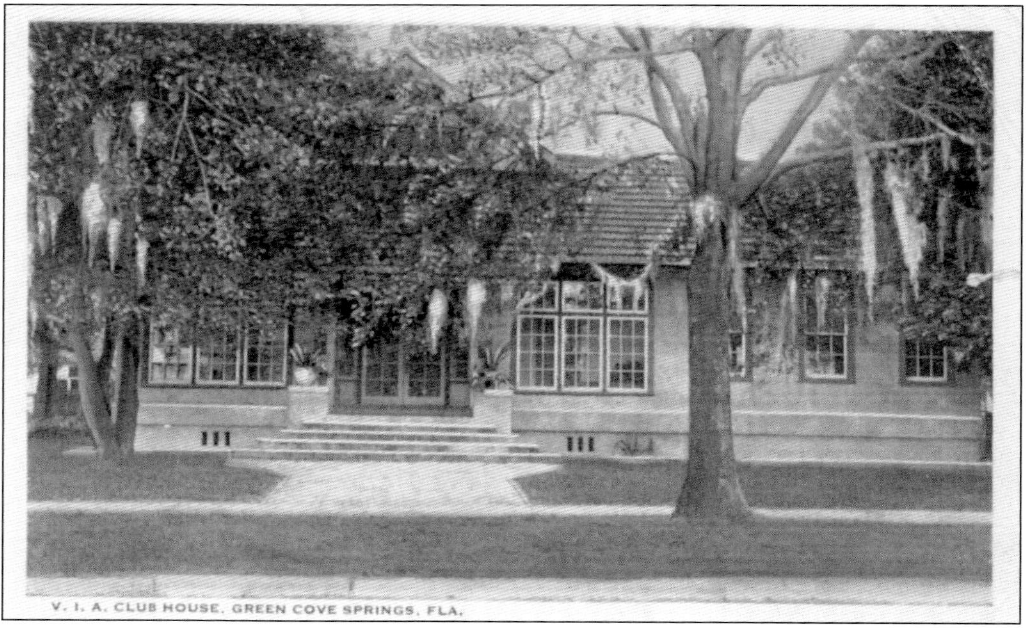

VIA Club House. The Village Improvement Association was organized in February 1883. The building pictured here was constructed in 1915 and is still in use by the organization. (Courtesy Clay County Archives.)

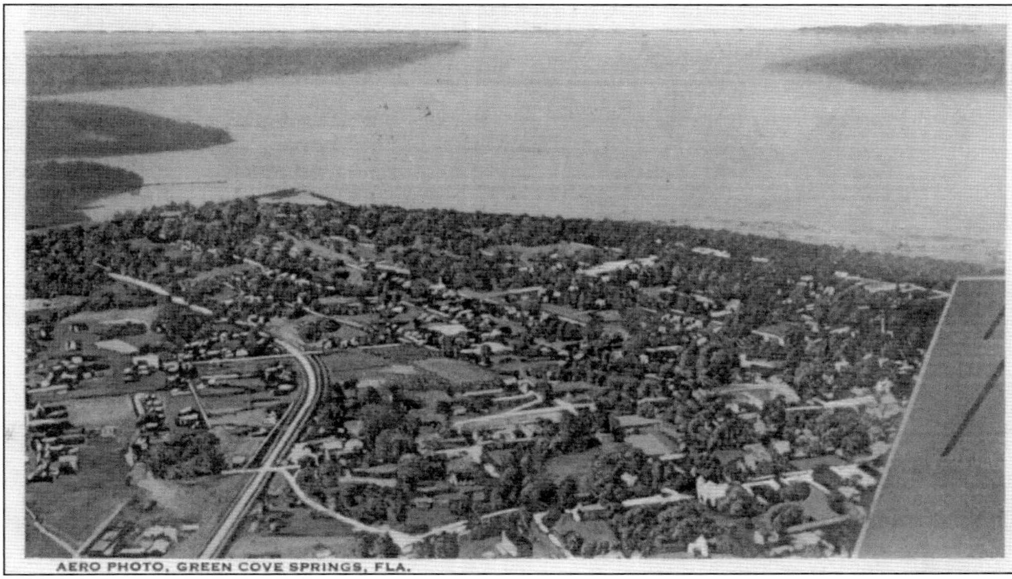

AREO-PHOTO OF GREEN COVE SPRINGS. By the early 1880s, the population of Green Cove Springs hovered around 850. One businessman wrote on November 2, 1883, that land "are at all prices from $1.25 to $100 an acre . . . but one would need only a few acres to cultivate if going into the vegetable business or planting an orange grove. Labor is mostly done by the blacks at wages from $1 to $1.25 a day." This postcard was mailed in March 1928.

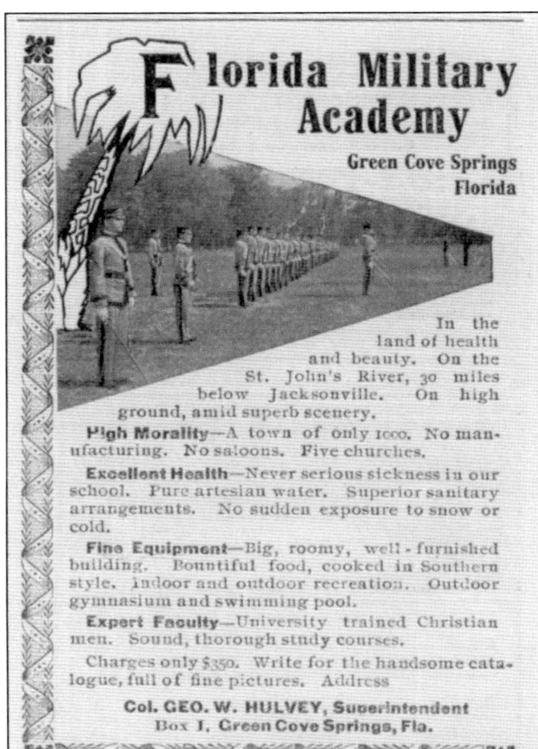

FLORIDA MILITARY ACADEMY. The Florida Military Academy established itself in Green Cove Springs around 1907. It was first located at the St. Elmo Hotel. It continued to reside there until 1916, when it moved to the Magnolia Springs Hotel.

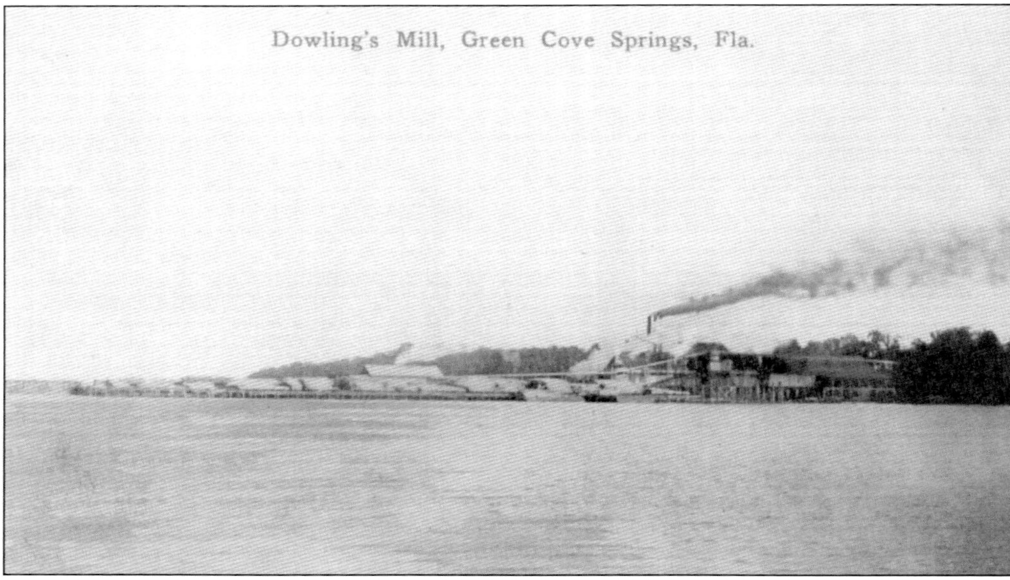

DOWLING'S MILL. After Dowling and Shands Mill merged the mill was associated with the Georgia-Florida Saw Mill Association. In 1913, there was a surplus of yellow pine, and the association wanted to cut the production of yellow pine lumber by 40 to 50 percent. If the majority of mills that were part of the association agreed to cut production, Dowling's Mill would shut down for 60 days on August 1.

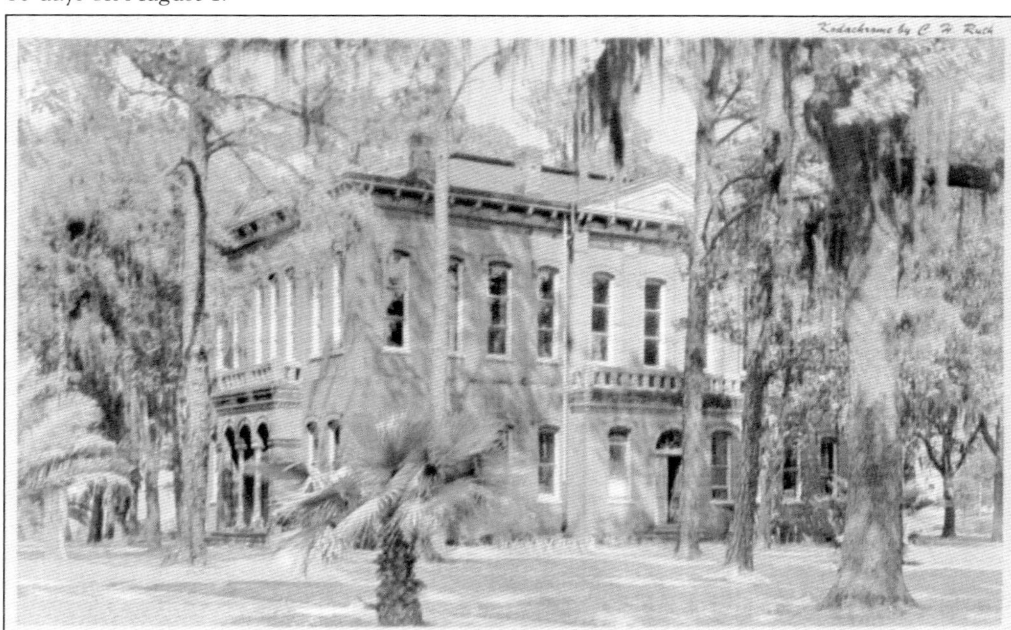

CLAY COUNTY COURTHOUSE. The old courthouse was used until 1973. In August 1957, a pigeon flew into the court of Judge W. A. Stanly and interrupted the session. Clerk of court George Carlisle tried in vain to shoo the bird out but only succeeded in frightening the bird. Judge Stanly then asked Sheriff John P. Hall to rid his courtroom of the pesky bird. Hall summoned a deputy with a .22 rifle. One shot; one dead bird.

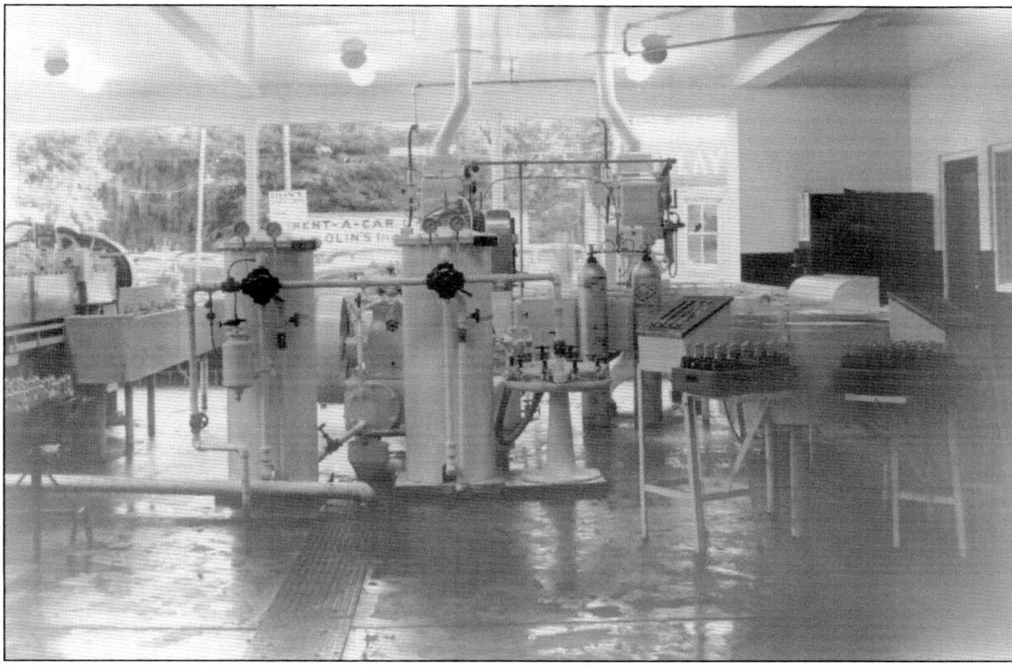

Interior View of Green Cove Springs Bottling Plant. The Green Cove Coca-Cola bottling plant was built at the end of World War II. It was primarily constructed because of the navy's influence. The plant closed its doors on November 1, 1971. (Courtesy Clay County Archives.)

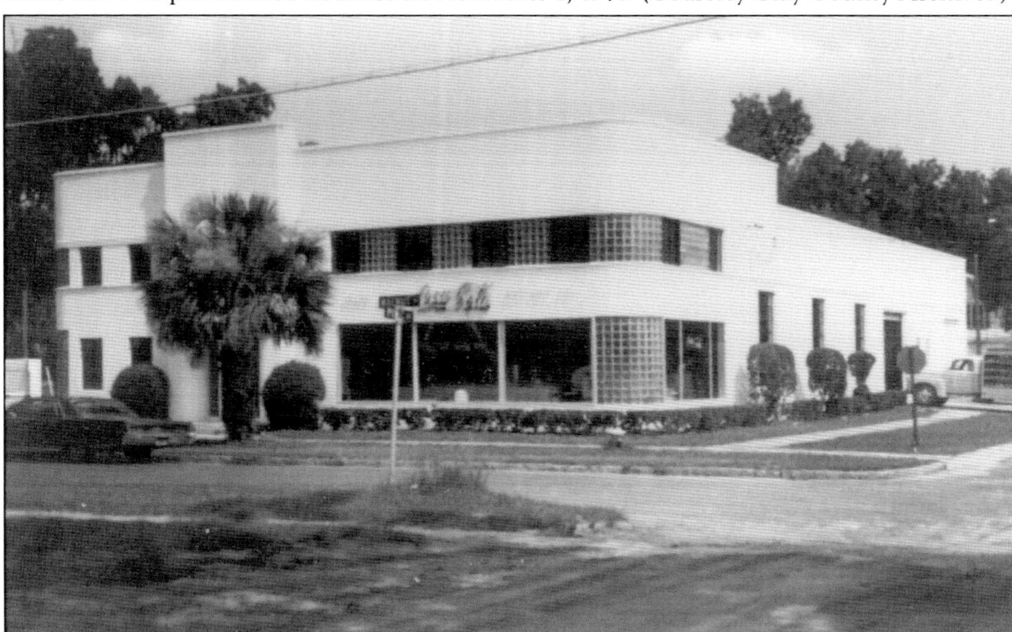

Green Cove Springs Coca-Cola Building. Although the Coca-Cola bottling operation had ceased, an ice plant still existed in the rear of the building. The ice plant continued to operate until 1994. Today the building is used by the city as a senior citizens center and a soup kitchen. (Courtesy Clay County Archives.)

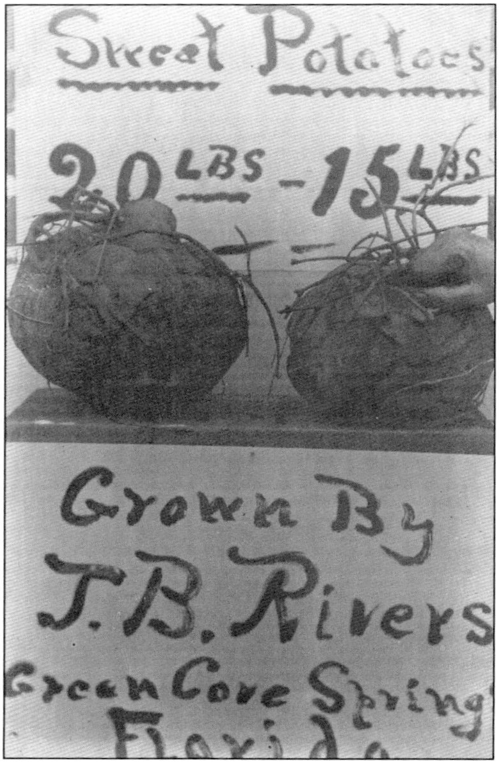

Sweet Potatoes. Pictured here are 20- and 15-pound sweet potatoes grown by J. B. Rivers in 1914. Notice a man's fist on the right providing perspective on how large the 15-pound potato is. This postcard was mailed on December 27, 1914.

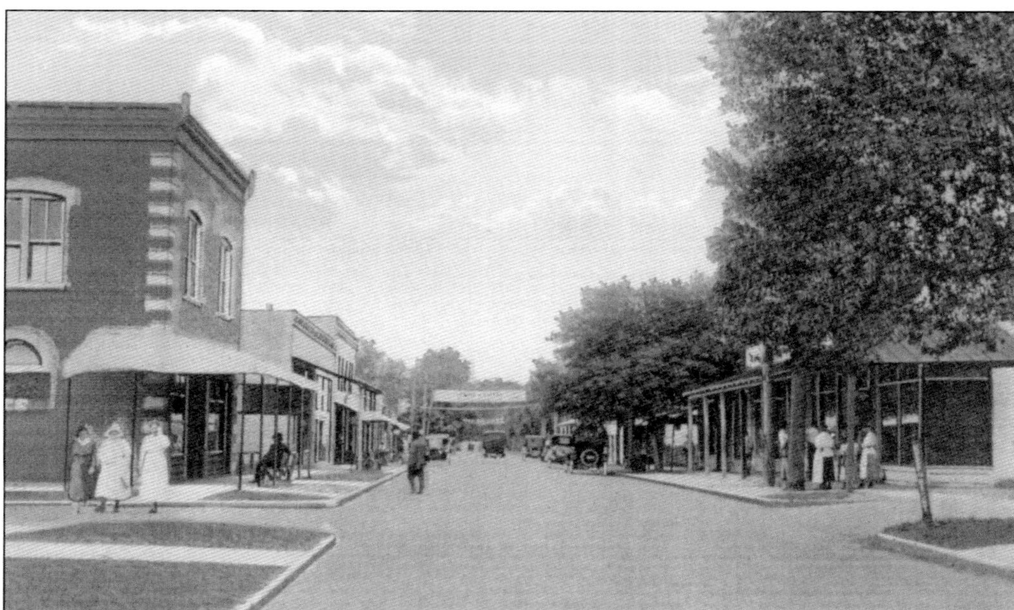

Walnut Street. This postcard shows Walnut Street looking west. In the center left was the post office along with a drug store, bakery, stationary shop, and shoe store. On the right was a barbershop; pool room and cigar factory; meats store; drugstore; general store; and the opera house and motion pictures.

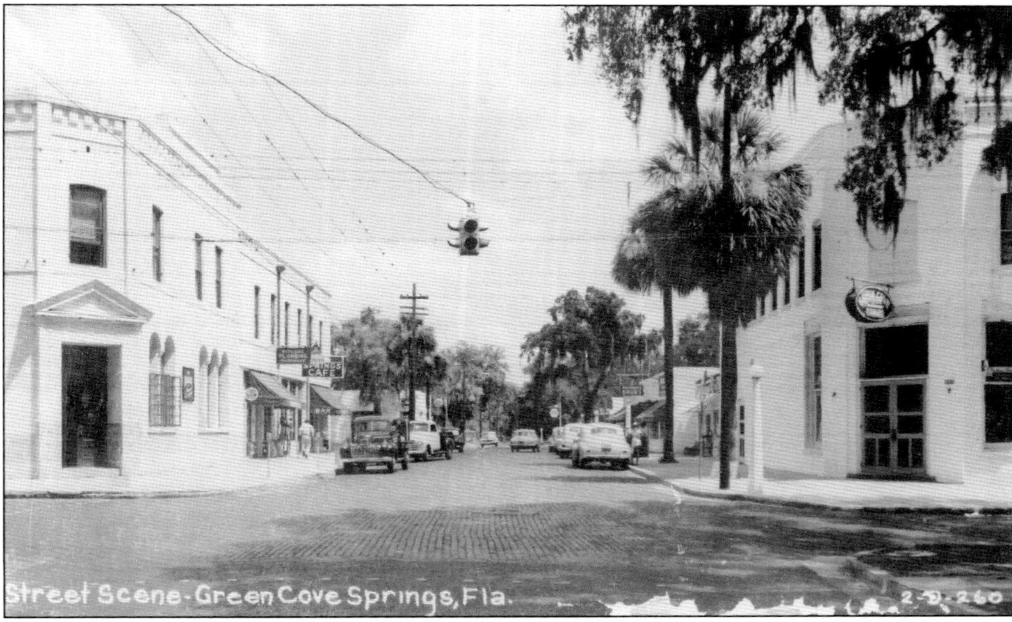

STREET SCENE. This photograph is looking north on U.S. Highway 17 and Walnut Street. Butlers Plumbing and Hardware is located on the left. Mayhugh's Drug Store, which is still in business, is located in the middle right.

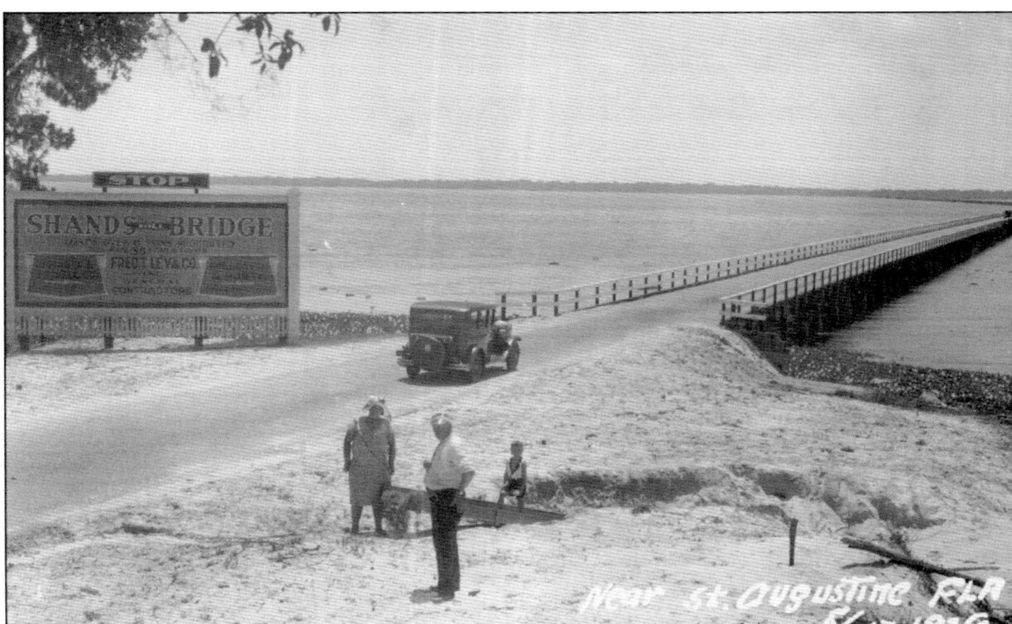

SHANDS BRIDGE. Built in 1929 at a cost of more than $500,000, the Shands Bridge became a local headache when it was struck by lightning and caught fire on July 23, 1939. The fire caused approximately 125 feet of the bridge, including the draw, to plunge into the St. Johns River. (Courtesy of Clay County Archives.)

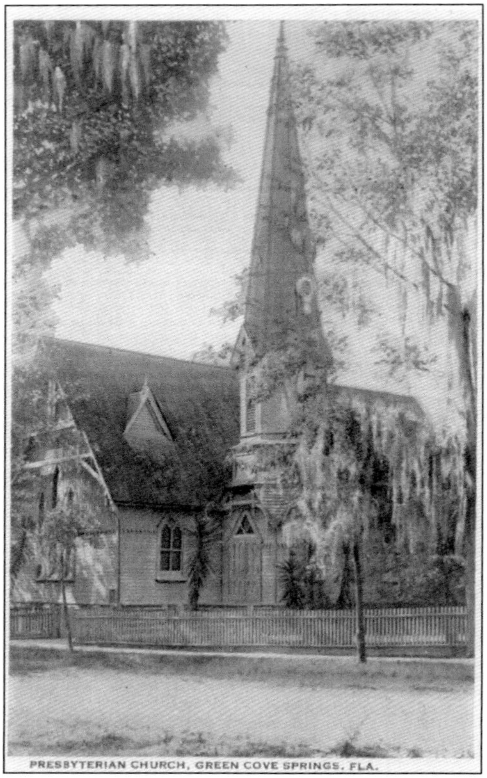

PRESBYTERIAN CHURCH. The church was first organized in 1884, and starting in 1893, the Rev. J. K. Wright would preach every winter at Green Cove Springs. Wright had been ordained in 1843 and had been preaching in Green Cove Springs for 15 years. This postcard was mailed in 1926.

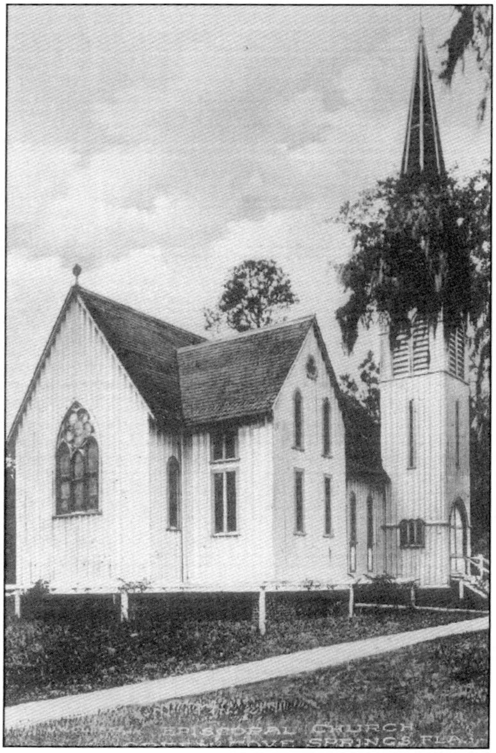

EPISCOPAL CHURCH. St. Mary's Episcopal Church was organized in 1878. In 1881, the interior of the church was said to be "finished in native wood and is really beautiful." In 1936, the building was valued at $4,700.

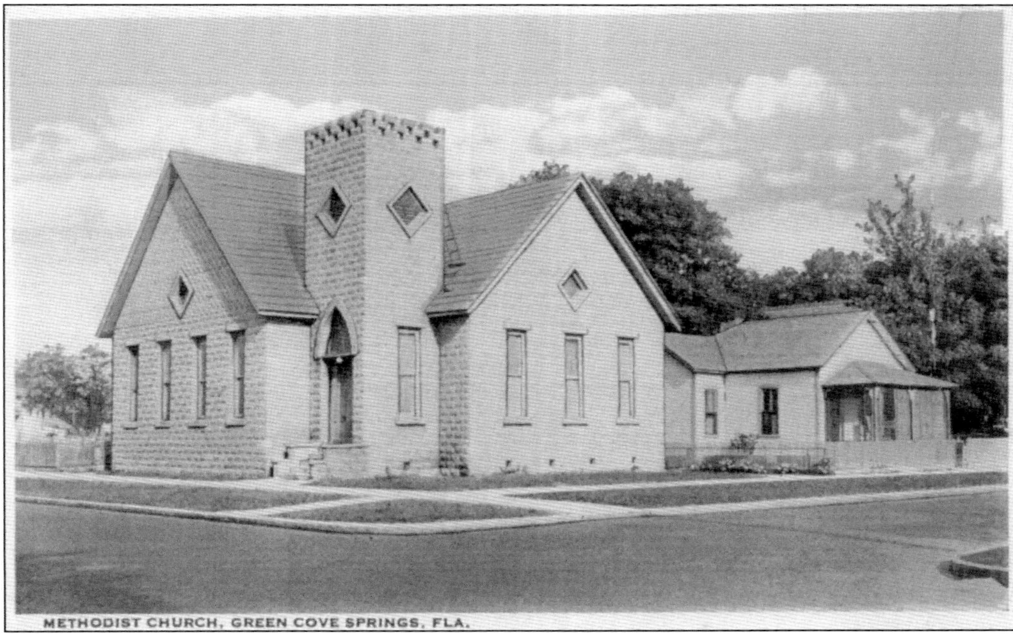

METHODIST CHURCH. The Methodist church in town was first organized in 1871 by the help of an affluent northern visitor. The Methodist circuit rider during the territorial period (1821–1845) was responsible for starting many of the Methodist churches in Florida. The original structure of this church was a wooden frame building.

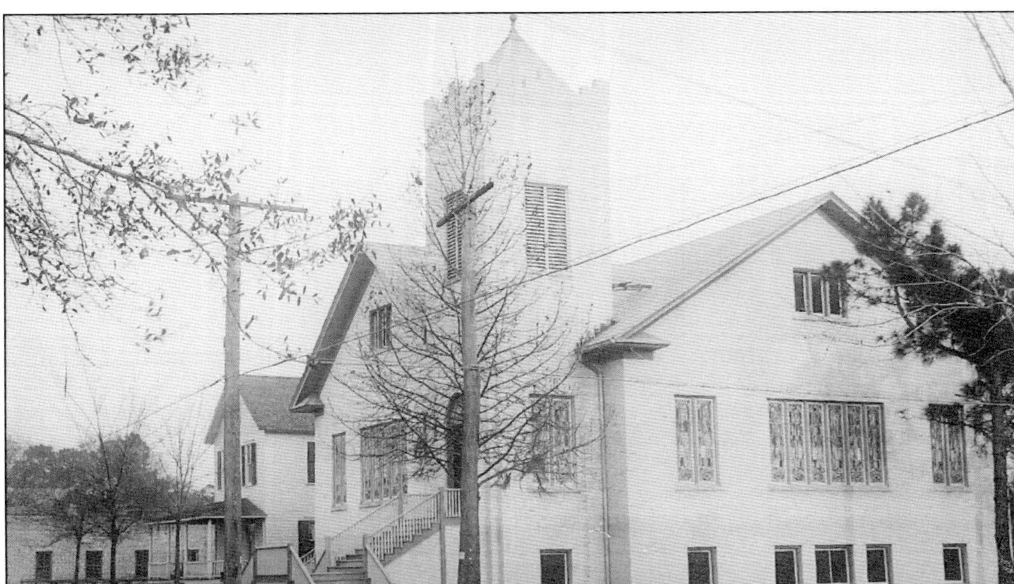

FIRST BAPTIST CHURCH. The current structure for this church was built in 1916 on Walnut Street and it is still in use. The Rev D. W. Glisson pastored this church in the late 19th century, and he was instrumental in helping start other Baptist churches. (Courtesy Clay County Archives.)

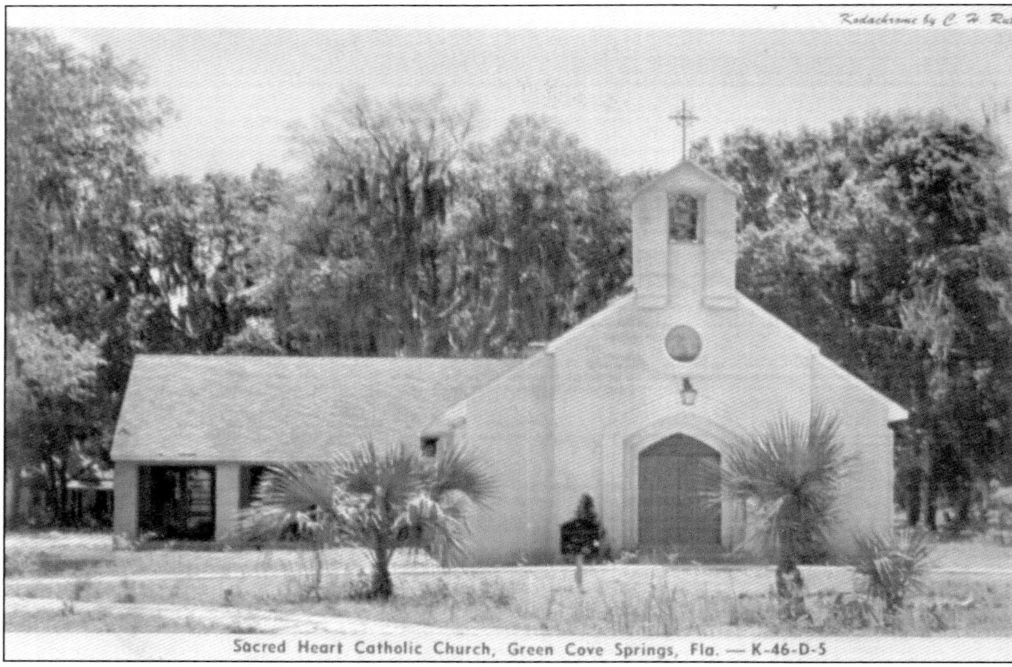

SACRED HEART CATHOLIC CHURCH. First organized in the late 19th century, the church constructed this building at the end of World War II.

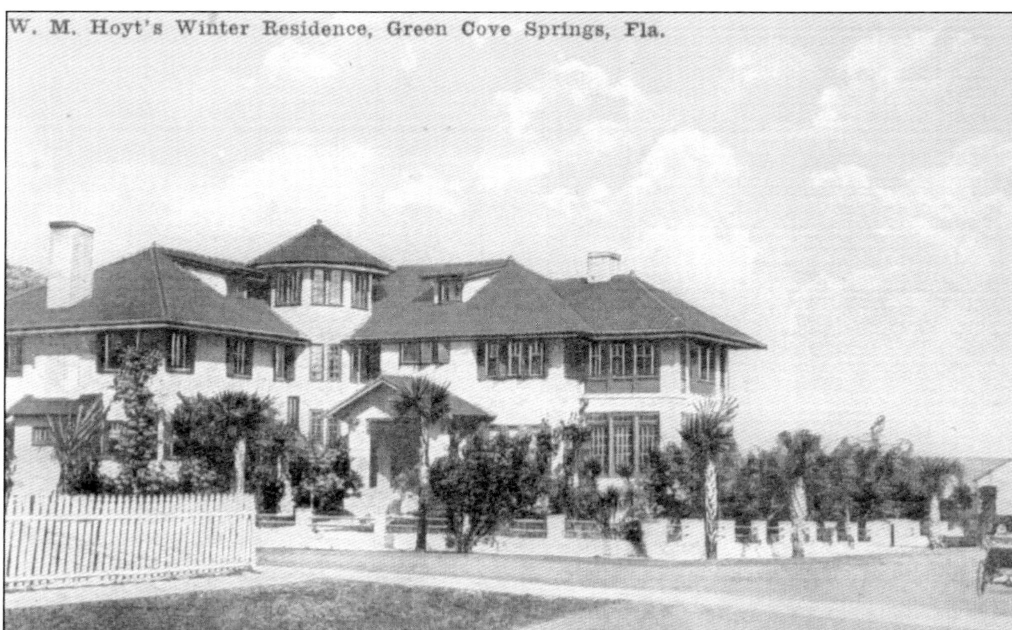

W. M. HOYT'S WINTER RESIDENCE. William Hoyt was a successful businessman in wholesale groceries, and he had large investments in Chicago real estate. His residence called "St. Johns Terrace" was completed around 1913. (Courtesy Clay County Archives.)

Seven

Isaac Haas, an Early Local Photographer

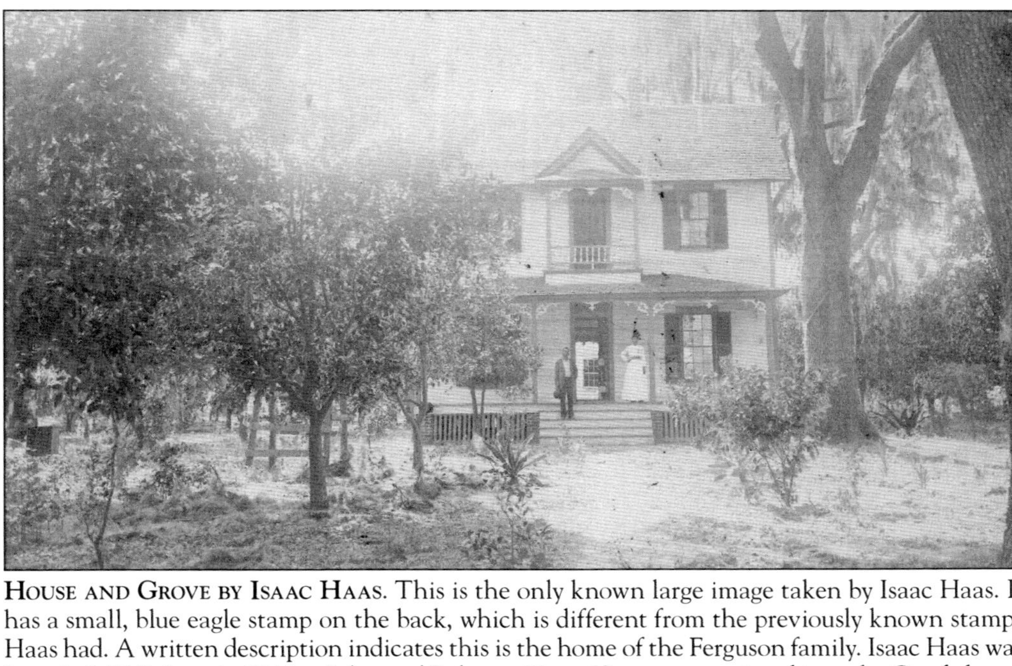

House and Grove by Isaac Haas. This is the only known large image taken by Isaac Haas. It has a small, blue eagle stamp on the back, which is different from the previously known stamps Haas had. A written description indicates this is the home of the Ferguson family. Isaac Haas was born in Middleburg in 1846 to John and Rebecca Haas. He was conscripted into the Confederate army in 1864 and remained in Florida to defend the state. After the war, Haas and his mother moved to Green Cove Springs, where he learned photography and opened his studio on Walnut Street. Haas primarily created stereoviews, and later in his career, he produced CDVs and cabinet cards. He died in 1902 and is buried in the old city cemetery.

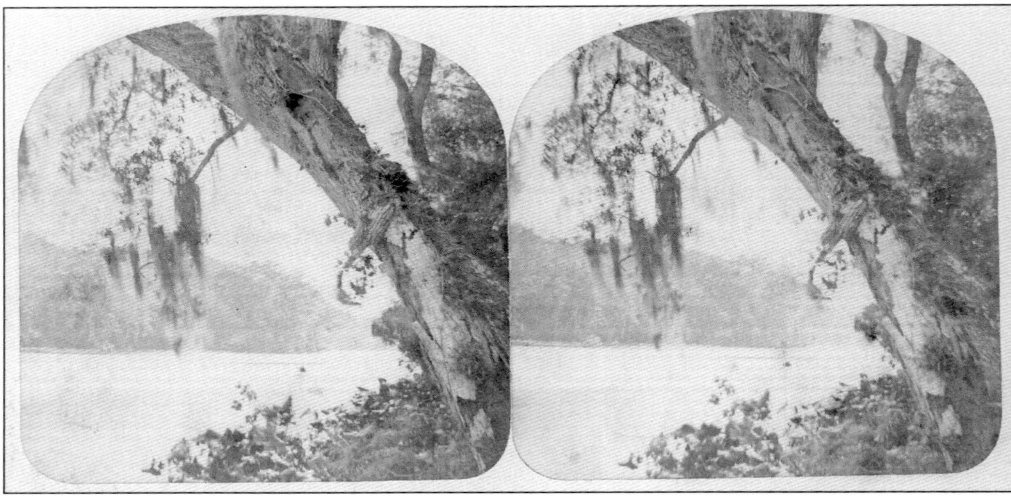

Black Creek by Isaac Haas. Isaac Haas spent his early years in Middleburg, and he would have seen a lot of Black Creek. Black Creek forks just above Middleburg. The creek was used by the military during the Second Seminole War (1835–1842) as a highway into the interior of Florida, and Fort Heileman, located on Black Creek, played a key role in providing quartermaster stores to the army during the war.

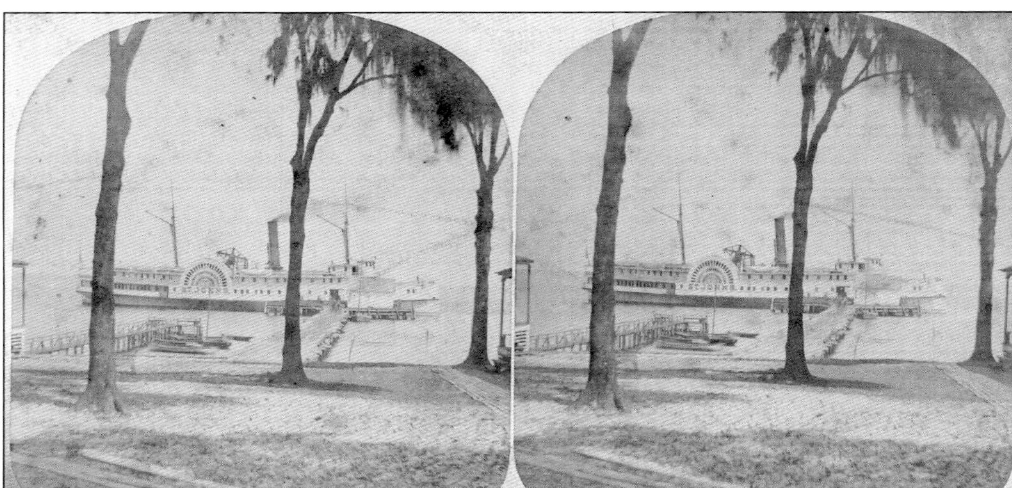

Landing at Green Cove Springs by Isaac Haas. Steamboats such as the *St. Johns*, pictured here, offered visitors the opportunity to travel the upper St. Johns. Excursions would go to Enterprise on Lake Monroe and then return, taking three days and allow the tourist to remain on the ship. This excursion was said to be "one of the most beautiful excursions in Florida."

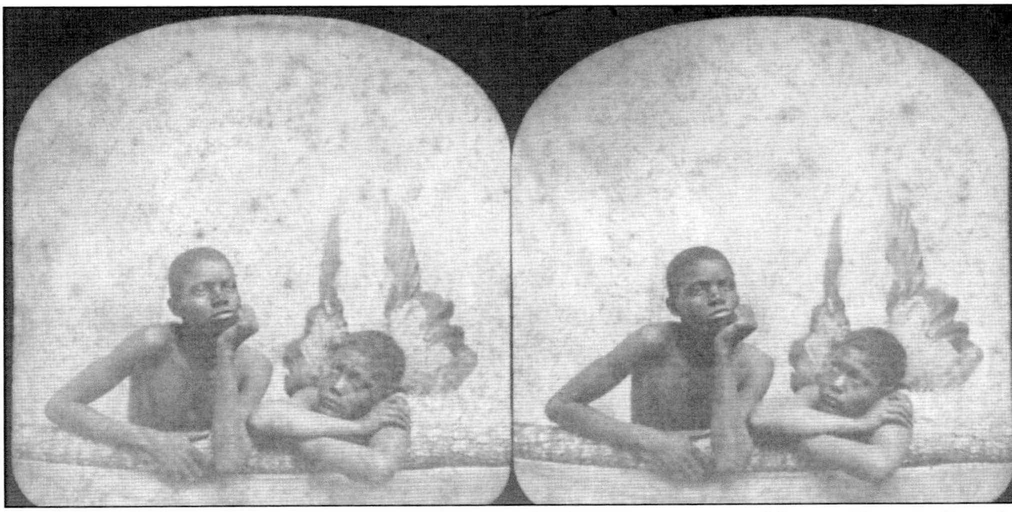

Cherubs by Isaac Haas. Haas was not known for his artistic views. He would typically take images of individuals in settings that would remind tourists of their trip to Green Cove Springs. It was not uncommon for Haas to employee the help of black boys, especially when photographing tourists in an ox cart. This image appears to have been taken in a studio with a painted backdrop of wings for the boy on the right.

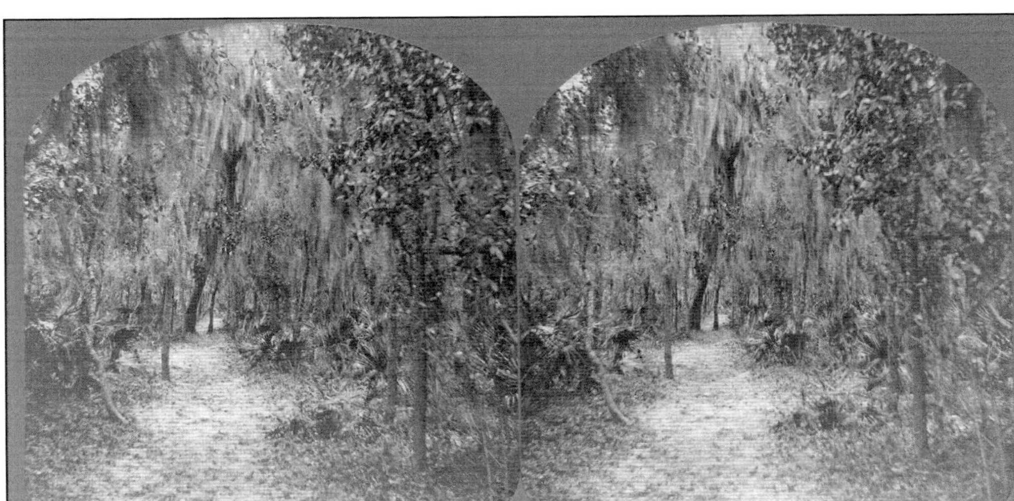

St. David's Path by Isaac Haas. Haas would take pictures of natural settings, which were often ignored by the more famous northern photographers who ventured south. Here Haas has captured the wilderness that enthralled the northern tourists. Spanish moss and palmettos are abundant along the path.

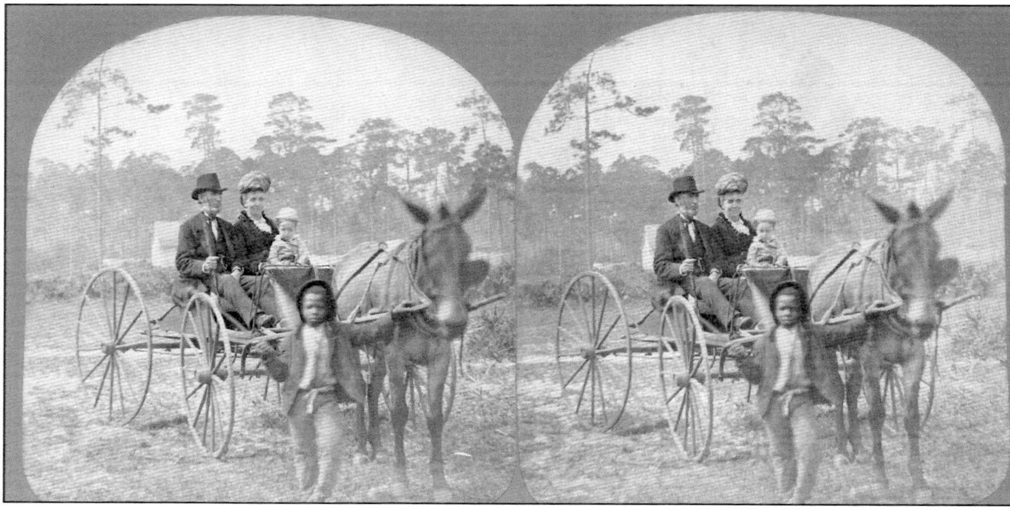

Mr. and Mrs. Robert Gilmore by Isaac Haas. While the exact location is unknown, Haas frequently used this location as a backdrop. Here the Gilmore family is photographed in a mule-drawn cart. Mr. Gilmore holds a walking stick in his right hand.

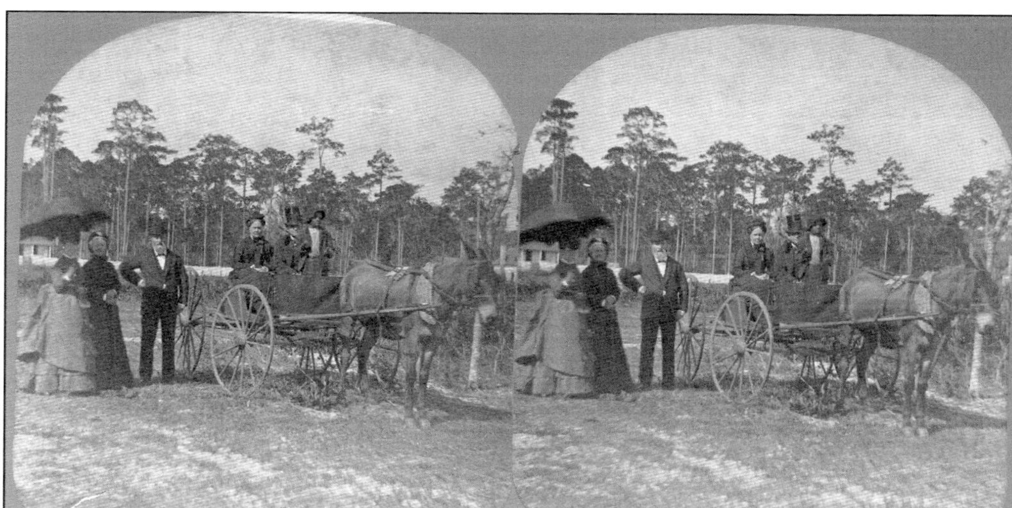

Tourists at Green Cove Springs by Isaac Haas. The location of this image is also unknown. Haas used the same cart and driver. Wagons were available to rent for 25¢ a day, so families and small groups could picnic in the woods on a nice, warm winter day.

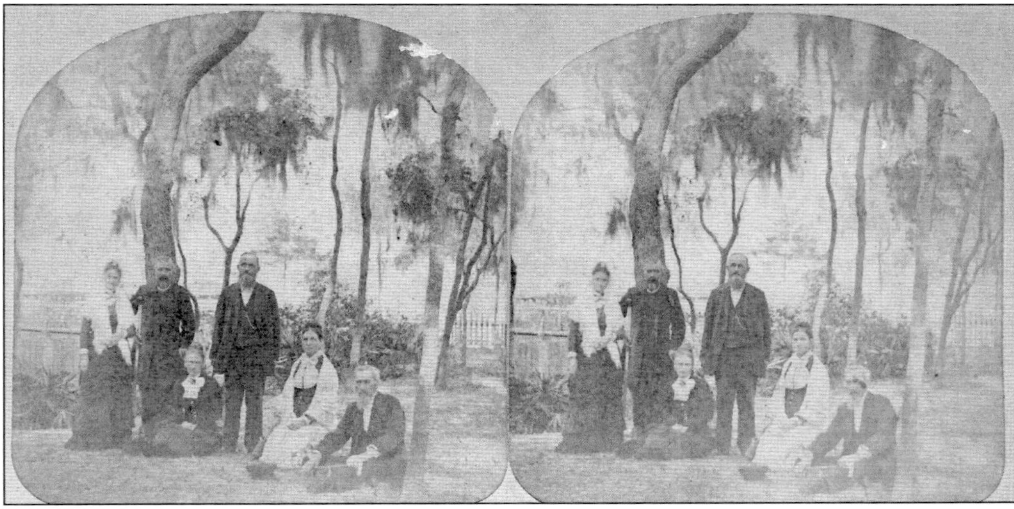

GROUP AT HOTEL BY ISAAC HAAS. This party of six appears to have been photographed along the river near the Riverside Hotel. The Riverside was located off St. Johns Avenue.

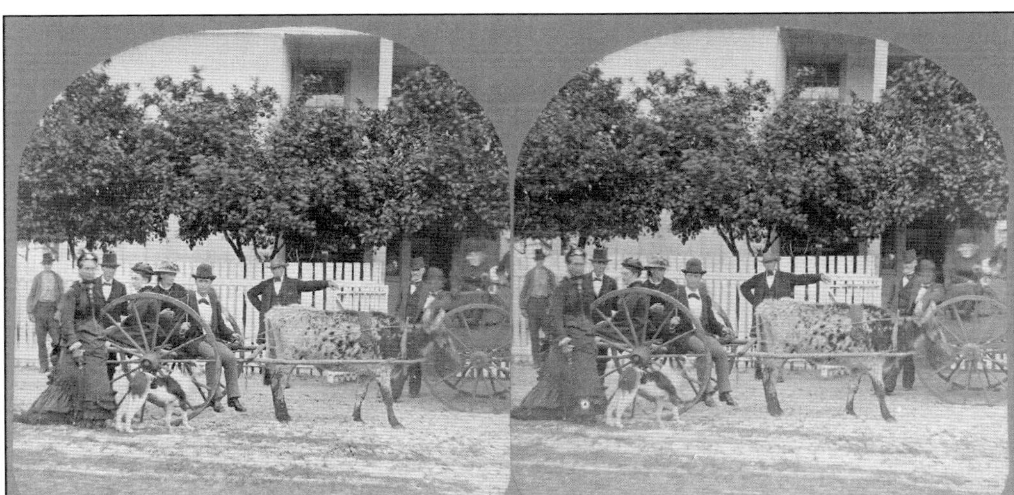

HOTEL GUESTS AT GREEN COVE SPRINGS BY ISAAC HAAS. A large group of tourists pose around an ox cart, which sometimes was referred to as the "Florida Express." The background setting is most likely the Clarendon Hotel. The trees in the background are citrus.

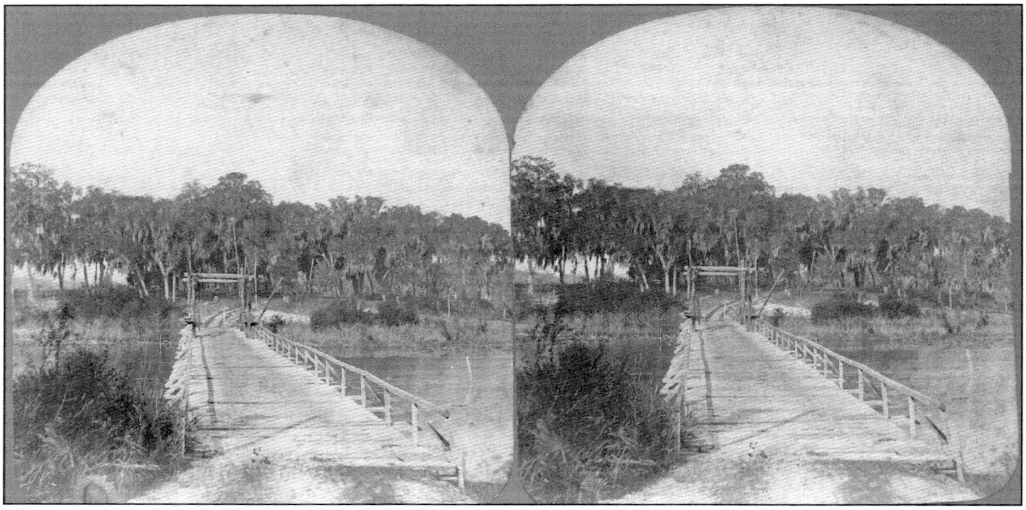

Governor's Creek Bridge by Isaac Haas. The bridge across Governor's Creek was an important artery connecting Magnolia Springs and Green Cove Springs. Before the bridge was built, a ferry was the only way to cross the creek.

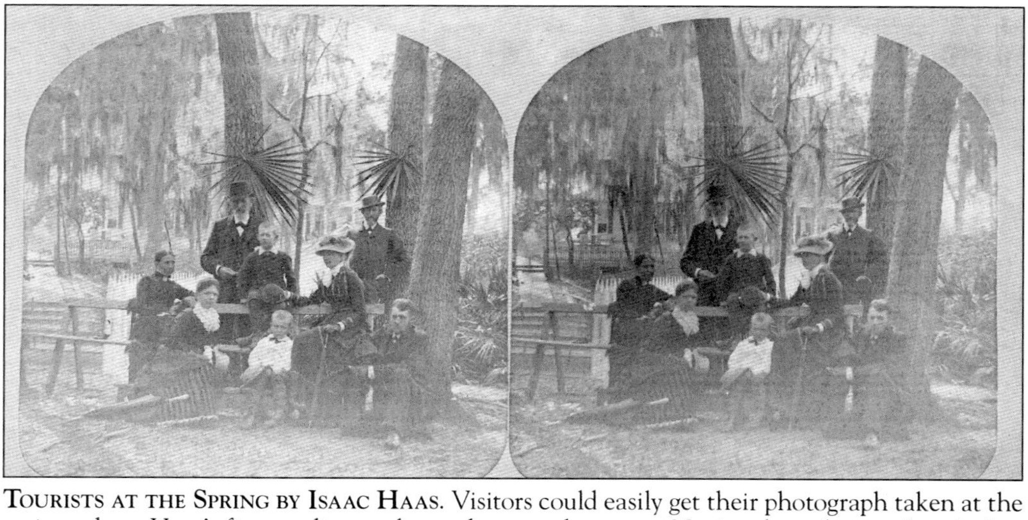

Tourists at the Spring by Isaac Haas. Visitors could easily get their photograph taken at the spring where Haas's first studio was located across the street. Notice the palmetto fronds that are tacked to the trees.

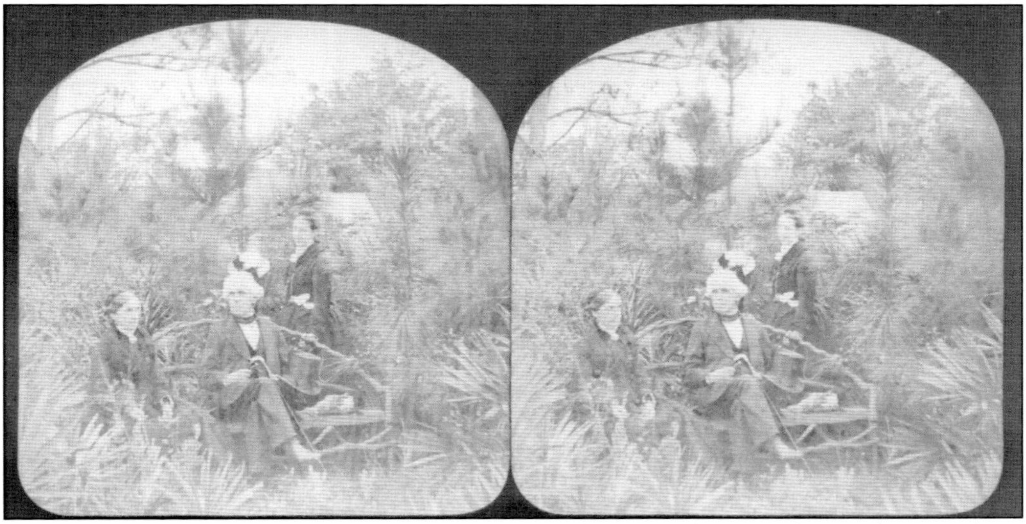

Tourists in Palmetto by Isaac Haas. This is another typical image of Haas showing three tourists standing in palmetto scrub and small, long leaf yellow pine. Haas was known to produce images at a "fair price." His studio was located off Walnut Street directly across from the swimming pools where he had a large sign stating, "Head Quarters for Florida Views Photography."

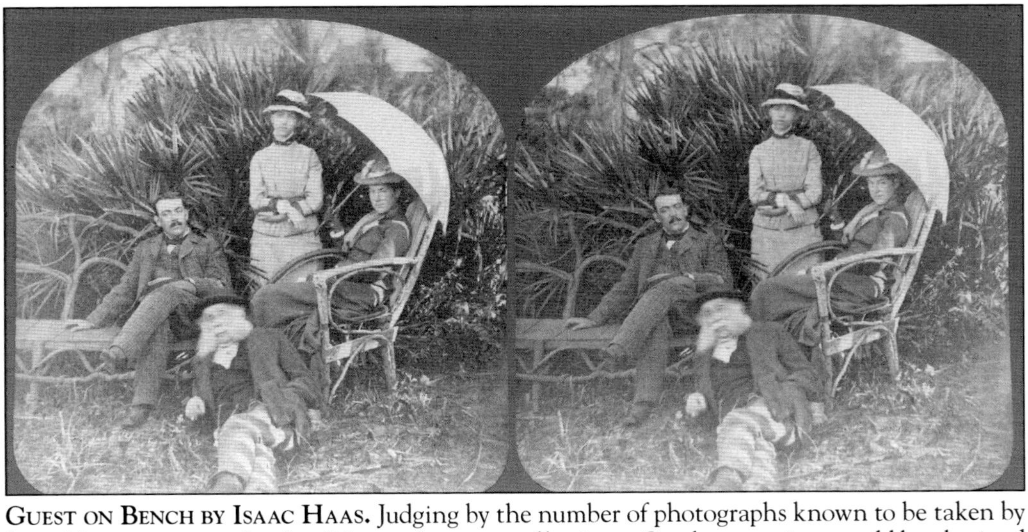

Guest on Bench by Isaac Haas. Judging by the number of photographs known to be taken by Isaac Haas, it appears that he did a good amount of business. Stock stereoviews could be obtained from 25¢ each to $1 for a dozen different views from a series. The man sitting on the ground appears to be Thaddeus Davids, who was mayor of Green Cove Springs.

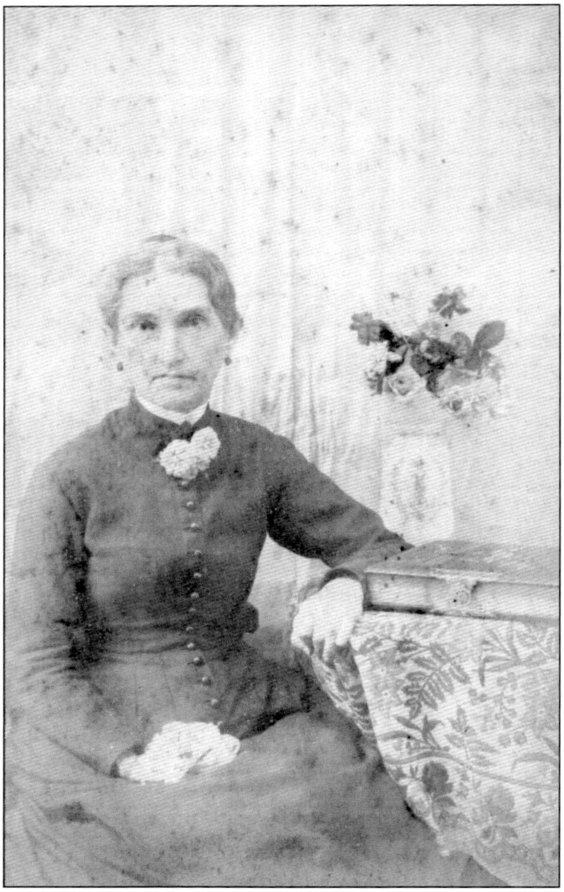

Portrait by Isaac Haas. This unknown lady sat for her likeness to be taken in the late 19th century. Included in this image are studio props that are not typically seen in Haas's photography. The beautiful tablecloth and the vase of freshly cut flowers add a nice touch to this image.

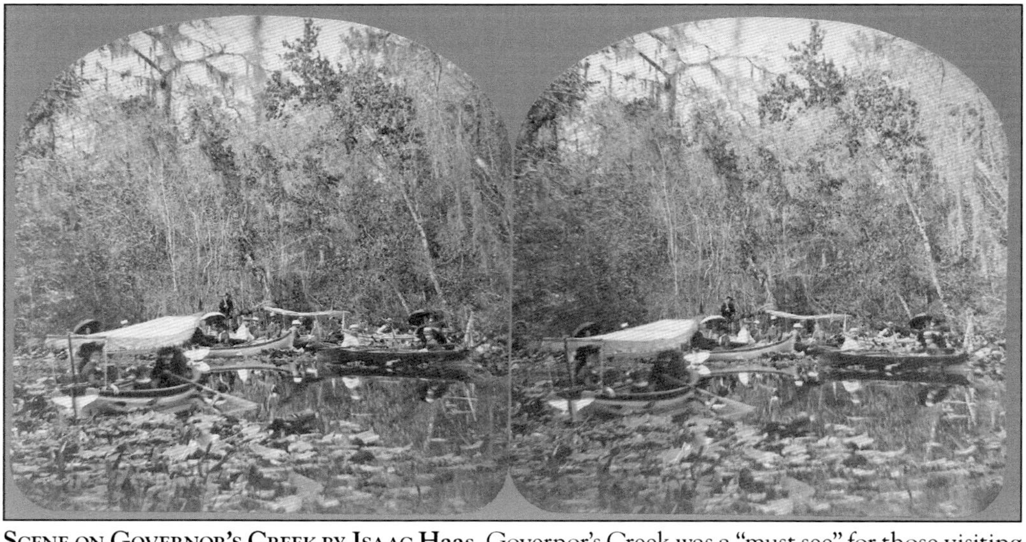

Scene on Governor's Creek by Isaac Haas. Governor's Creek was a "must see" for those visiting Magnolia and Green Cove Springs. Many of the hotels offered small rowboats for a nominal fee so their guest could enjoy the tranquil scenery that the creek provided.

Boy by Isaac Haas. Photographs of this size are uncommon by Haas. The small CDV-sized cards have a gilt edge and are of better quality than most photographs taken by Haas. This little boy appears to have not wanted his picture taken while he is holding a wood boat.

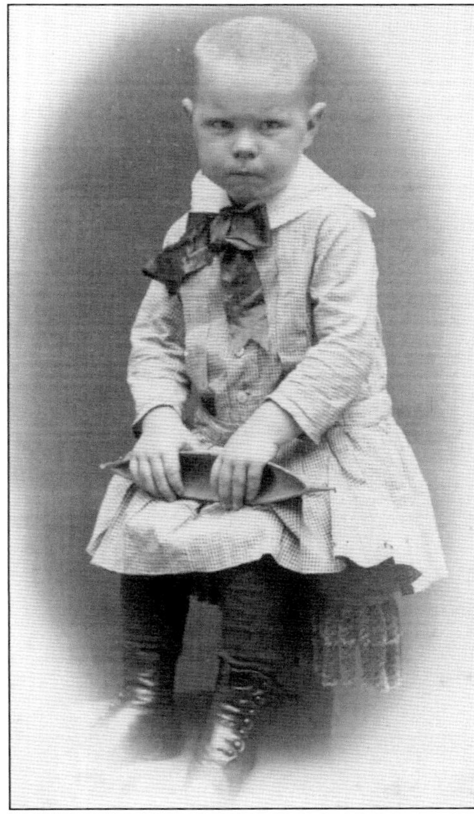

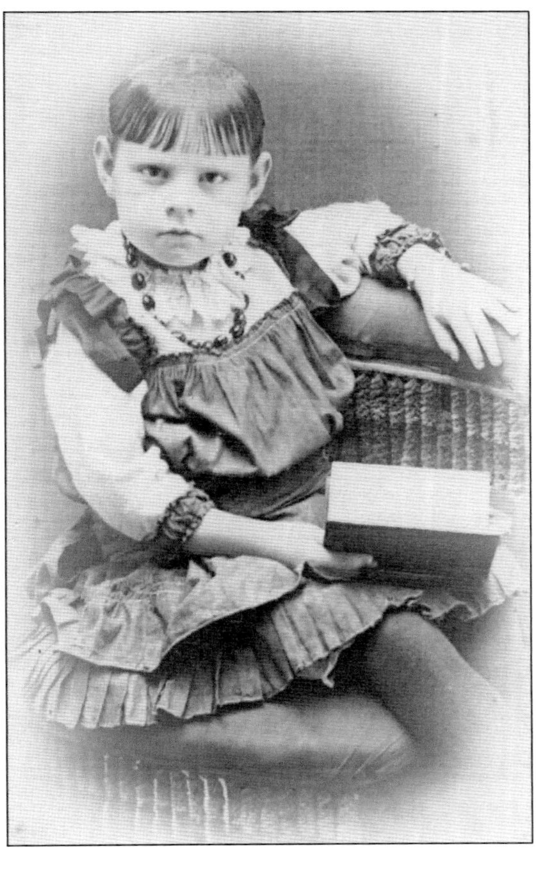

Girl by Isaac Haas. It is not known when Haas ceased to be a photographer. After the Crocker Block was built at the corner of Walnut Street and St. Johns Avenue, Haas moved his studio out to the corner of Palmetto and Springs Streets away from center of the hotels. This high-quality CDV was most likely produced in the late 1880s.

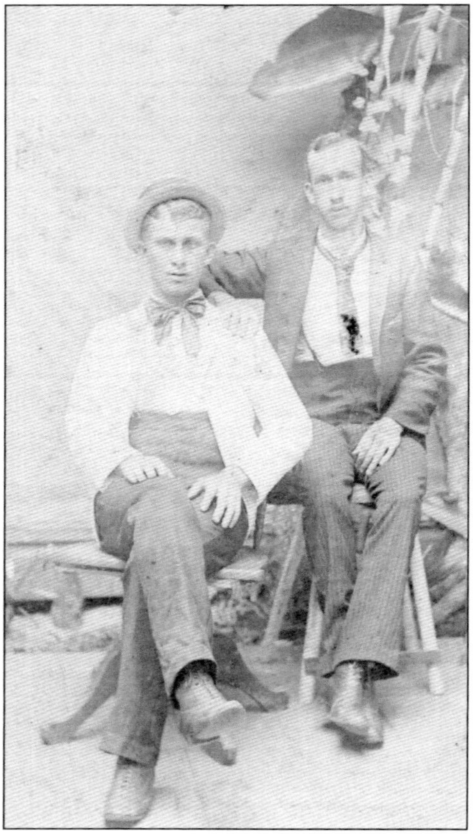

WASHINGTON BRANNING AND GEORGE HULL BY ISAAC HAAS. Washington Branning, during the Civil War, carried the mail twice a week from Middleburg to Baldwin on Florida Route 1502. Branning was paid $416 annually and signed a contract on May 15, 1863. Both the Branning and Hull families lived in Middleburg.

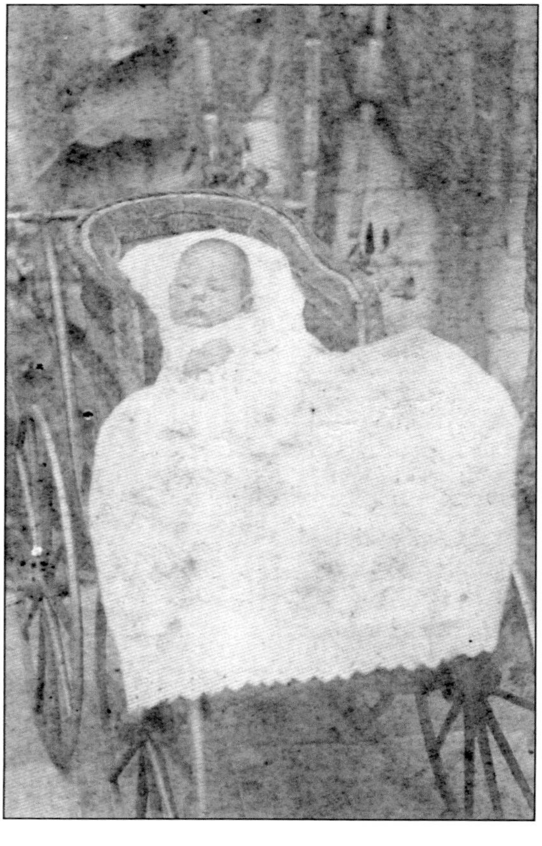

JOHN HANFORD BY ISAAC HAAS. Unlike the photographs on the preceding page, this photograph exhibits the typical qualities associated with Haas's photography. This image of John Hanford is tied to Haas by a simple stamp in block letters with the photographer's name.

Eight

Lee Field and NAAS Green Cove Springs

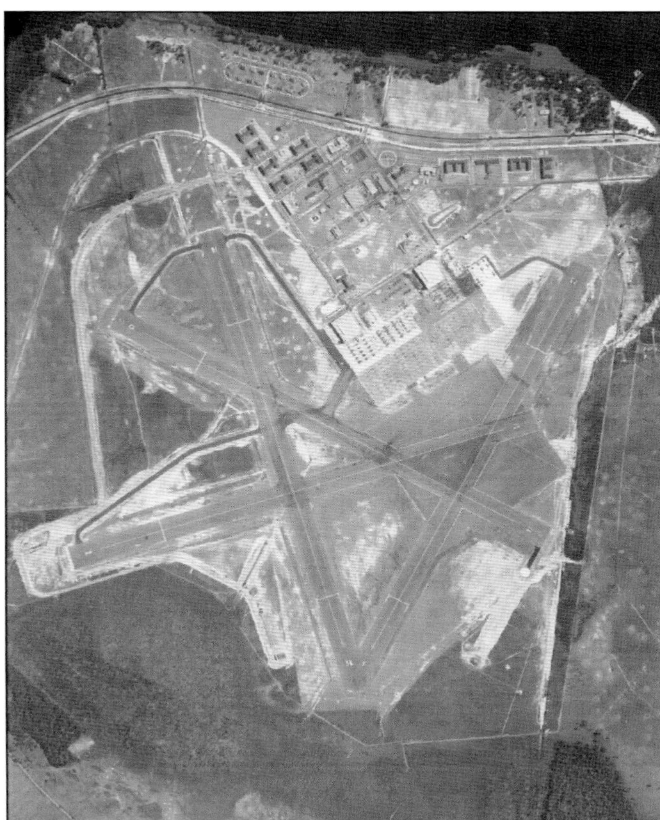

Lee Field at 8,750 feet. An airfield was created at Green Cove Springs to help facilitate the storage of planes being sent to NAS Jacksonville. The airfield officially opened on September 11, 1940, and was later named Lee Field in honor of Benjamin Lee who lost his life in a crash at Killingholme, England, during World War I. Lee had lived in Jacksonville for a short time. As early as 1938, the navy had been looking at Green Cove Springs as a possible site for a naval base. (Courtesy National Archives, College Park, Maryland.)

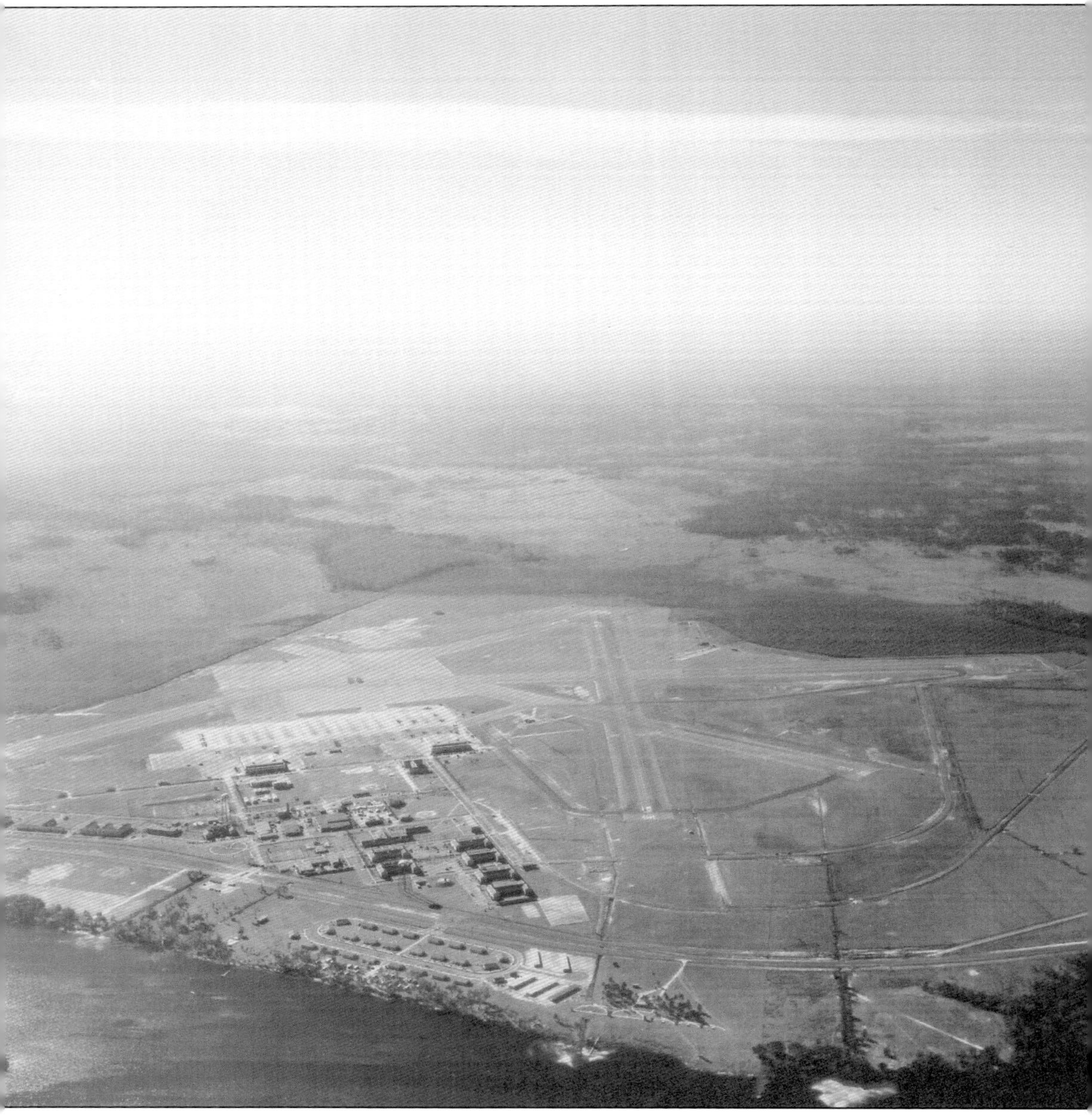

Lee Field. Ens. Benjamin Lee was killed in a seaplane crash on October 28, 1918. On that morning, he and two other pilots took off for a mission in the North Sea. His aircraft was the first to take flight and circled in air waiting for the other two aircraft. As the other two aircraft became airborne, Lee spiraled down to take his position in the formation. His commanding officer, an eyewitness, described what happened next. In the middle of the turn, for some unknown reason, the machine suddenly went into a side slip and spin. He pulled out of the spin, straightened out into a dive, and it appeared for an instant that he had a small chance of recovering, but there was insufficient height, and the machine dove into the Humber River. Lee would later be awarded the U.S. Navy Cross. (Courtesy National Archives, College Park, Maryland.)

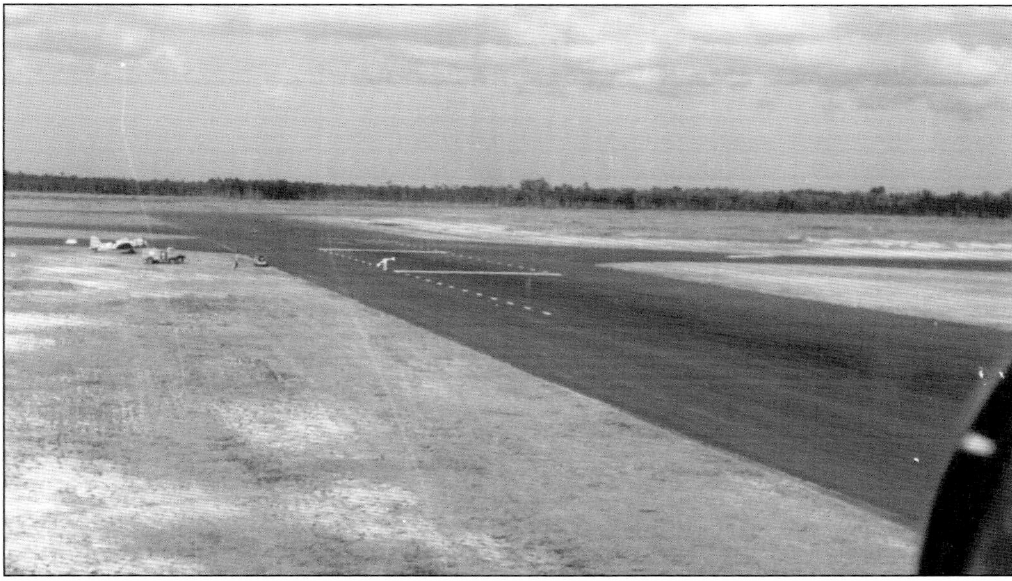

Practice Carrier Approach at Lee Field. Later in the war, Naval Auxiliary Air Station Green Cove Springs or NAAS Green Cove Springs was used to train new pilots for carrier landings. Newly commissioned 2nd Lt. Ed McMahon was sent to Green Cove Springs to learn how to fly the F4U Corsair. This image, dated April 5, 1944, shows the approach to the rectangle on the runway that represents the landing area on an aircraft carrier. (Courtesy National Archives, College Park, Maryland.)

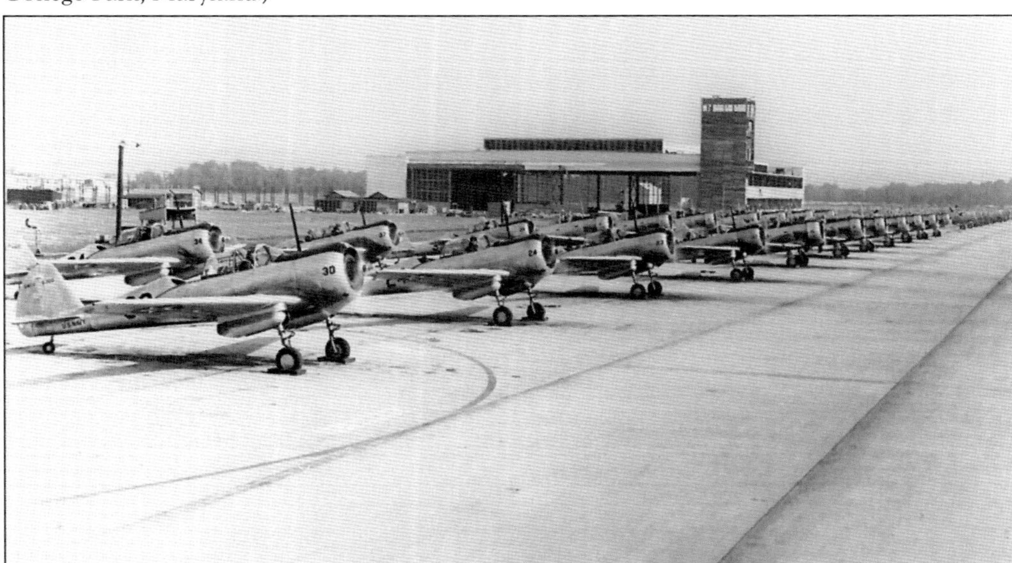

Aircraft at Lee Field. Even before the attack on Pearl Harbor on December 7, 1941, the military had already expended $82 million on various navy and army bases located in Florida. By March 1941, the navy had spent $1.8 million on Lee Field. It had quarters for 40 officers and 200 enlisted men. The Florida lime rock mines reported record sales in 1940. The lime rock used to build the runways at Green Cove Springs were mined at Kendrick and Redick, Florida. (Courtesy Clay County Archives.)

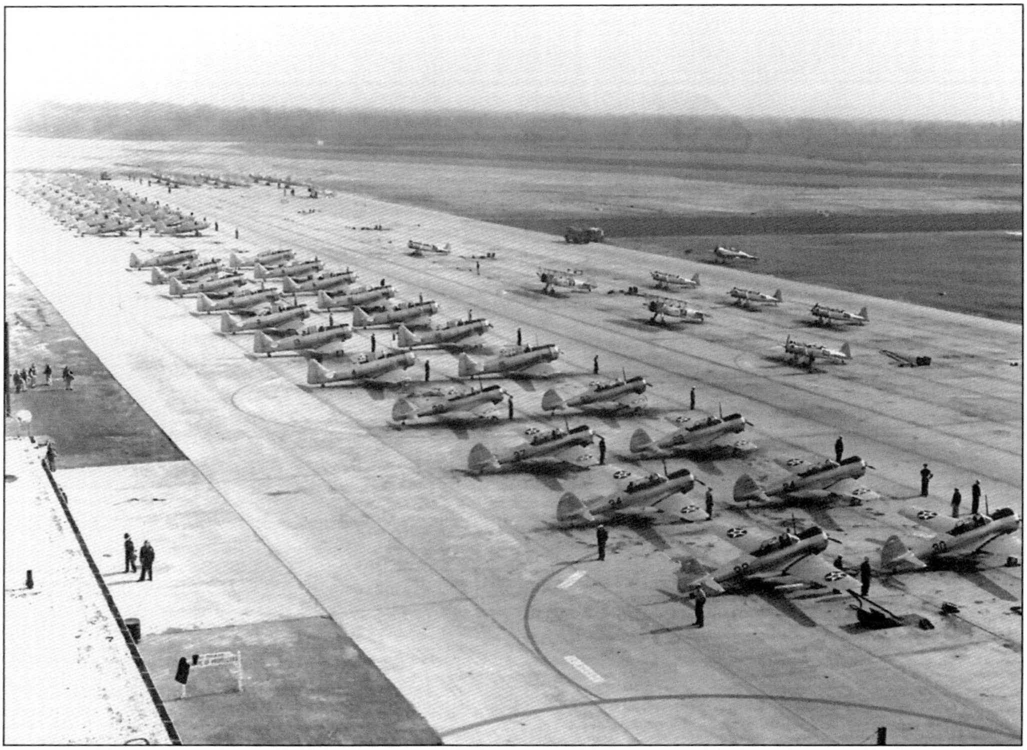

AIRCRAFT AT LEE FIELD. During the war, many of the instructors at Lee Field were combat-tested veterans. Lt. Elbert S. McCuskey of Stuttgart, Arkansas, an instructor, had shot down five Japanese aircraft at the Battle of Midway—three dive bombers and two Zeroes. The aircraft pictured here were used for training. (Courtesy Clay County Archives.)

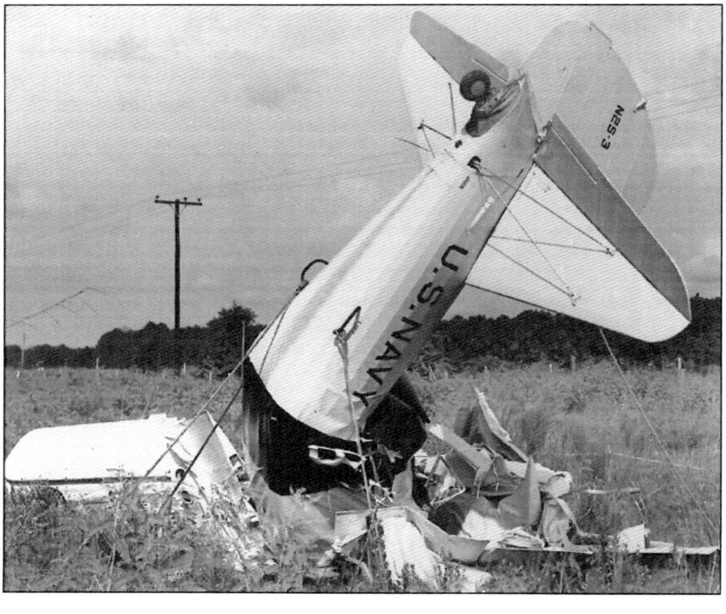

CRASH OF N2S. With several airfields and bombing ranges nearby, accidents were bound to happen. Crashes while training at night were frequent, and planes even crashed in the St. Johns. In April 1942, four men were killed when the bomber crashed in the river near Green Cove Springs. This picture shows an N2S Stearnman that crashed near Green Cove Springs. (Courtesy Clay County Archives.)

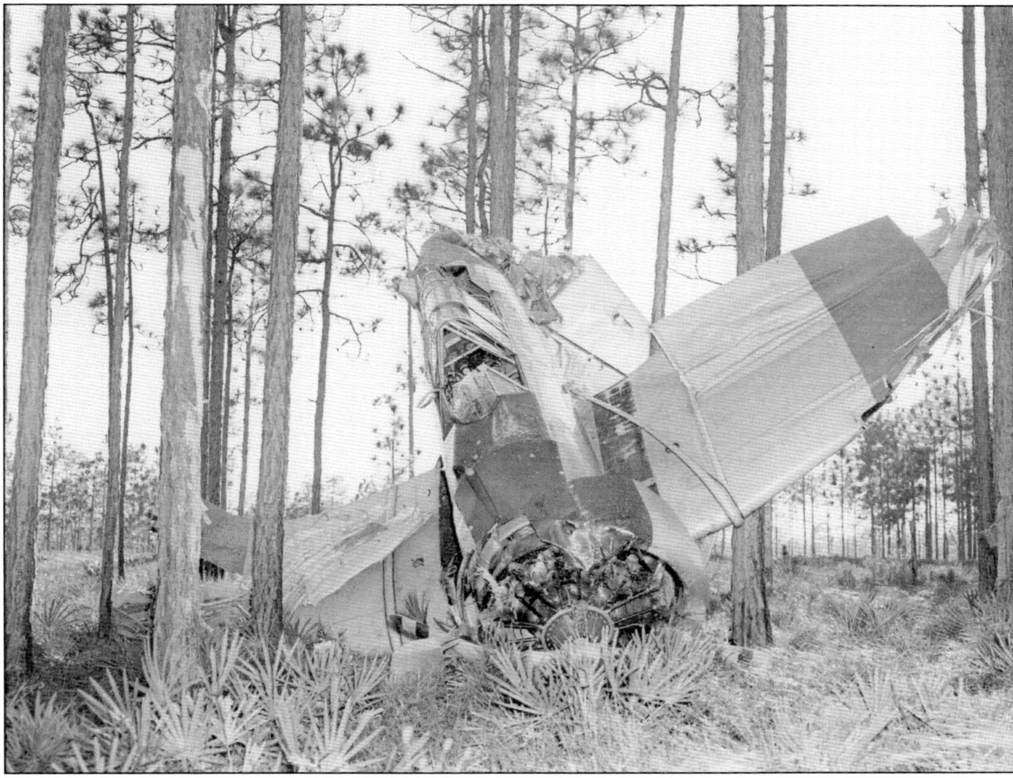

Crash of SNJ-4. Crashes at Lee Field were not uncommon when the airfield was first opened. On November 24, 1942, Ens. Alexander William Felix (USNR), 24, of Cincinnati, Ohio, was instantly killed Tuesday when his plane crashed near Lee Field. Pictured here is an SNJ-4 Texan, that crashed near Lee Field. (Courtesy National Archives, College Park, Maryland.)

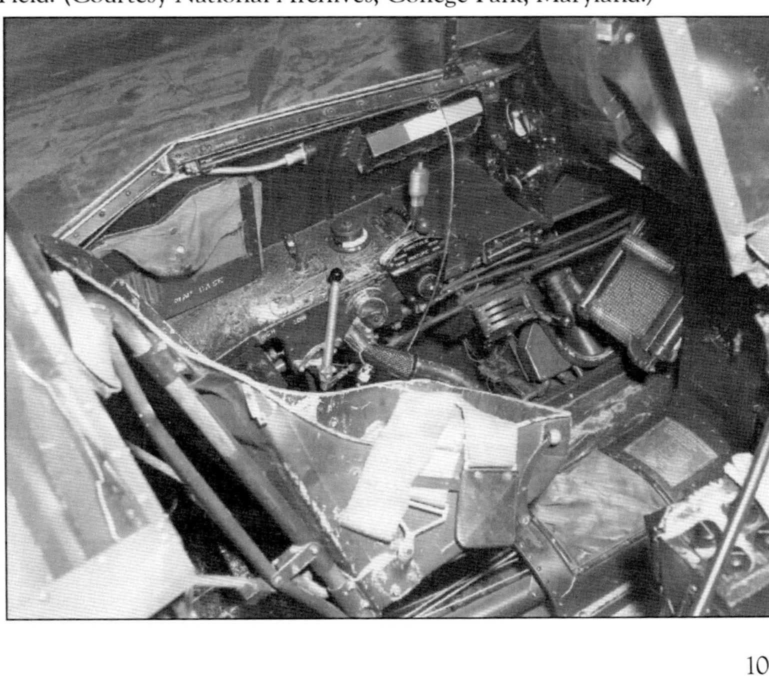

Crash F4F-3. This photograph shows the cockpit of an F4F-3 that crashed near Green Cove Springs on November 22, 1942. Known as the Wildcat, this fighter was used primarily by the U.S. Navy and Marines during the first two years of the war. It was phased out and replaced by the F6F, the Hellcat. (Courtesy National Archives, College Park, Maryland.)

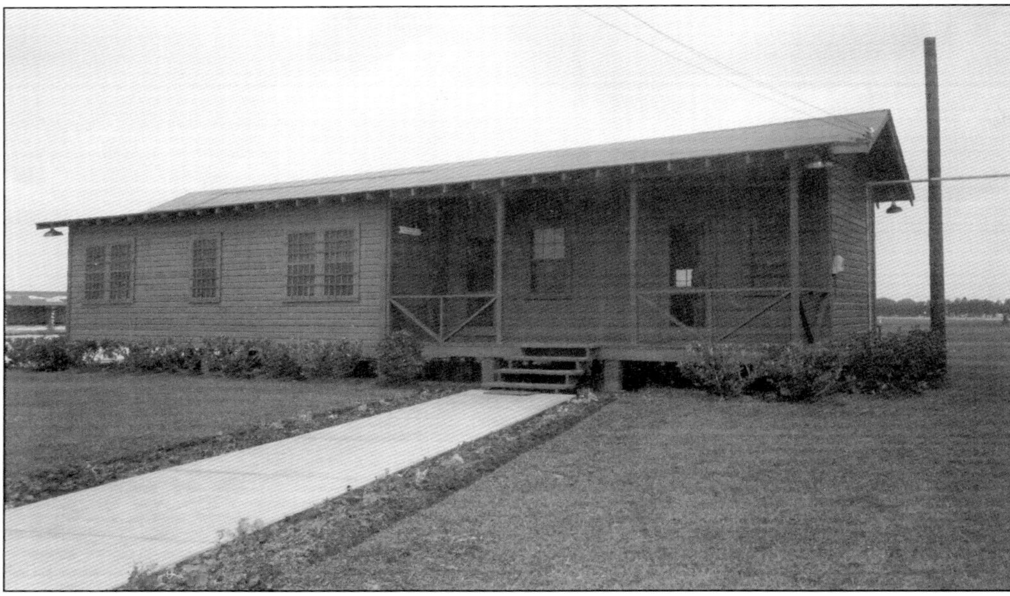

The Brig at Lee Field. The navy, with permission from the county and City of Green Cove Springs, created a shore patrol office in the city near the courthouse. Typically the sailors were held at the shore patrol office waiting transportation to the brig. The chief cause for confinement was excessive drinking. (Courtesy National Archives, College Park, Maryland.)

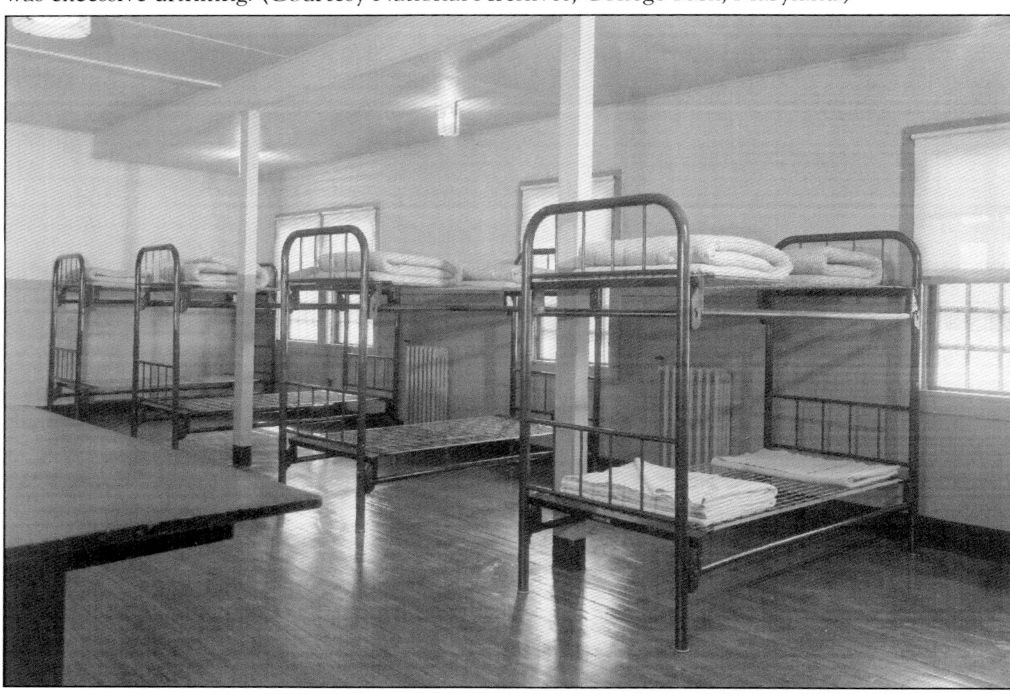

Interior of Brig at Lee Field. Sailors appreciated the larger quarters on land than those aboard ship. One sailor said the bunks were wider and the lockers more spacious; however, those bunks pictured here would not be enjoyed, since they were located in the brig. This photograph was taken on April 4, 1944. (Courtesy National Archives, College Park, Maryland.)

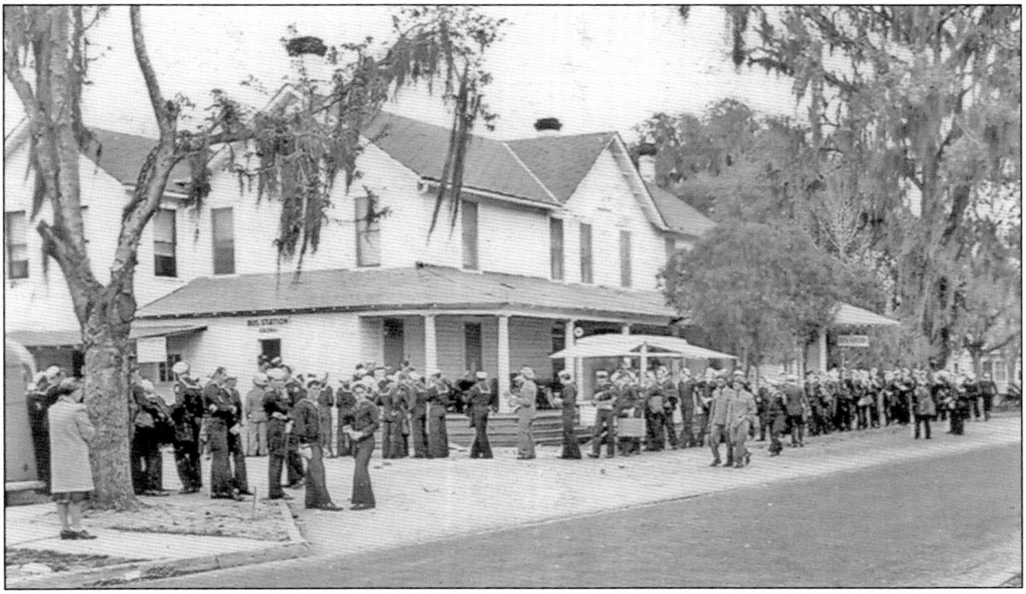

Bus Stop at Green Cove Springs. Sailors are waiting for the bus at the old Mohawk Hotel during World War II. Sailors would travel to Jacksonville to be entertained, and those wanting to spend a little more money would travel to Daytona Beach to enjoy the beaches. With the quick pace at which the airfield was expanding, the state put a fast track on rebuilding the Shands Bridge, which had been closed due to a fire caused by lightning. The repair helped to facilitate travel to St. Augustine and Daytona. (Courtesy Clay County Archives.)

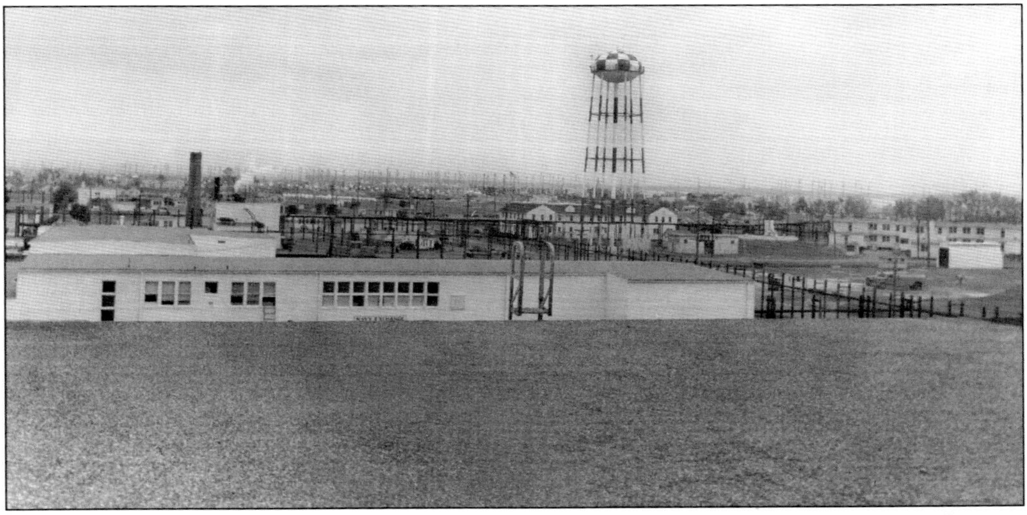

Reserve Fleet Berthing Area. On August 17, 1961, Gov. Farris Bryant held a press conference. One topic during the conference was Green Cove Springs. The governor, having visited the navy base that morning, called it a "beautiful facility." He said it "has a sewage facility; water facilities; housing of varying classes; it can feed 1,500 men and 80 officers; it has a wonderful dock facility there, one of the finest I have ever seen . . . there are 1,500 acres, an airstrip with four or five thousand foot strips on it, a really marvelous facility that we or the Federal government must in some way find a use for. It would be a crying shame to let it go to waste." This image is dated January 4, 1951. (Courtesy National Archives, College Park, Maryland.)

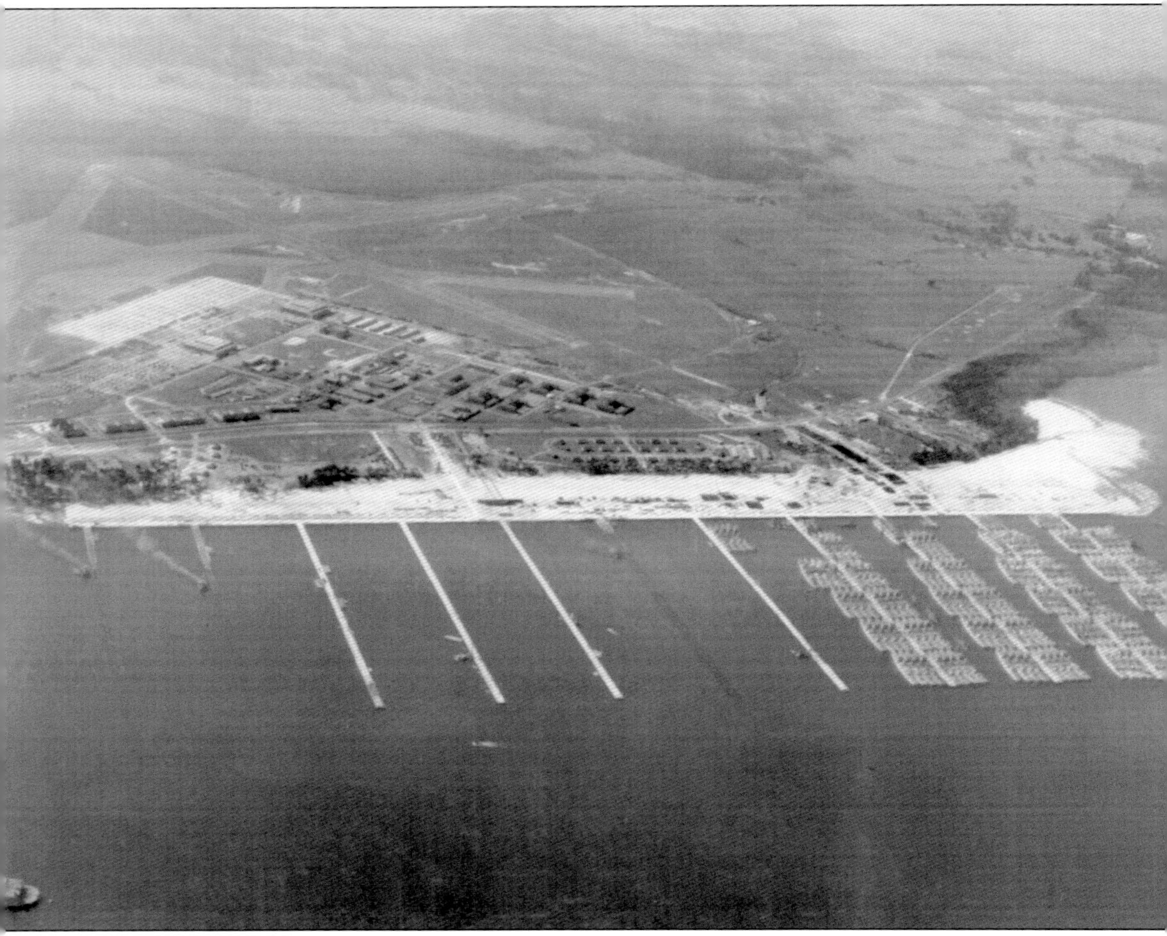

Area of Immobilized Ships at NAAS Green Cove Springs. This photograph shows piers 6, 10, and 11 under construction. With the influx of ships to be mothballed, the 11 piers could not sufficiently house all ships so a floating dock was built near Red Bay and called Able dock. This photograph was taken at an altitude of 4,000 feet on January 23, 1947. (Courtesy National Archives, College Park, Maryland.)

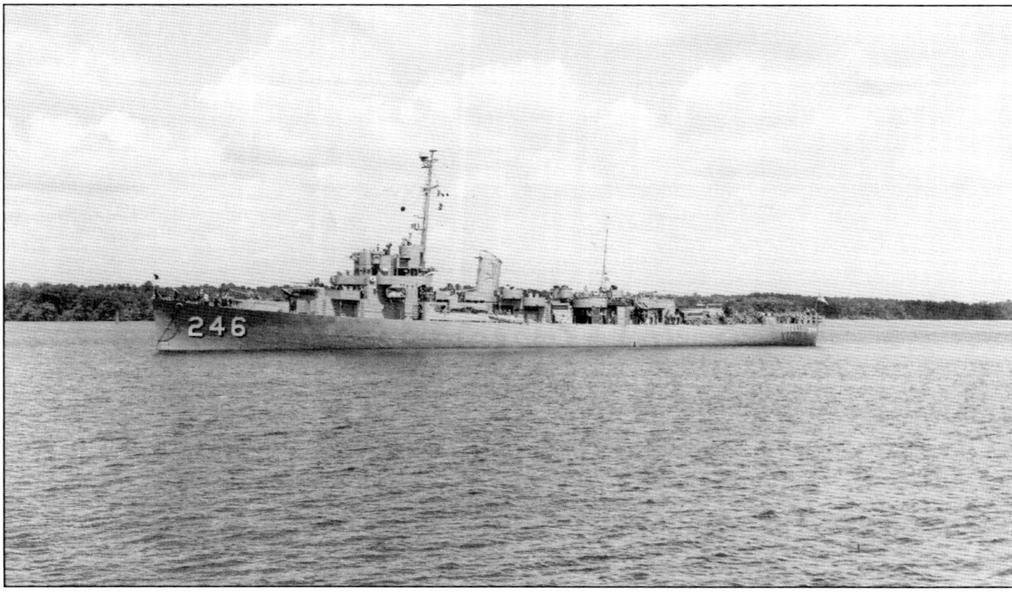

USS Snowden. The *Snowden* spent a few days cruising the St. Johns River after she was recommissoned on June 6, 1951. The *Snowden's* keel was laid on December 7, 1942, and during World War II she earned three battle stars. The destroyer escort was used as a target and sunk June 27, 1969. This photograph was taken on June 13, 1951. (Courtesy National Archives, College Park, Maryland.)

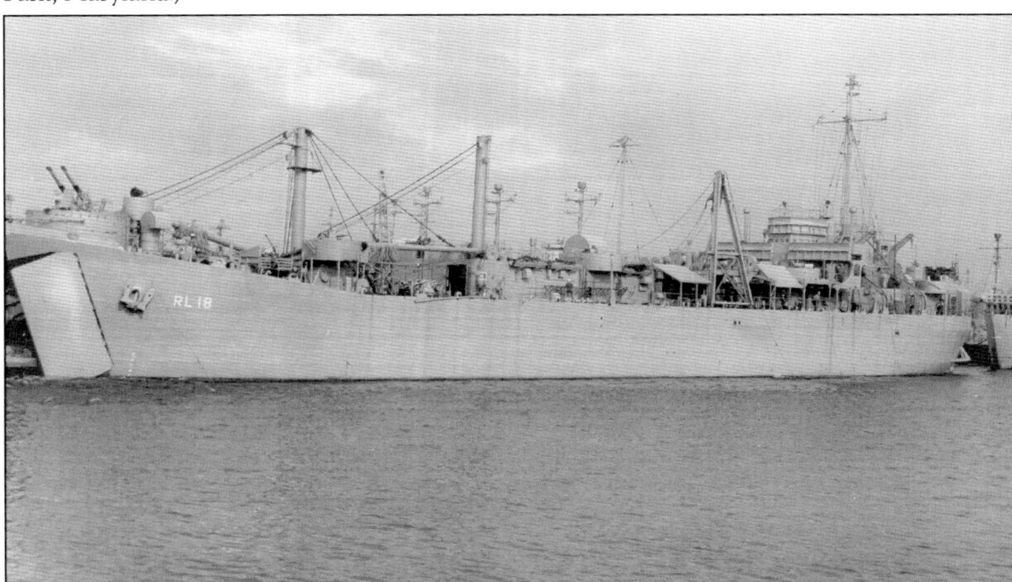

USS Pandemus. Its keel was laid July 20, 1944, and it was to become a tank landing ship. However, it was changed to a landing craft repair ship. Launched in October 1944, she set sail for New Orleans where she would get the final conversion for a repair ship. The *Pandemus* earned one battle star during World War II seeing action in the Pacific. In 1969, she was used as a target and sunk. This photograph is dated December 14, 1951—the day she was recommissioned. (Courtesy National Archives, College Park, Maryland.)

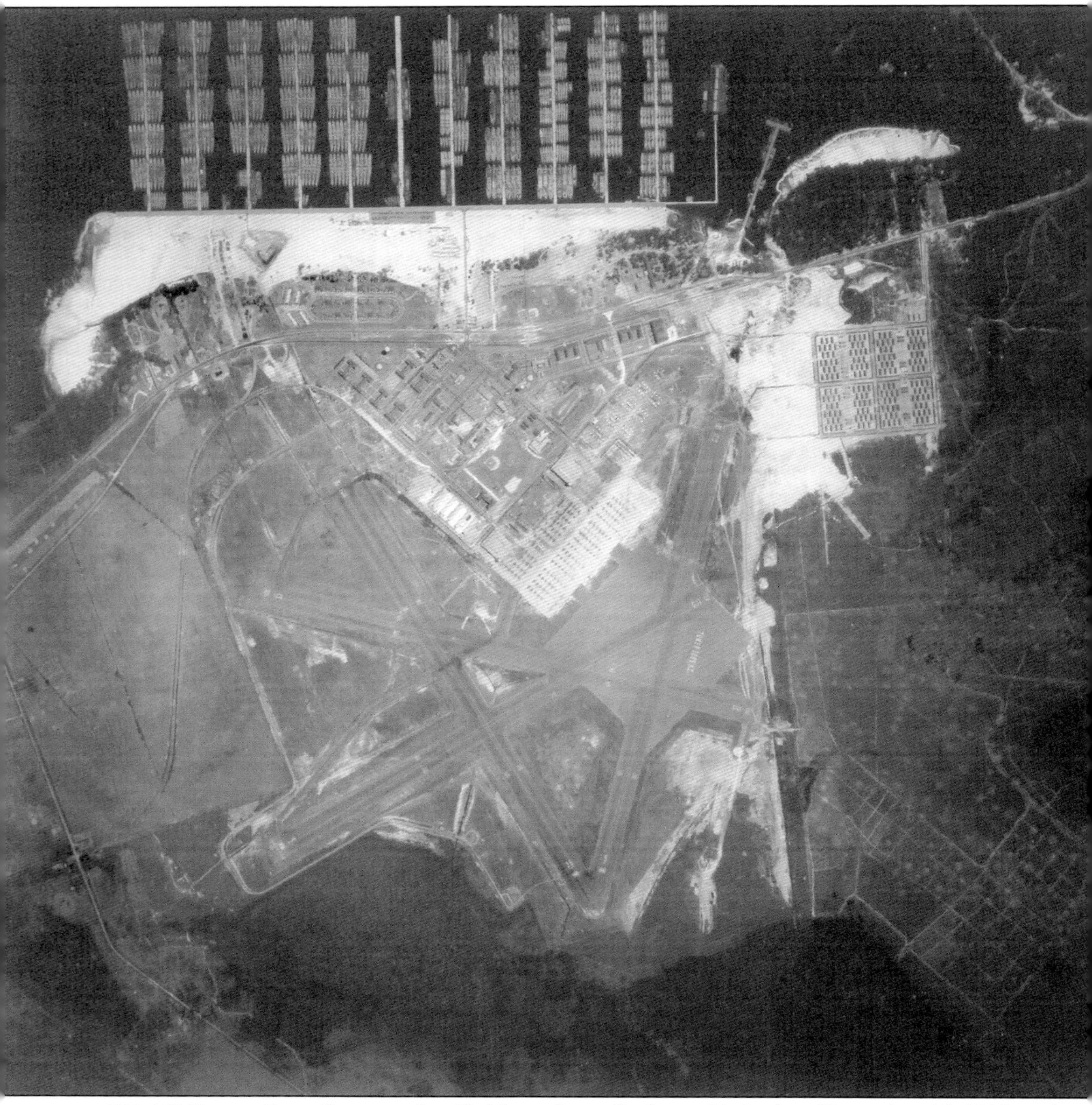

NAAS Green Cove Springs. Lee Field was formally disestablished on December 15, 1945, and transferred to the Inactive Fleet Berthing Area. The runways were transferred to NAS Jacksonville as an outlying field for limited-training operations. This image shows all 13 piers, which houses approximately 470 vessels. During the Korean War, more than 155 vessels were recommissioned at the base. (Courtesy National Archives, College Park, Maryland.)

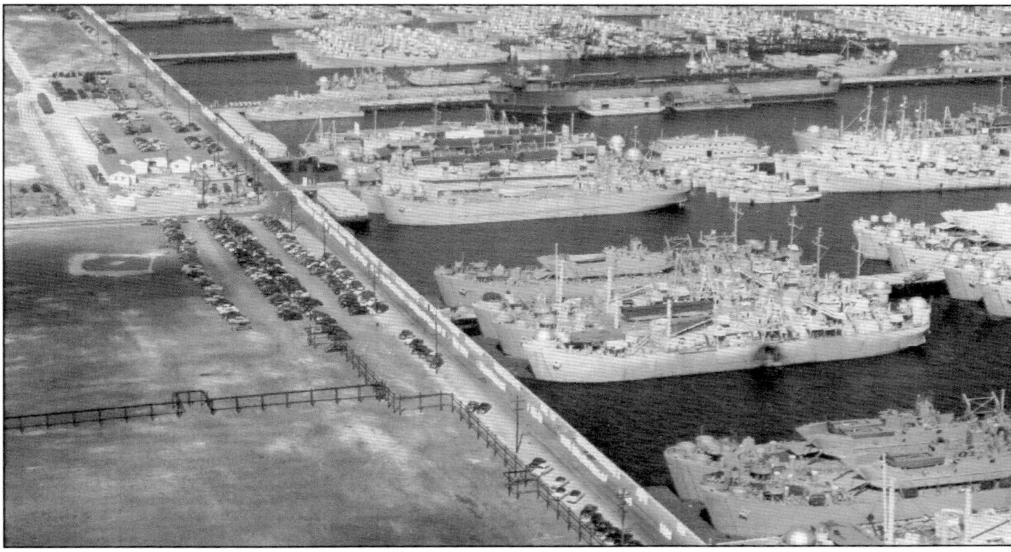

"Mothball Fleet" at NAAS Green Cove Springs. In March 1961, U.S. Secretary of Defense John McNamara announced that it would be closing the reserve fleet activities at Green Cove Springs. The local newspapers reported that it would mean the loss of a payroll in excess of $5 million to Clay County. The closure would mean that most of the current 325 civilian employees would be out of work, and the 734 enlisted men and officers would be transferred. This photograph was taken on October 14, 1950. (Courtesy National Archives, College Park, Maryland.)

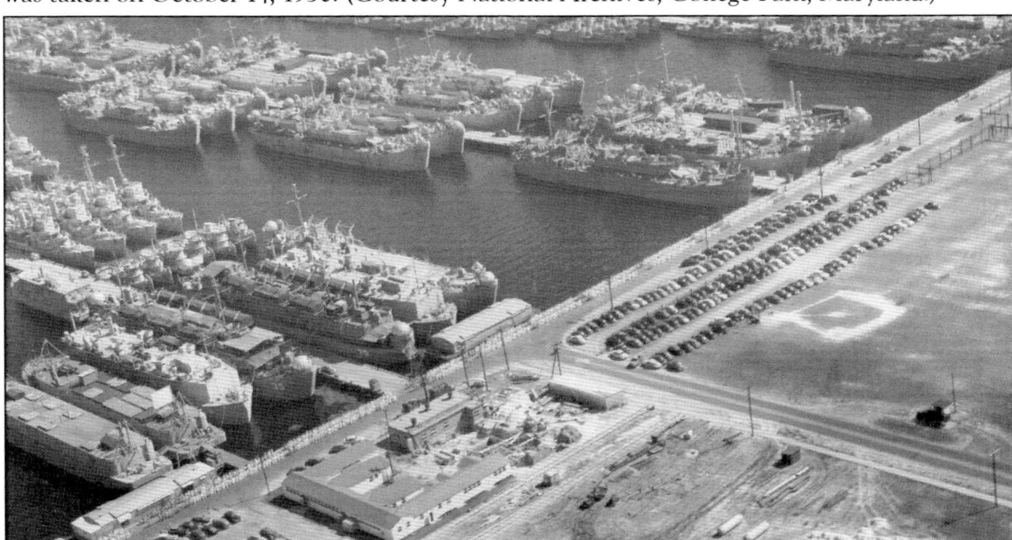

Aerial Commission of Ships Ceremony, Capt. Chauncey Moore Commanding. After the announcement that the navy base would be closed, there were 231 ships moored in the St. Johns River ranging from auxiliary floating dry docks and destroyer escorts down to small service craft. Capt. G. K. Hudson, commander of the Florida Group, said activities at the station will be closed out by June 30, 1962. The remaining ships were sent to Orange, Texas, and Norfolk, Virginia. Many of the civilians employed were transferred to Jacksonville Naval Air Station and Mayport Naval Station. This photograph was taken on October 14, 1950. (Courtesy National Archives, College Park, Maryland.)

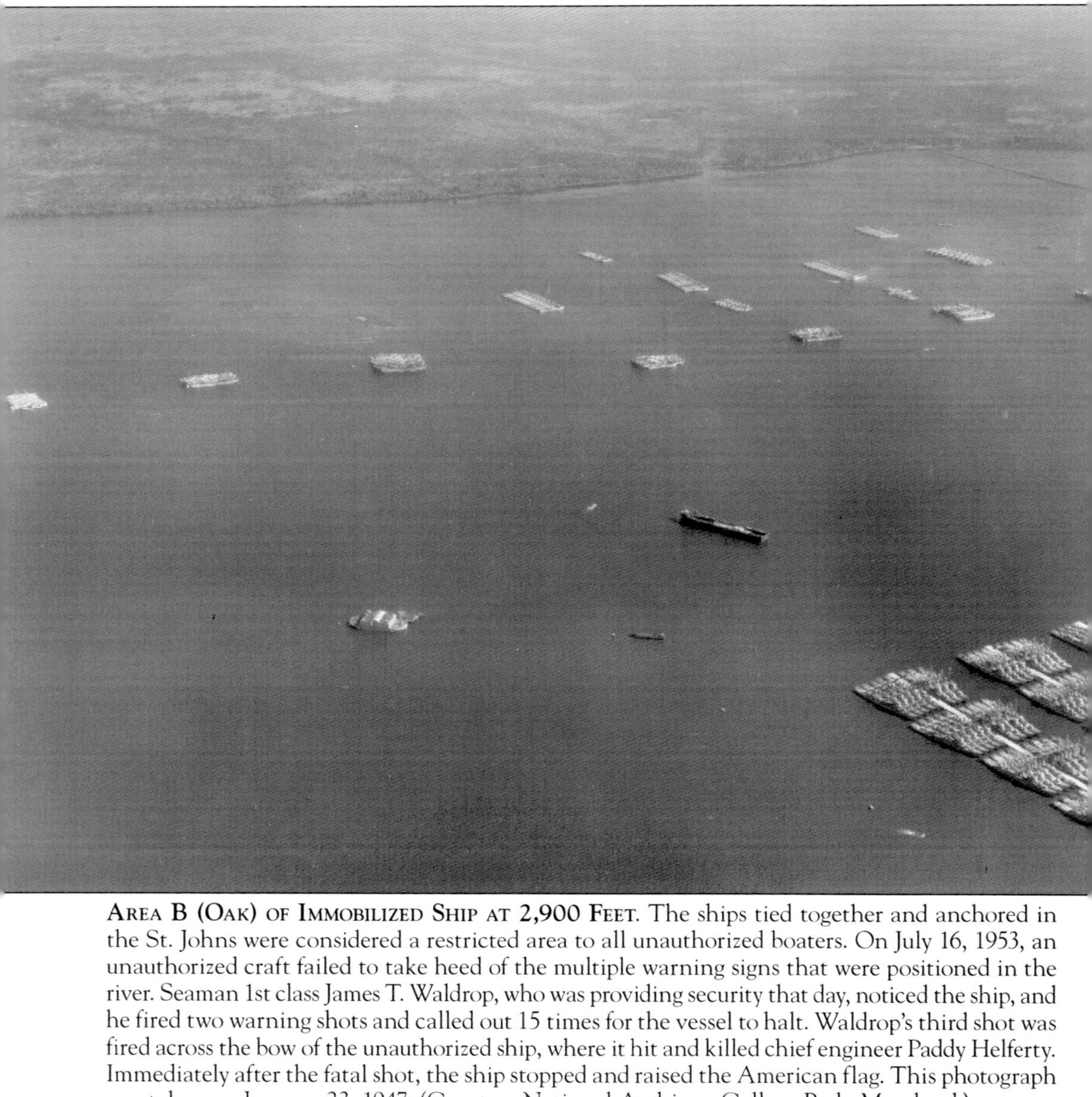

Area B (Oak) of Immobilized Ship at 2,900 Feet. The ships tied together and anchored in the St. Johns were considered a restricted area to all unauthorized boaters. On July 16, 1953, an unauthorized craft failed to take heed of the multiple warning signs that were positioned in the river. Seaman 1st class James T. Waldrop, who was providing security that day, noticed the ship, and he fired two warning shots and called out 15 times for the vessel to halt. Waldrop's third shot was fired across the bow of the unauthorized ship, where it hit and killed chief engineer Paddy Helferty. Immediately after the fatal shot, the ship stopped and raised the American flag. This photograph was taken on January 23, 1947. (Courtesy National Archives, College Park, Maryland.)

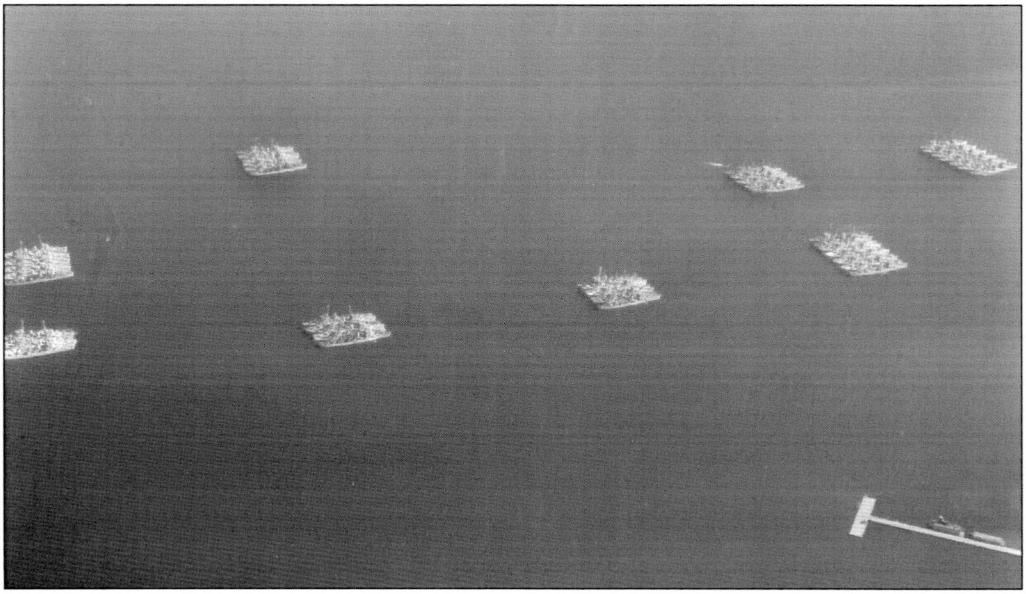

Area of Immobilized Ship. In 1954, a sailor described Green Cove Springs as a "mossy, snug little place located two miles from the base . . . it has two theaters . . . several gas stations, and a few drug stores . . . it also had several bars. The residential section is shaded by tall trees hung with Spanish moss . . . from the shore near town one can see an endless number of gray Navy ships, neatly nestled together." (Courtesy National Archives, College Park, Maryland.)

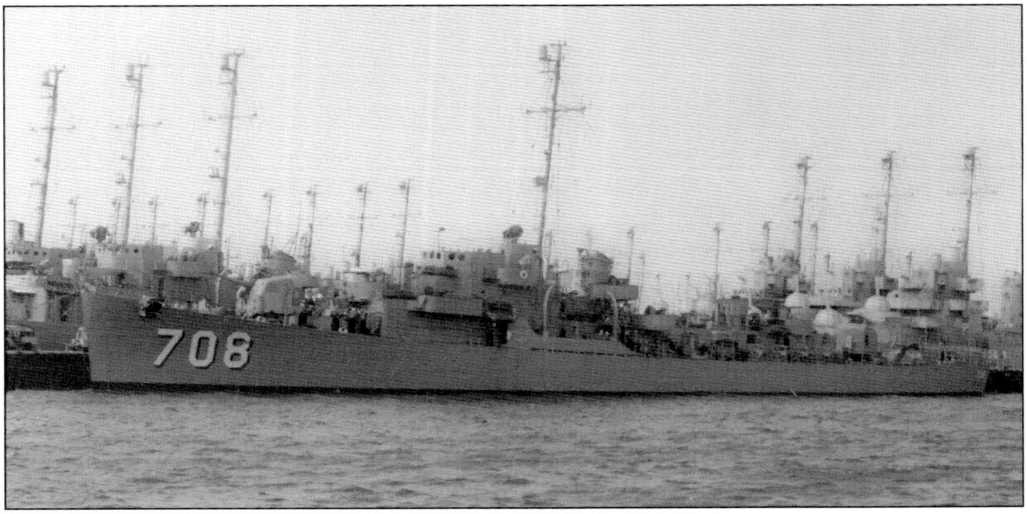

USS *Parle* (DE-708). The ship was named after Ens. John Parle, who, during the invasion of Sicily, July 9–10, 1943, entered a boat containing ammunition after a smoke pot had been accidentally ignited. Ensign Parle was unable to extinguish the smoke pot, and he took the smoke pot with his hands and threw it overboard. A week later, he died after inhaling poisonous fumes and smoke. "Ensign Parle's heroic self-sacrifice prevented grave damage to the ship and personnel and insured the security of a vital mission. He gallantly gave his life to service of his country." Ensign Parle was awarded the Congressional Medal of Honor. This photograph was taken March 2, 1951, when the ship was recommissioned at Green Cove Springs. (Courtesy National Archives, College Park, Maryland.)

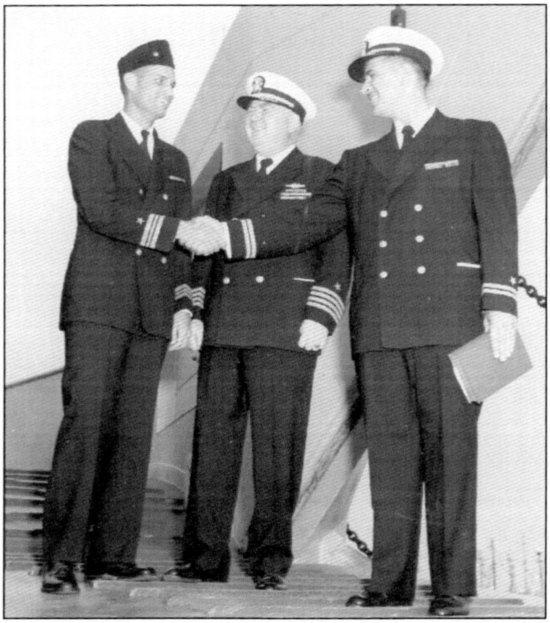

Commission of LST-32 at Green Cove Springs. Gardnar Mulloy, pictured on the left, was a professional tennis player and the commanding officer of LST-32. Mulloy won the U.S. doubles championship in 1942, 1945, 1946, and 1948 with Bill Talbert. In 1957 at the age of 43, he won at Wimbledon with doubles partner Budge Patty. Mulloy graduated from the University of Miami, and he was inducted into the International Tennis Hall of Fame and the Florida Sports Hall of Fame. Mulloy was the commanding officer of LST-32, which was recommissioned on March 7, 1951. This photograph is from the recommissioning ceremony. Also pictured with Mulloy are Capt. Chauncey Moore (middle) and Lt. J. W. Leonard (left). (Courtesy National Archives, College Park, Maryland.)

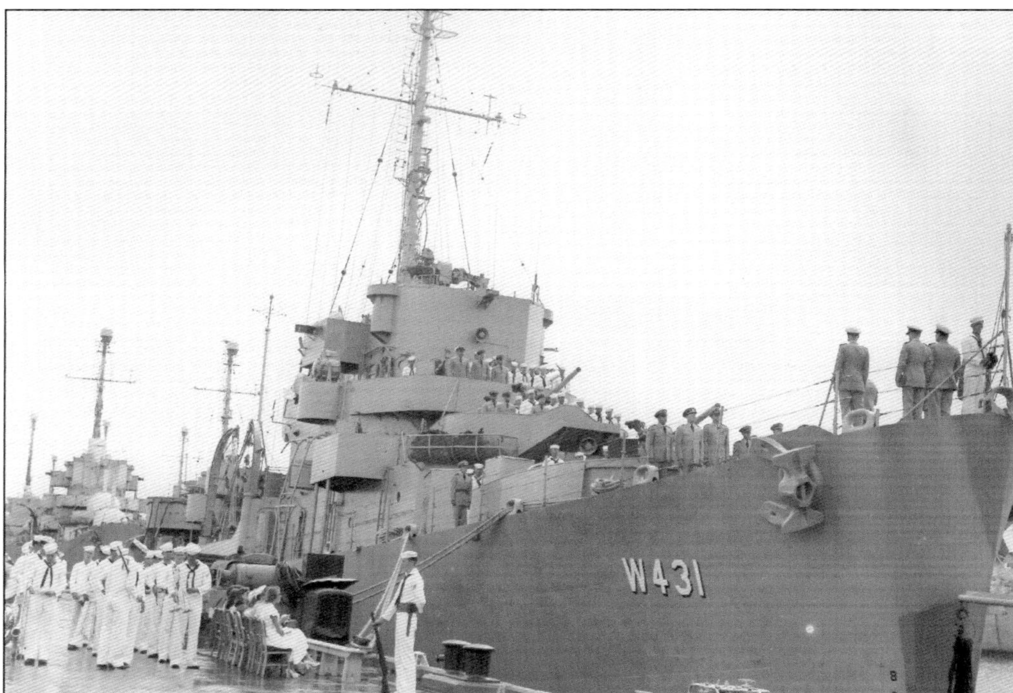

USS *Koiner*. "Between 1946 and 1951, American taxpayers put out only $213 million to maintain over 2,000 ships in the country's reserve fleet—approximately one-half of one percent of the original cost of building these ships," said Capt. Chauncey Moore, fleet commander. Chauncey said that original cost of the ships of the fleet was approximately $12,863,500,000 and to replace them today in 1951, it would cost $26,994,500,00. Here the USS *Koiner* (WDE-431) is recommissioned for the Coast Guard on June 20, 1951. (Courtesy National Archives, College Park, Maryland.)

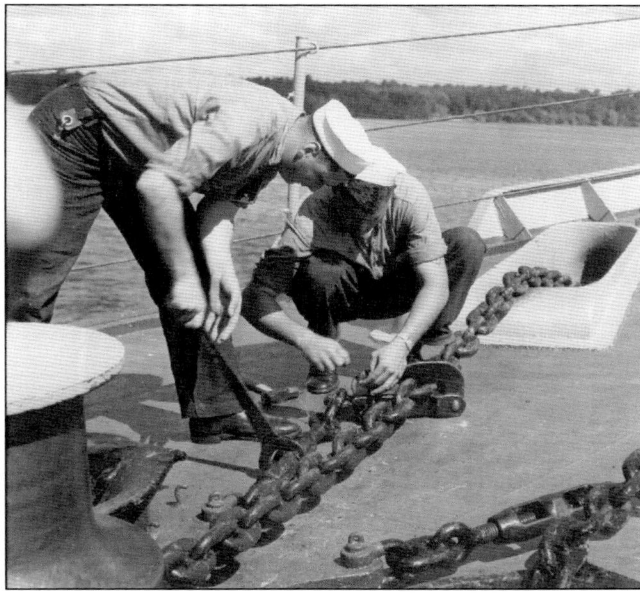

Crewmen Attaching a Chain Stopper. The typical day of a sailor at sea in Green Cove Springs was to rise at 6:30 a.m. and meet for quarters on the pier by 7:25 a.m. At 7:45 a.m., the crew was at the office huddled around the coffee maker, and they worked until 11:15 a.m. After lunch, work resumed at 12:30 p.m. and would continue until 3:40 p.m., when they would clean up and stop work by 4:00 p.m. Taps would sound at 10:00 p.m. This photograph was taken onboard the USS *Snowden* on June 13, 1951. (Courtesy of National Archives, College Park, Maryland.)

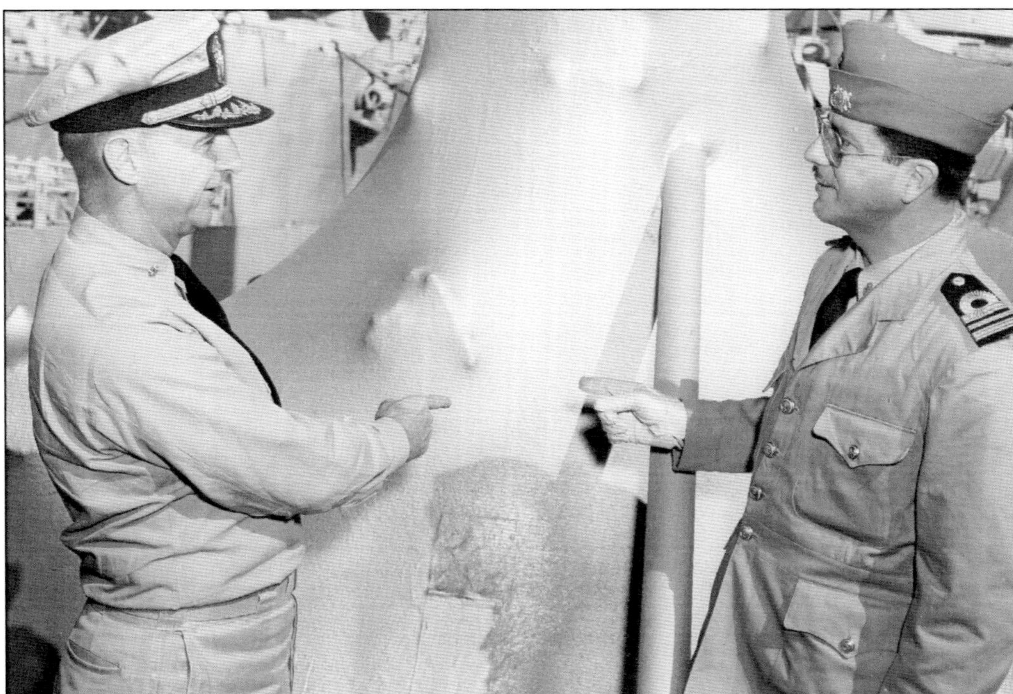

Inspecting Preservation. During the Korean War, the navy started taking some of its ships out of mothballs. Vice Adm. Oscar Badger of New York, commander of the Eastern Sea Frontier and the Atlantic Reserve Fleet, visited Florida in August 1950. Between 20 and 30 ships will be activated, Admiral Badger said. This work sent an additional 1,800 men to Green Cove Springs to help ready the ships for activation. Here Lt. Comdr. Pablo Bonilla on the right from the Venezuelan Navy and Comdr. Arthur A. Goodhue of the U.S. Navy on the left inspect the preservation of a destroyer escort on January 26, 1951. (Courtesy National Archives, College Park, Maryland.)

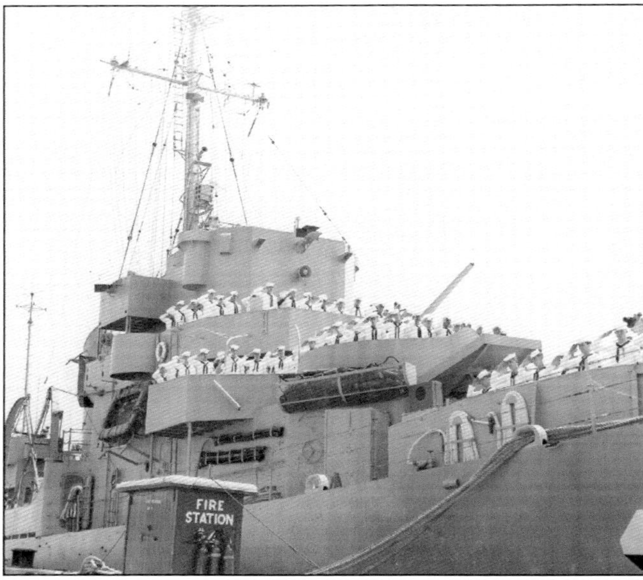

USS *STURTEVANT* DE-239. The *Sturtevant* was commissioned on June 16, 1943. The destroyer escort helped to provide defense for the Atlantic conveys. In June 1945, the ship was overhauled and quickly set sail for the Pacific. Finding the war over, the *Sturtevant* was decommissioned and sent to Green Cove Springs were she would remain for 6 years until recommissioned on August 3, 1951. In 1973, she was sold for scrap metal. This image shows the recommissioning ceremony on August 3, 1951. (Courtesy National Archives, College Park, Maryland.)

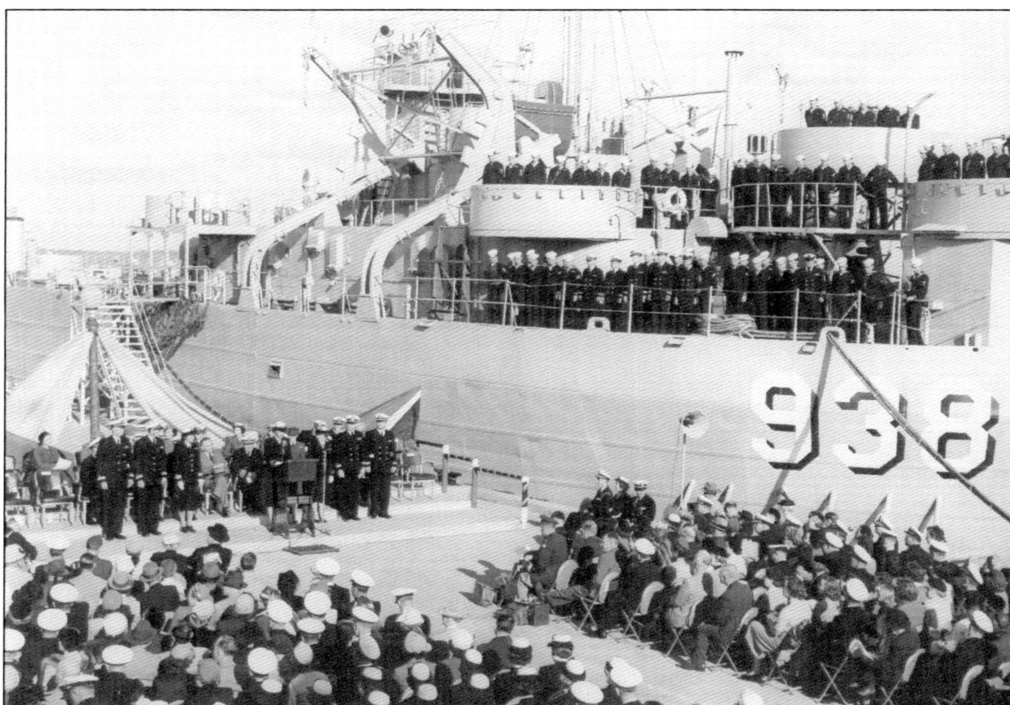

RECOMMISSIONING OF LST-938. The keel for this ship was laid July 14, 1944, and she was commissioned on September 9, 1944. In January 1945, LST-938 spent several months in the Phillipines after it was liberated. Later the ship would transport troops of the Australian 7th Infantry Division where it landed at Borneo. The ship received two battle stars during World War II, was decommissioned December 1949, and sent to Green Cove Springs. This photograph, dated December 14, 1951, shows the ship getting recommissioned. (Courtesy National Archives, College Park, Maryland.)

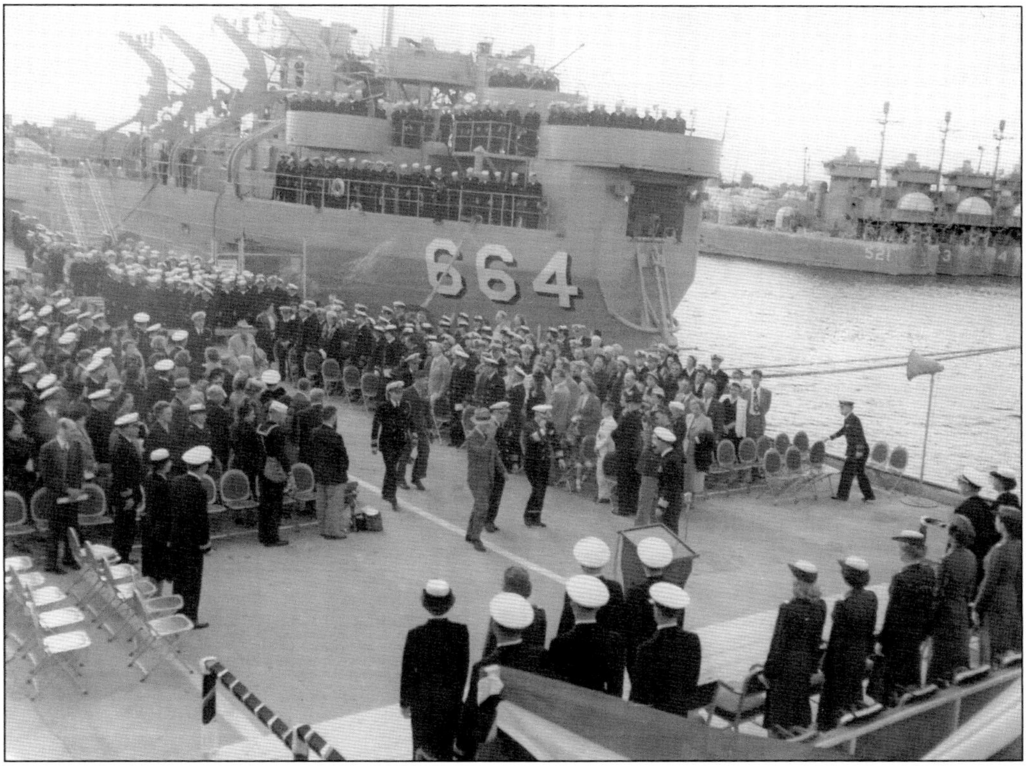

Recommissioning Ceremonies of USS *LST 664-528-938*. December 14, 1951, found the navy busy at the piers. On that day, four ships were recommissioned: *LST 528*, *664*, *938*, and the USS *Pandemus*. U.S. Undersecretary of the Navy Francis P. Whitehair attended the ceremonies. Whitehair unsuccessfully ran for Florida governor in 1940. He served as U.S. undersecretary of the navy from August 7, 1951, to January 2, 1953. (Courtesy National Archives, College Park, Maryland.)

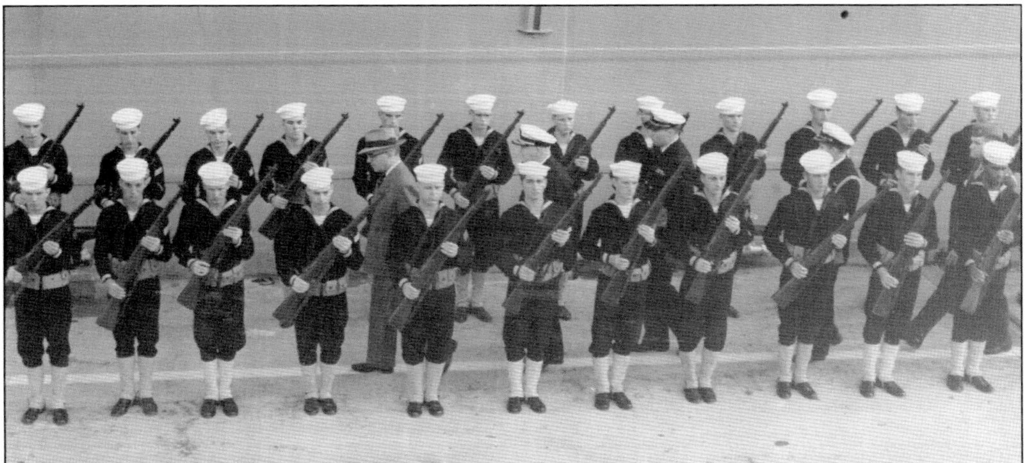

Inspection of Sailors by U.S. Undersecretary of the Navy Francis P. Whitehair. During the recommissioning of *LST 528*, *664*, *938*, and the USS *Pandemus*. U.S. Undersecretary of the Navy Francis P. Whitehair inspected the sailors who would be assigned to these ships. This photograph is dated December 14, 1951. (Courtesy National Archives, College Park, Maryland.)

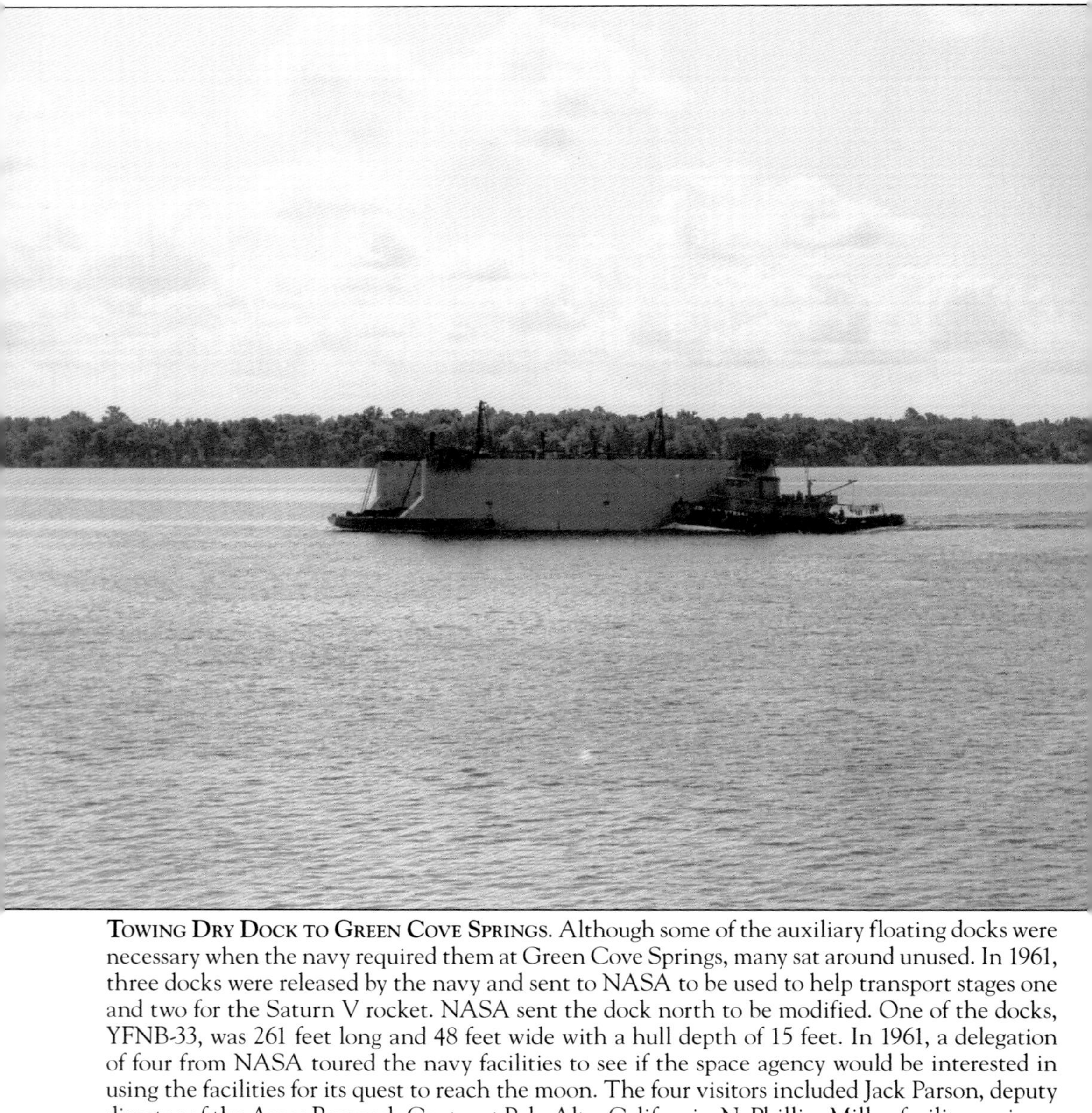

TOWING DRY DOCK TO GREEN COVE SPRINGS. Although some of the auxiliary floating docks were necessary when the navy required them at Green Cove Springs, many sat around unused. In 1961, three docks were released by the navy and sent to NASA to be used to help transport stages one and two for the Saturn V rocket. NASA sent the dock north to be modified. One of the docks, YFNB-33, was 261 feet long and 48 feet wide with a hull depth of 15 feet. In 1961, a delegation of four from NASA toured the navy facilities to see if the space agency would be interested in using the facilities for its quest to reach the moon. The four visitors included Jack Parson, deputy director of the Ames Research Center at Palo Alto, California; N. Phillips Miller, facility engineer at the Goddard Space Flight Center in Greenbelt, Maryland; Martin Byrnes, staff assistant to the director of NASA's space task group at Langley Air Force Base, Virginia; and Ed Camphena, NASA construction engineer. (Courtesy National Archives, College Park, Maryland.)

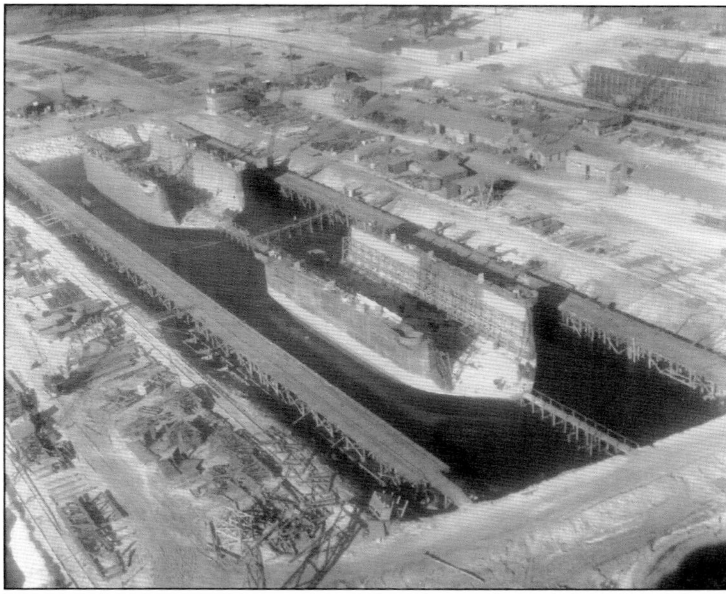

Construction of Mobile Floating Dry Docks at Jacksonville. Dry docks used at Green Cove Springs were built at NAS Jacksonville and transported south. These auxiliary floating docks displaced 1,000 tons and needed to be towed. Pictured here are the USS *AFD-18* and USS *AFD-19* under construction in 1944. (Courtesy National Archives, College Park, Maryland.)

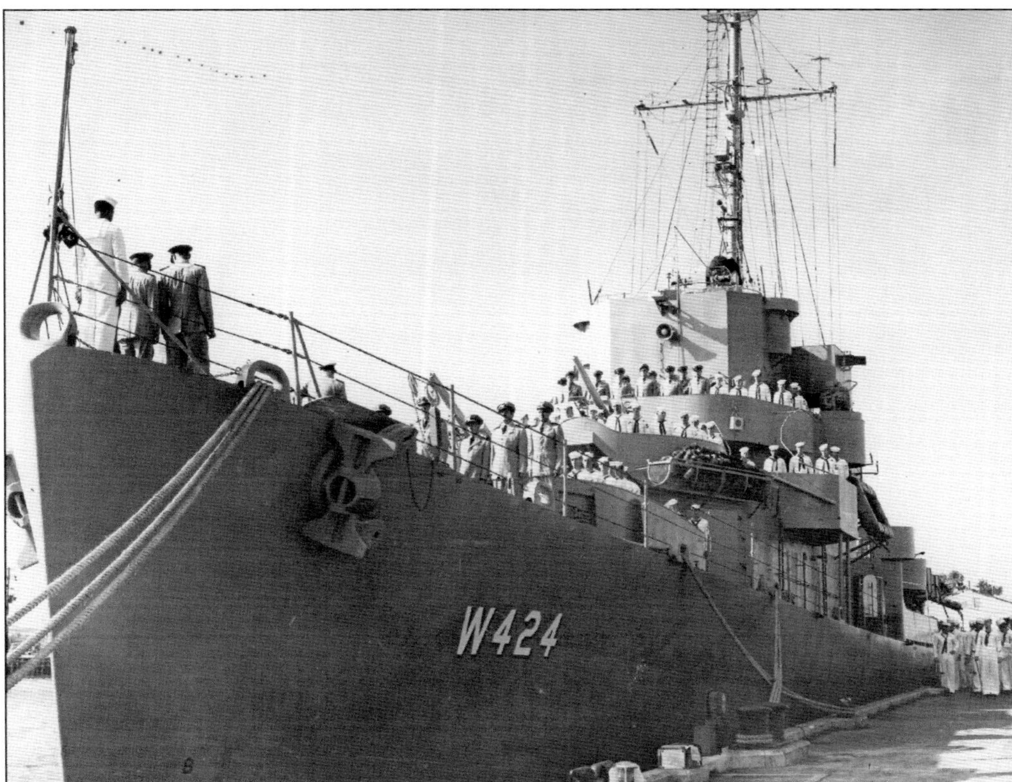

USS Falgout. The destroyer escort *Falgout* was commissioned November 13, 1943. On August 24, 1951, the *Falgout* was loaned to the Coast Guard and recommissioned as *WDE-424*. In 1977 off the coast of California, she was sunk after being used for target practice. This photograph was taken on August 24, 1951. (Courtesy National Archives, College Park, Maryland.)

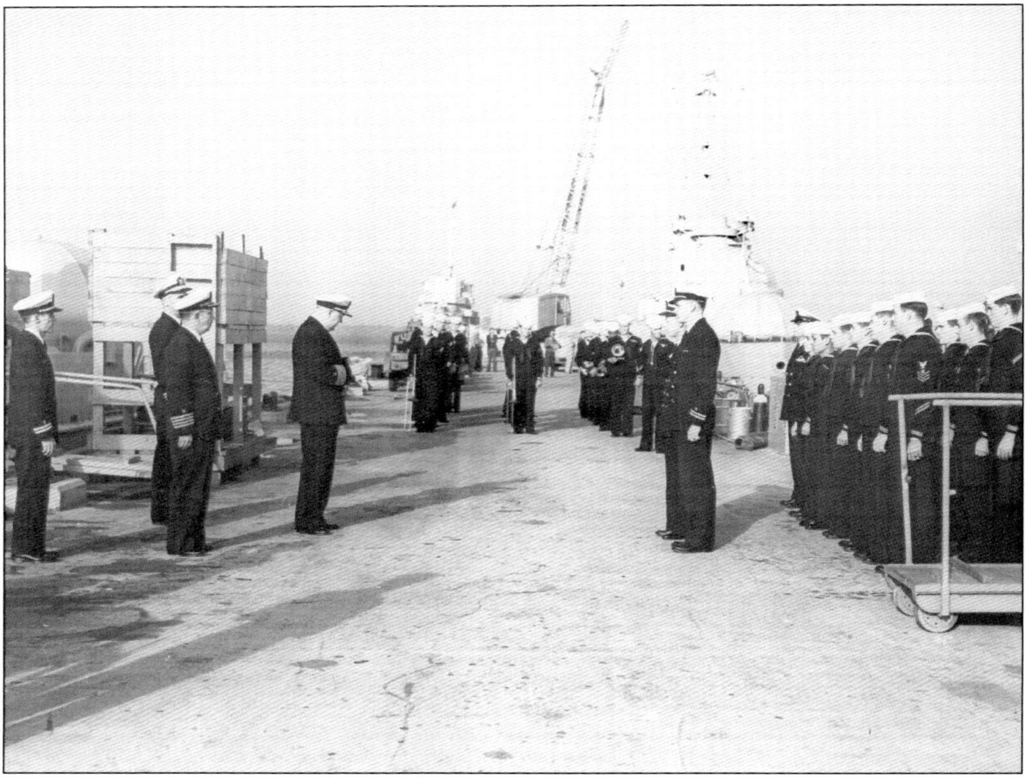

The Recommissioning of *LSSL-57* and *LSSL-120*. The recommissioning ceremonies for these two ships took place on November 30, 1951. Each of these ships participated in the assault and occupation of Okinawa. In the early 1950s, both ships were temporarily transferred to the Japanese Navy. (Courtesy National Archives, College Park, Maryland.)

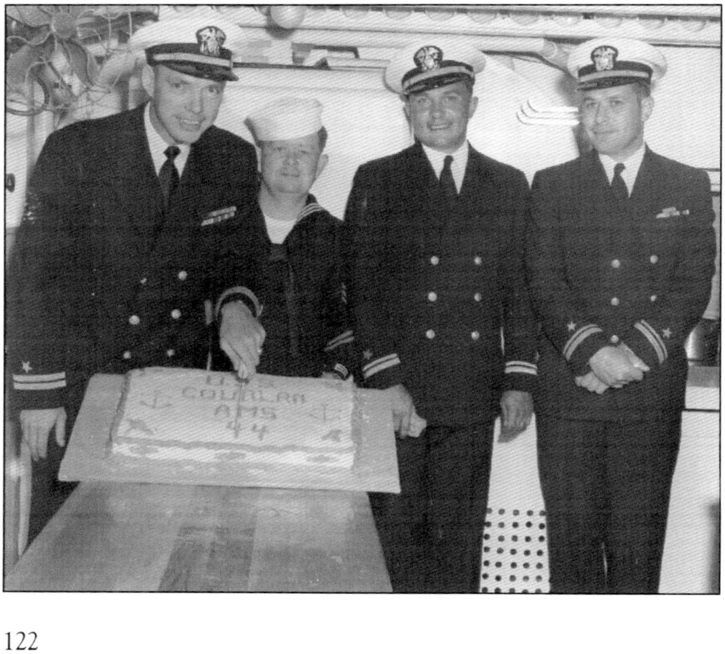

USS *Courlan*. This ship was originally named the *YMS-114*. Built in San Diego, California, and commissioned in August 1942, the ship served as a minesweeper. In January 1947, it was renamed the USS *Courlan*. On March 10, 1951, it was recommissioned at Green Cove Springs. Pictured here is the commanding officer of the ship, Lt. C. W. Loree, after the recommissioning ceremony. (Courtesy National Archives, College Park, Maryland.)

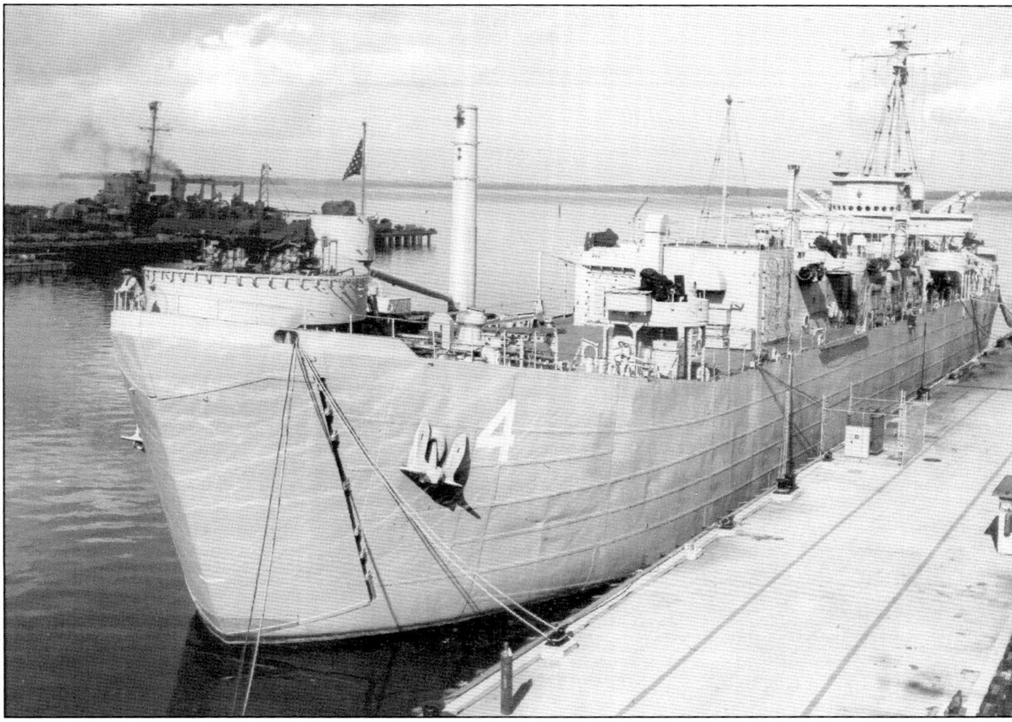

USS Chloris (ARV (E) 4). The *Chloris* was built toward the end of World War II and commissioned on June 19, 1945. A year later, it arrived at Green Cove Springs and was decommissioned where it sat until it was recommissioned on January 5, 1951. The USS *Chloris* was an aircraft engine repair ship. This photograph was taken on October 24, 1951. (Courtesy National Archives, College Park, Maryland.)

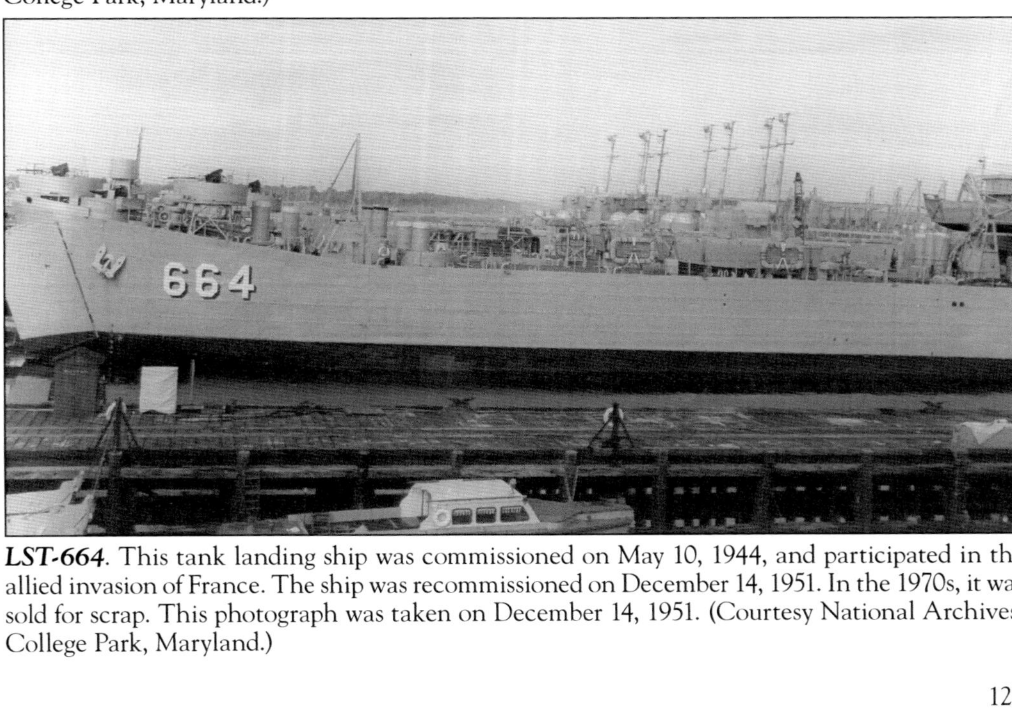

LST-664. This tank landing ship was commissioned on May 10, 1944, and participated in the allied invasion of France. The ship was recommissioned on December 14, 1951. In the 1970s, it was sold for scrap. This photograph was taken on December 14, 1951. (Courtesy National Archives, College Park, Maryland.)

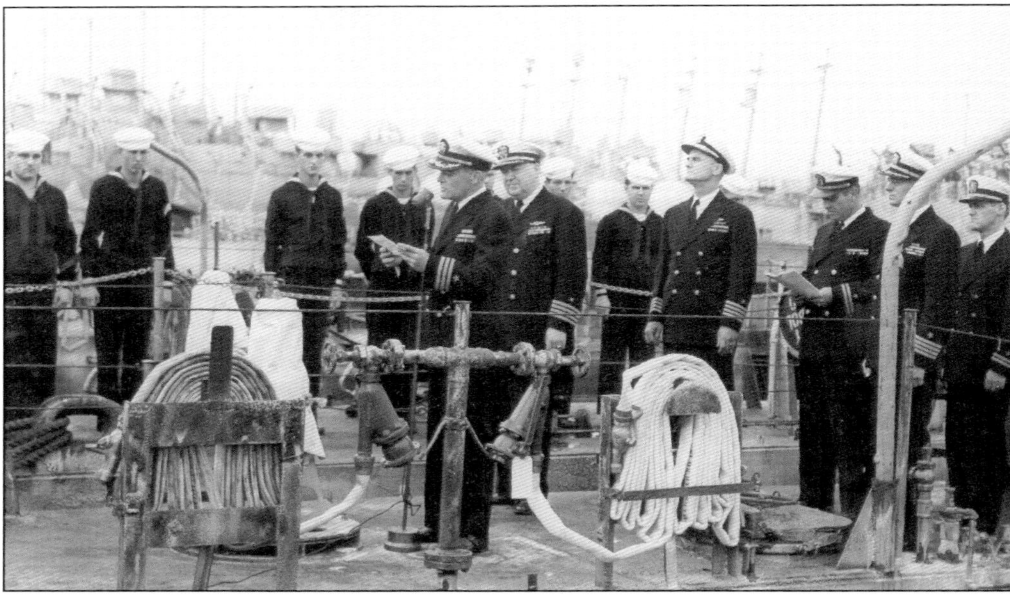

***LSM-492* and *LSM493*.** Both of these landing ships had similar service records. Each participated in the Pacific Theater during World War II. After the war, both ships were converted to minesweepers and transferred to Norway and then Turkey. *LSM-492* was decommissioned by the Turkish Navy in 1996. This photograph is dated January 21, 1952, when they were recommissioned. (Courtesy National Archives, College Park, Maryland.)

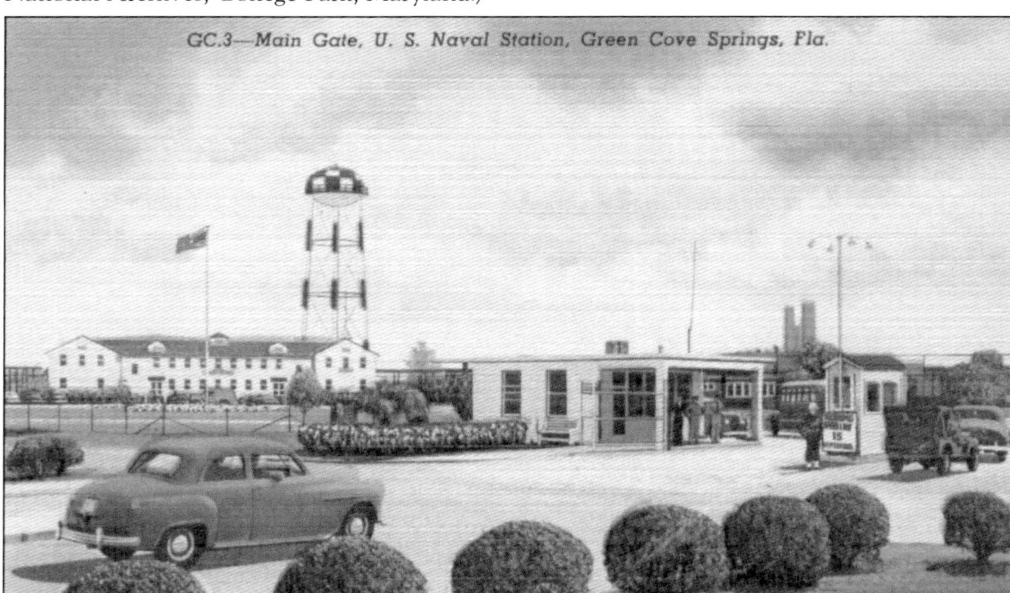

Main Gate, U.S. Naval Station Green Cove Springs. New housing was constructed on base due to a shortage of available housing in town. Typical complaints were "poor housing" and "high rents." In the early 1950s, the federal government built some housing for families; however, it appeared destined that the navy base would not be long lived as several housing projects were cancelled. This postcard is dated March 16, 1953.

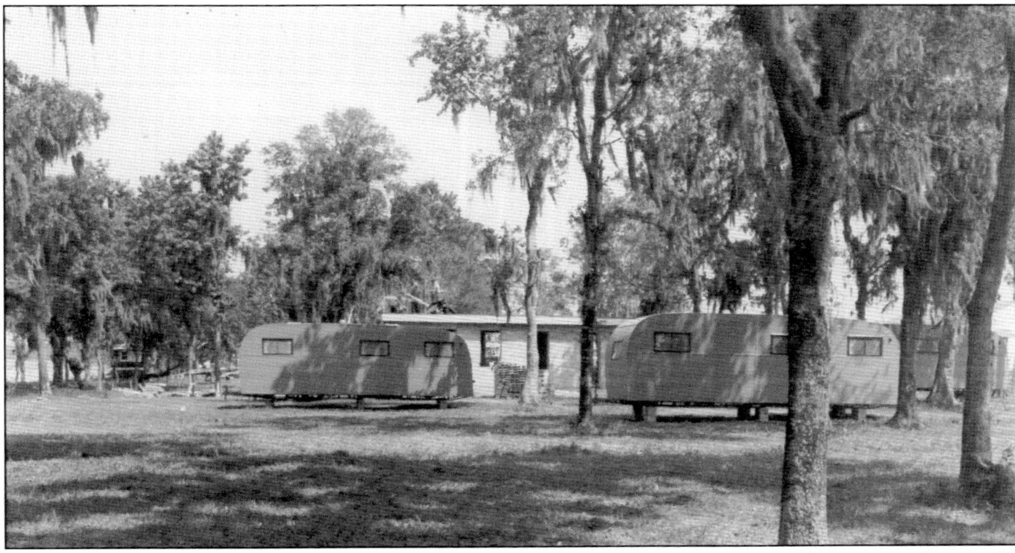

Trailer Facilities at Lee Field. House trailers were used for temporary housing. The trailer program was started at Green Cove Springs in 1947, and it ceased in October 1953. In May 1953, two trailers were shipped to NAAS Glynco, Georgia, and in 1957, those trailers that could be salvaged were shipped to Charleston, South Carolina. The others were demolished. The trailer facility, building 210, was constructed in 1947 for $4,000. (Courtesy National Archives, College Park, Maryland.)

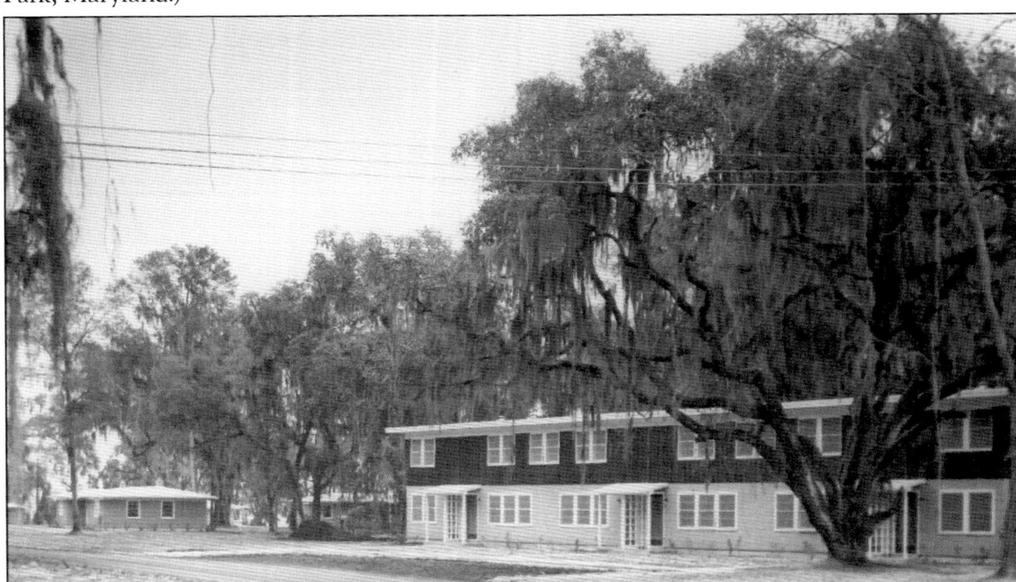

Magnolia Springs Housing. On August 1, 1952, the U.S. government, under Title VIII of the National Housing Act, entered into agreement with the Magnolia Springs Apartments, Inc., to furnish 392 family units for civilian and military personnel assigned to the Green Cove Springs Navy Base. The apartments were designed and built by March and Saxelbye of Jacksonville. The Magnolia Springs Apartments, Inc., took out a mortgage of $2,567,900. (Courtesy National Archives, College Park, Maryland.)

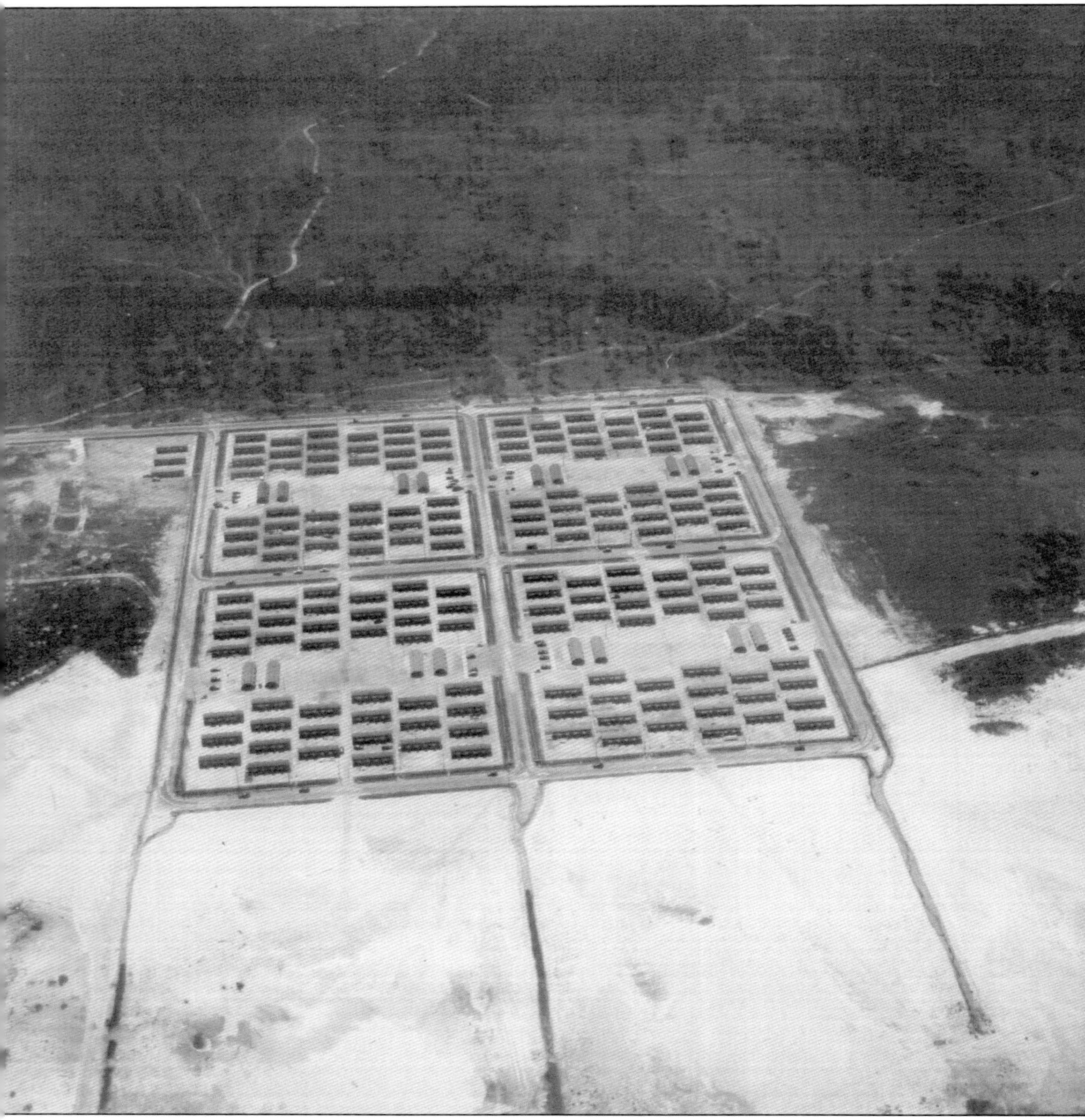

MARRIED, ENLISTED PERSONAL HOUSING. When the federal government announced in 1961 that it would close the base, there were only 325 civilian employees, 734 navy personnel, and 231 ships. The City of Green Cove Springs pursued the acquisition of the base in 1963; however, three taxpayers filed suit to prevent the purchase. Circuit judge John M. McNatt ruled that a 1963 legislative act gave the city the right to borrow money for the purchase; however, the city could only repay the loan by money collected from cigarette tax, utility revenue, and money from the lease of the land and buildings at the old base. The city purchased the property for $750,000, and within a few months after its purchase, the city sold the property to J. Louis Reynolds for $925,000. Reynolds had indicated that he would develop the property to attract new business; however, he simply used the property as a tax write-off. (Courtesy National Archives, College Park, Maryland.)

BIBLIOGRAPHY

Barbour, George M. *Florida for Tourists, Invalids, and Settlers*. New York, NY: D. Appleton and Company, 1881.

Bill, Ledyard. *A Winter in Florida*. New York, NY: Wood and Holbrook, 1869.

Blakey, Arch Fredric. *Parade of Memories: A History of Clay County, Florida*. Jacksonville, FL: Clay County Bicentennial Steering Committee, 1976.

Cahn, Julius. *Julius Cahn's Official Theatrical Guide Vol 5*. Empire Theater Building, New York, NY: 1900.

Cope, Edward D and Packard, A. S. ed. *The American Naturalist. Vol XVIII* January, 1884. Philadelphia, PA: Press of McCalla and Stavely, 1884.

Harris, John T. *Seeing the Sunny South*. Philadelphia, PA: J. B. Lippincott Company, 1921.

Hartfield MD, Marcus P. and Palmer MD, Geo. Thos. Ed. *The Chicago Clinic and Pure Water Journal*. Chicago, IL: The Geo. Thos. Palmer Company, 1907.

Hooper, Kevin S. *The Early History of Clay County. A Wilderness that Could be Tamed*. Charleston, SC: The History Press, 2006.

Mitchem, Jeffrey M. The *East Florida Expeditions of Clarence Bloomfield Moore*. Tuscaloosa: The University of Alabama Press, 1999.

———. *Cases Argues and Adjudged in the Supreme Court of Florida during the Years 1881-82, Vol. XVIII*. Tallahassee, FL, 1882.

———. *The Federal Reporter. Volume 33, January – May 1888*. St. Paul, MN: West Publishing Company, 1888.

———. Mineral Resources of the United States. Washington, D.C.:Government Printing Office, 1911.

National Archives, College Park, Maryland. Records of the Bureau of Yards and Docks, 1784–1963.

Poor, Henry Varnum. *Manual of the Railroads of the United States, Volume 22*. H. V. and H. W. Poor, 1889.

Schafer, Daniel L. *Thunder on the River. The Civil War in Northeast Florida*. Gainesville, FL: University Press of Florida, 2010.

Tyler, Daniel F. *Where to Go in Florida*. New York, NY: Hopcraft and Company, 1881.